ILLUMINATING THE ALBERTA ORDER OF EXCELLENCE

ILLUMINATING THE ALBERTA ORDER OF EXCELLENCE

Edited, with an Introduction by Allison Sivak

Illustrations by Cora Healy-Tobin

Gutteridge
BOOKS
An Imprint of The University of Alberta Press

Published by

The University of Alberta Press
Ring House 2
Edmonton, Alberta, Canada T6G 2E1

Copyright © 2008 The University of Alberta Press

LIBRARY AND ARCHIVES CANADA CATALOGUING IN PUBLICATION

Illuminating the Alberta Order of Excellence / Allison
Sivak, editor ; Cora Healy-Tobin, Illustrator.

(University of Alberta centennial series)
ISBN 978–0–88864–485–5

1. Alberta Order of Excellence. 2. Alberta—Biography.
I. Sivak, Allison II. Healy-Tobin, Cora III. Series.

CR6257.I55 2008   929.8'17123   C2007–907568–1

The University of Alberta Press gratefully acknowledges the support received for its publishing program from The Canada Council for the Arts. The University of Alberta Press also gratefully acknowledges the financial support of the Government of Canada through the Book Publishing Industry Development Program (BPIDP) and from the Alberta Foundation for the Arts for its publishing activities.

CONTENTS

Message from the Lieutenant-Governor *vii*

Message from the Premier *viii*

Message from the Chair of The Alberta Order of Excellence *ix*

Message from the Vice-Provost and Chief Librarian, University of Alberta *x*

Foreword *xi*

Editorial Note *xviii*

Introduction: The Work of Cora Healy-Tobin in Context *xiii*

Chancellors of the Alberta Order of Excellence *2*

Members of the Governing Council *3–7*

Chronological Listing of Members

1981
>   Senator The Honourable Ernest Charles Manning *8*

1982
>   Dr. Walter Hugh Johns *10*
>   The Honourable Dr. J.W. Grant MacEwan *12*

1983
>   The Right Honourable Charles Joseph Clark *14*
>   Dr. Mary Percy Jackson *16*
>   Dr. Chester A. Ronning *18*

1984
>   Dr. Alexander Johnston *20*
>   The Honourable Ronald Martland *22*

1985
>   Dr. David S.R. Leighton *24*
>   Dr. G. Richard A. Rice *26*
>   Dr. Winnifred M. Stewart *28*

1986
>   Dr. John Carter Callaghan *30*
>   Leonard Kane Haney *32*
>   Herbert Thomas Hargrave *34*
>   Dr. Esther Robins *36*

1987
>   Dr. C. Fred Bentley *38*
>   Dr. James H. Gray *40*

1988
>   Dr. Arthur T. Jenkyns *42*
>   Margaret E. Southern *44*

1989
>   The Honourable Peter Lougheed *46*
>   Dr. Maxwell William Ward *48*

1990
>   Dr. Raymond Lemieux *50*
>   Dr. Joseph H. Shoctor *52*

1991
>   Dr. Norbert R. Morgenstern *54*

1992
>   Dr. Howard V. Gimbel *56*

1993
>   Dr. Thomas Benjamin Banks *58*
>   Dr. Robert Bertram Church *60*

1994
>   Dr. Helen Isabel Huston *62*

1995
>   Dr. Stanley A. Milner *64*
>   Dr. Francis G. Winspear *66*

1996
>   Dr. A. Ernest Pallister *68*
>   Dr. John Snow *70*

1997
>   Ian Malcolm Macdonald *72*
>   Arthur Ryan Smith *74*

1998

Harley Norman Hotchkiss 76
June Louise Lore 78
Sandy Auld Mactaggart 80
Dr. Donald Russell Stanley 82

1999

Donald Ross Getty 84
Stanley George Reynolds 86
Dr. Shirley M. Stinson 88

2000

Jenny Belzberg 90
Dr. Chester R. Cunningham 92
Dr. D. Lorne J. Tyrrell 94

2001

Louis Armand Desrochers 96
Colonel (Retired) Donald S. Ethell 98

2002

Dr. Steven K.H. Aung 100
James K. Gray 102
John Murrell 104

2003

The Right Honourable Donald F. Mazankowski 106
Audrey Attril Morrice 108
James Simpson Palmer 110
Leonard Peter Ratzlaff 112

2004

Alvin Gerald Libin 114
M. Ann McCaig 116
Eric Patrick Newell 118
Bryan Perkins 120
Barbara Caroline Poole and John Edward Poole 122

2005

Robert W. Chapman, Sr. 124
Dr. Gerald Warren Hankins 126
Dr. Margaret (Marmie) Perkins Hess 128
Elsie Kawulych 130
Ronald Neil Mannix 132
Father Charles Michael McCaffery 134

2006

Dr. William A. Cochrane 136
Bertha (Berdie) Fowler 138
Richard F. Haskayne 140
Harry Hole 142
James Deverell Horsman 144
The Honourable Samuel Sereth Lieberman 146
Dr. Raymond V. Rajotte 148
Dr. Matthew Warren Spence 150
Ian Tyson 152

2007

Evelyn L. Buckley 154
Chief Victor Stanley Buffalo 156
Lt. General Donald C. Laubman 158
David W. Leonard 160
Gary William (Wilcox) McPherson 162
Douglas H. Mitchell 164
Patrick R. Nixon 166

MESSAGES

IT BRINGS ME GREAT PLEASURE to present this landmark book, which celebrates the Alberta Order of Excellence. These awards, in turn, celebrate the unparalleled achievements of Albertans. I am inspired by the unique contributions that have been made by each and every one of the members of the Order of Excellence; their stories read as embodiments of the Alberta spirit: a great vision for the community, a singular determination, and the knowledge and ability to make that vision reality. For their achievements, they are awarded the province's highest honour.

The Alberta Order of Excellence serves not only to recognize these citizens, but to demonstrate what is possible through an individual's leadership. I hope these stories serve as a source of encouragement, inspiration and enjoyment for all Albertans.

The Honourable Norman L. Kwong, CM, AOE
Lieutenant-Governor of Alberta

IT IS AN HONOUR AND A PLEASURE for me to present *Illuminating the Alberta Order of Excellence*. This book is a tribute to those individuals who have dedicated their lives to realizing the opportunities they saw to create better communities for so many Alberta citizens. I believe this potential exists within all Albertans. Over one hundred years ago, my grandparents arrived in what would become the Province of Alberta. They settled on a homestead near Andrew with little more than their hopes and dreams of creating a good life for themselves and future generations of their family.

As we begin our province's second century, Albertans have these same hopes and dreams, whether they are new arrivals to the province, or those who have lived here for generations. This land has offered an abundance of resources and opportunities that have helped to build the province. However, these opportunities would have meant little without the vision and determination of those people who saw their potential.

The Alberta Order of Excellence is our highest provincial honour, recognizing those who have contributed to the province in so many ways. In their stories, we see how they have seized opportunities to achieve greatness in industry, culture, human service, and community development. The recipients of the Order have contributed so much to Alberta in its first century. I hope they serve as inspiration to all our citizens of what we can achieve in the second.

Premier Ed Stelmach

WHERE DOES OUR PROVINCE FIND LEADERSHIP if not from our citizens? This book contains the stories of Albertans who have contributed immeasurably to the success and quality of life within our communities. As chair of the Alberta Order of Excellence Council, it is my privilege to oversee the induction of new members; each year, I learn about the many contributions inductees have made to this great province, and the impact these contributions have made in the lives of many others. This inspiring and beautiful book will allow readers to learn about them as well.

Between the covers, you will encounter stories of the members' perseverance through hardship, dedication to community service, and innovative ideas. You, or someone you know, may very likely have received the benefit of their good works. I believe you will be amazed and inspired by the impact one person, with a great vision and the courage to attain that vision, can have on society. We have been so fortunate in this province to have had these leaders who have seen beyond what is to what could be, who have the generosity to contribute themselves and their belief in excellence to the province and the people of Alberta.

Robert C. P. Westbury, PhD, LLD (*HON*)
Chair, Alberta Order of Excellence Council

IN THE UNIVERSITY OF ALBERTA'S PLAN, *Dare to Discover: A Vision for a Great University*, President Indira Samarasekera presents the four cornerstones of our vision: Talented People; Learning, Discovery, and Citizenship; Connecting Communities; and Transformative Organization and Support. Drawn from the founding principles of the University, these cornerstones anchor our vision "to inspire the human spirit through outstanding achievements in learning, discovery, and citizenship in a creative community, building one of the world's great universities for the public good." This vision of inspiration and achievement is exemplified in the work of the members of the Alberta Order of Excellence.

So many of the Alberta Order of Excellence members have contributed to the University of Alberta as students, professors, researchers, members of the Senate, members of the Board of Governors, and supporters. The University has grown to be a leading post-secondary institution in no small part due to the work of such citizens. We are proud to foster excellence through teaching, learning, research, and community service. As a university, we seek to sustain our students, faculty, staff, and volunteers through their own journeys of discovery, and to encourage and inspire them to leadership in all areas of their lives. Throughout this book, we see the achievements of Alberta leaders past and present; we believe it is the University of Alberta's responsibility to help create the leaders of the future.

Such a book is the product of many. I would like to extend my gratitude to the University of Alberta Press for its fine work, evident in the quality of this book. Cora Healy-Tobin generously gave of her limited time between pressing family and professional commitments so that the story of her life and work could be told. Allison Sivak has created a vivid and engaging portrait of Cora in her introductory essay. In particular, I would like to express special thanks to Dr. Margaret (Marmie) P. Hess, a member of the Alberta Order of Excellence, who first drew my attention to Cora's art. Among her many accomplishments, Dr. Hess has served as one of our most knowledgeable and dedicated advocates for Albertan and Canadian art; her suggestion that Cora's scrollwork merited greater recognition was the beginning of this beautiful volume.

I thank the lieutenant-governor, The Honourable Norman Kwong, for allowing us the privilege of telling the story of the Alberta Order of Excellence and its members. Dr. Robert C.P. Westbury has been instrumental to the project, supporting our goal of bringing these stories to Albertans and the world. Gayle Stannard, executive secretary of the Alberta Order of Excellence Council, has provided valuable guidance throughout the process of creating this book.

Ernie Ingles, FRSC
Vice-Provost and Chief Librarian, University of Alberta

FOREWORD

AS THE UNIVERSITY OF ALBERTA LOOKS FORWARD to its centennial in 2008, it is time also to look back at the history of this campus. The University of Alberta Centennial Series celebrates the University's 100 years of academic excellence with a variety of books about the people and events that have shaped this institution.

This third volume to appear in the Series, *Illuminating the Alberta Order of Excellence*, pays tribute to the many people who have been honoured for their contribution as citizens and for the examples of individual citizenship they provide for fellow Albertans. The book showcases Cora Healy-Tobin's artwork for the scrolls given to individuals who have been invested into the Alberta Order of Excellence. Allison Sivak's introductory essay gives the reader an insight into the life and work of the artist whose illuminated scrolls have been presented to each recipient of Alberta's highest civic award.

The books in the University of Alberta Centennial Series reflect the rich and varied history of this University: the first is Donald G. Wetherwell's *Architecture, Town Planning and Community: Selected Writings and Public Talks by Cecil Burgess, 1909–1946*. Cecil Burgess was appointed by Henry Marshall Tory as resident architect and professor of Architecture in 1913. Burgess influenced the planning and development of our campus for many years and he would be proud to know that his work remains highly valued to this day.

"I Was There:" A Century of Alumni Stories about the University of Alberta, 1906–2006 is oral history at its best. Ellen Schoeck's labour of love captures the spirit and soul of a century-old institution. She has done so with a rigour for accuracy, and with a passion for its people.

Lois Hole Speaks: Words that Matter, gathers in one volume the speeches Lois Hole made as lieutenant-governor. This commemorative volume captures the wit, humour and wisdom of a much-loved public figure.

Commissioned specifically for the University's centennial, Professor Rod Macleod's *All True Things: The University of Alberta, 1908–2008*, delves into the community of scholars, researchers and students at the University of Alberta over the past century. Dr. Macleod states that to be able "to reflect on the history of your own institution is a real privilege."

In the centennial year, the University of Alberta will host conversations with the six living individuals who have served as prime minister of Canada. The final book in the University of Alberta Centennial Series intends to bring together in one collection these conversations with our national leaders. The collection will provide readers with unique insights into the way national leaders, past and present, have responded to challenges from members of the higher education community.

As honorary editor of this fine series, I am delighted to present our collective history to our alumni, students and staff in these and other new books planned in this series as we lead up to our celebrations in 2008.

James S. Edwards, PC
Board Chair Emeritus, University of Alberta

INTRODUCTION
The Work of Cora Healy-Tobin in Context

CORA HEALY-TOBIN IS A WOMAN WITH A QUICK AND SWEET SMILE, and an Irish lilt that has softened after almost forty years in North America. She will greet strangers warmly, as if she has known them for years, and can establish a quick and easy intimacy within minutes through what she calls her "gift of the gab." She is a humanitarian who maintains a strong belief in using her talents and knowledge to contribute to her community. She is also one of the premier calligraphers and illuminators in North America, whose prized scrolls are held in the collections of government, royalty, and other dignitaries throughout the world.

Her career has taken a number of interesting twists and turns from her formative years with her family in Cork, Ireland, where an aptitude for drawing led her to pursue an education in the fine traditional arts of calligraphy, illumination, and heraldry. Her desire to work as an artist is matched by her desire to help others through her career and her voluntarism. Pair these passions with a strong practical streak and a keen interest in people, and you can see how she easily moves between very different worlds: from the solitary life of the artist to a fast-paced job providing information to hospital visitors, from working with disadvantaged children to cultivating friendships with some of our most honoured and eminent Albertans. She sets extremely high standards for her own scrollwork and yet expresses a sense of wonder and honour at the pleasure with which her work is received. She indeed seems to live by the words of the seminal calligraphic artist Edward Johnston, who wrote that practicing the art of writing and illuminating is *"making an honest attempt to achieve a simple end."*

Cora was born and grew up in Cork, Ireland as the third of six children. The Healy family were deeply religious with a strong pride in their Celtic heritage and valued the expression of those beliefs through traditional and fine handwork. Both her parents were artistic: her mother designed elaborate fireplace screens, and her father's hobby was decorative woodworking. He also drew frequently, focussing on Celtic designs and religious themes.

Cora shared an aptitude for sports with her three brothers and her two sisters, due in part to her excellent hand-eye co-ordination. But she differed in that at a young age, she developed a strong interest in art. "I knew all of my childhood that I wanted to go to a college of art," she says. Even though her own talents were the exception amongst her siblings, this made Cora

feel special, rather than out of place. She recalls winning a prize from the Cork newspaper for drawing. "It made me feel I was the best in the world," she says. She received a box of paints from her parents the following Christmas. "They thought I was talented, that I had a gift for art."

Her parents encouraged her further; she was the only one of her siblings allowed by her mother to spend extended periods of time in the family parlour, painting at the table. It was a haven of solitude that allowed young Cora the space and silence to concentrate, when compared to the busy kitchen where the rest of the family gathered and worked. Today, her brother in Ireland, who is also an artist, has kept some of the art she made as a young woman. "When I look at it," Cora says, "I think, Oh God. But they love it, and they think it's beautiful."

Art was also about play for Cora, who would incorporate almost any material she could find. "We would get the wrappers from sweets and make our own designs and coloured papers." When they visited their seaside cottage, they would draw and paint on shells they found on the beach. Cora made her own paper dolls and designed their clothes, and painted her own Christmas cards.

At the age of 14, she started attending a Catholic boarding school in London. One of her aunts, a nun, told Cora about Mother Monica, a Sister who was a skilled calligrapher and artist; Mother Monica took a strong interest in Cora's abilities and continued to encourage her as her parents had done previously.

At boarding school, Cora had her first experience of meeting people from a broad cross-section of cultural and social backgrounds. But she was not intimidated in the least, she remarks: "In that school we had boarders from all over the world—ambassadors' daughters...when I met them, I felt how much alike we were."

Her family's strong Catholic faith prompted them to be very active in their church and community. Cora belonged to the Legion of Mary as a young adult, which provided support for the elderly and disabled, scrubbing their floors or running their errands. "'Twas just the way we were brought up, to help people," she says.

After her high school graduation, Cora attended the Hornsey College of Art in London, today the Cat Hill Campus of the University of Middlesex. She majored in heraldic illuminated arts and calligraphy in a small and exclusive program with only 16 students enrolled in her class. Cora excelled within this environment, quickly moving from the beginner class into the advanced. She also learned other fine crafts, including blackwork, a complex embroidery technique of the Elizabethan era, in which black silk thread is worked in geometric designs. During visits to the British Museum Library (today the British Library) with her class, she saw, for the first time, the Lindisfarne Gospels and the original art work from the Book of Kells (temporarily on loan from Trinity College, Dublin). The manuscripts made an indelible impression on her for their intricate designs and scripts.

She also studied modern art. Cora recalls first seeing Salvador Dali's 1937 painting *Metamorphosis of Narcissus* at the Tate Gallery, and looking with amazement at the brilliance of the light reflecting off the knife. While the work of Dali may seem an incongruous favourite for one who practices such traditional arts, it is true that illumination is primarily concerned with colour and light. Indeed, when talking about her interest in other artists, such as the Impressionsists, she speaks about them in terms of the commonalities that her own work shares with theirs, making use of light and shade. Her ability to draw connections between such disparate artwork attests to her quick visual imagination, and her artistic open-mindedness.

While she had much respect for her instructors, she also believed in doing things her own way. Once, an instructor brought in what looked to the class to be a finely-executed scroll, on which Cora was struck by the use of colour gradation in the illumination. The instructor asked if they saw any errors in its appearance. "We all looked at it," Cora remembers, "and couldn't find a fault. I spoke up, and said in the Irish way—back to front—'Oh, it's

the two-tone.' And before I could finish my sentence he said, 'You've hit the nail on the head. The ink was too runny.' But I liked it, you see." She will still paint this effect into her illuminations as a hallmark of her style.

After receiving her diploma, she was at a crossroads in terms of her career. "You couldn't find full time work providing calligraphic scrolls. And London was expensive.... I felt unless I could make a full living from it, it wasn't going to be feasible." So she began a two-year diploma in Business Administration from the City and Guilds of London Institute, thinking it would give her an additional set of skills to work in the corporate sector. "In England, you couldn't make much of a living through art unless you went into an advertising agency," Cora muses. But she found it difficult to fit her own high standards for design work into a set billing process within a busy workplace: "There were so many demands that you had to price the art on the time [spent on the work]. I couldn't create that way."

Drawing on her strong belief in altruism that her parents had fostered in her, she attended the University of London to pursue studies in social work. It brought Cora a powerful satisfaction that her career would be helping others: "[When] I studied social work, I felt I was doing something positive with my life; I was contributing to humanity," she says. Upon graduation, she began to work with youth at risk, and even managed to incorporate art into her work with the children; this was a method of focussing their energies, as well as helping them to develop their talents. Cora took this teaching seriously, as a part of the children's education: "I taught them everything I knew."

She emigrated to Canada with her then-husband in 1969, leaving behind "the crowding" in London for the great amount of space in Alberta and the expanses of the Rocky Mountains which had captured their imaginations. The couple settled first in Edmonton and then moved to the vibrant Franco-Albertan community of St. Paul. They moved frequently throughout the province, living for periods in Lethbridge and Medicine Hat, as well as living in San Francisco for a short time. Eventually, Cora settled in Calgary with her son, Gerard, and daughter, Noeleen.

She was no longer doing social work, and felt the need for a change of career; the stress of youth intervention work had proved itself to be draining. She began to accept commissions for calligraphy and illumination in the corporate sector. Healy-Tobin's first commissions came from the corporate sector, writing certificates for Nova Alberta Gas Trunkline, the American-based J. Walton Thompson Advertising Agency, and several advertising agencies in Calgary: Francis Williamson Johnson, Baker Lovick, and Ogilvie Mather.

When she first approached the advertising agency Francis Williams and Johnson in 1979, computers were just starting to be used for graphic design. When the agency art directors saw her portfolio, they were impressed with the quality of this little-practiced art. She was immediately offered work creating scrolls and other projects that required a fine hand. Her reputation for fine work grew, and other agencies began to contact her.

Certainly, advertising work was a far cry from the calligraphy that she studied in school. She admits that it meant "some mundane work at first," but it also allowed her to complete a range of contemporary projects that she would not have been able to do otherwise. She has never advertised her craft; clients have instead sought her out after seeing examples of her projects. For example, a Calgary-based printing company that contracted her to design a cover for an art auction led to projects for such firms as Baker Lovick, Fording Coal and, ultimately, the Government of Alberta. Her first provincial government contract was to do the design and calligraphy for the Alberta Achievement Awards. She has also completed work for several international companies and for the City of Calgary.

Her career in fine hand-drawn work had taken off, although it was not quite enough income on which to raise a family. And while art was her passion and vocation, it involved many solitary hours at her drawing table. She still had a strong inclination do work that served others. Ultimately, she says, "I'm a people person. I need to interact with people."

The Foothills Hospital gave her that opportunity: Cora has worked at the front desk of the Foothills General hospital for the last twenty years. "I felt I wanted to do something where I could help people," she says. "It should be your priority, to make it so you are giving back something." She has combined her desk job with her reputation to lead to other projects, such as the request from Dr. Rene Lafrenière to create the heraldry for the Canadian section of the International College of Surgeons.

Cora has created scrolls and other documents in honour of a great number of dignitaries and events. These have included a provincial commission for the visit of Pope John Paul II, the City of Calgary's guest book page for visitors like Mikhail Gorbachev, and the Princess of Thailand. The lieutenant-governor's office commissioned a scroll in honour of Her Majesty Queen Elizabeth II, Prince Charles and Princess Diana, the King and Queen Noor of The Hesemite Kingdom of Jordan, and Queen Margarethe and Prince Henrik II of Denmark. She also completed a scroll for Princess Takamado of Japan to mark the 75th Anniversary of diplomatic relations between Japan and Canada, and the Government of Canada had Cora create scrolls in English and French for the Winter Olympic Games in Lake Placid (1980), Sarajevo (1984), and Calgary (1988), as well as for the Canadian Judicial Council. One of the highlights of her artistic career was to be commissioned by the Supreme Court of Canada to design retirement scrolls for Supreme Court Judges. She has also accepted commissions for many societies and non-profit associations.

Such prestigious commissions bring with them great pressure and high expectations, even considering Cora's own exacting standards. She can recall one instance where late in the project, the organization requested a change in the scroll size. "I was up for three nights before the deadline," she laughs. Her hand was so tired that she had to ask her daughter to hold it steady while she was burnishing the scroll with gold. Even under extreme pressure, she will accept no less than a flawless result.

Her high artistic standards and her belief in community suggest that it is particularly fitting that she has spent the last quarter century paying tribute to those Albertans who have made key contributions to the social, economic, artistic, and political spheres of this province through the Alberta Order of Excellence scrolls. Cora has designed and illuminated the scrolls since the beginning of the Order in 1981. In the first years of

the awards, she would conduct an in-depth interview with each of the recipients to gain a closer understanding of not only their achievements, but the recipients as individuals. When she talks about those whom she has interviewed, such as Dr. Robert J. Church and Francis Winspear, she reveals her deep respect for their accomplishments, but also for them as people. She speaks of their friendliness, their personableness, their humility. She says, "The calibre of the people was such that I felt it was an honour for me to design scrolls for them."

The personal interviews also have allowed her to delve beyond a brief biography of the recipient and to collect some of the details of their lives; she could then incorporate very personal images into the scroll designs.

She draws on numerous sources for the scrolls' visual references, both published works as well as artifacts. For the scroll presented to Elsie Kawulych, who is of Ukrainian heritage, Cora studied the intricately hand-painted Ukrainian Easter eggs so that she could see examples of traditional designs. But she does incorporate her own perspective into such details to ensure cohesion in the overall design.

She looks to the text and the language to determine the appropriate calligraphic style; a contemporary text will be written in a more free flowing hand. While she is expert in many calligraphic scripts, her preferred is the English roundhand, which she believes is most conducive to some modification and allows her greater artistic license. She has great admiration for such calligraphers as Edward Johnston, who wrote his treatise on hand-lettering and design, *Writing and Illuminating, and Lettering* in 1906. She also appreciates the work of Eric Gill, the English typographer and printmaker, and a student of Johnston's.

Many years of experience have built her artistic expertise, but they do not necessarily make the work easier Cora says, "The artwork is...difficult for me. It is labour intensive, careful measuring and working as a draftsman as well as an artist." Her preparatory work is careful and extensive: she repeatedly sketches the text on paper until she is satisfied that she has achieved the design she wants. She then traces the final design onto the parchment, drawing a final version and inking it in.

Cora uses thick waterproof Indian inks that stand up to the test of time and minimize fading due to light exposure. The line is varied through her choice of pen; for very fine writing, she uses a mapping nib, which has an open tip. For thicker lines, she employs the brouse nib, which has a reservoir at the top to hold the ink and make for smooth flow. The illumination is painted with watercolour and gouache, an opaque water-based paint that has the effect of reflecting light and heightening the colour. She also uses rotring inks and 24-carat gold to add brilliance to all her scrolls. Cora paints on an opaque thick vellum, which has been increasingly hard to source.

A steady hand and a steady eye are key to the slow, exacting process of illumination and calligraphy. "It takes one hundred percent concentration," Cora says. The calligraphy itself is very much about visual presentation; Cora seeks to achieve elegance and consistency in her work. "But once your hands or eyesight go, it's no good," she cautions.

She does have a few tricks up her sleeve; one is a pair of surgical eye-glasses given to her by Order of Excellence recipient, Dr. Howard Gimbel. Cora tells the story: "I had interviewed him and his wife for the scroll. He came into the hospital one day, and was surprised to see me there—I told him I couldn't be doing artwork all day long!" As they talked, she mentioned that she had to have her own eyes checked, and he suggested she make an appointment with his office and to make sure he knew when she was coming in. At Dr. Gimbel's clinic, Cora expressed interest in his professional equipment, particularly the surgical glasses. He promptly offered her the glasses that he used when he first began his work in eye surgery. Cora uses them to do a final quality check on her work.

Cora notes that many people do not have the patience for the painstaking work involved in her artistic process. She has remained a one-person

The trellis for Dr. Robert J. Church, for example, is a string of DNA, alluding to his groundbreaking work in molecular genetics.

A side effect of the increasing numbers of who are deemed to be honoured by the province is that such an intimate knowledge of the lives of the Order of Excellence recipients is no longer feasible. Some honourees have, however, specifically requested a meeting with Cora as she is preparing their scrolls. Dr. Margaret (Marmie) Hess, Cora notes, had a strong interest in the art of calligraphy, and so asked to meet the artist. Other Order recipients invariably write to Cora to express their pleasure at receiving the scroll. The scrolls are drawn as an official commemorative document, but the honourees see this fine work as a very individual form of recognition, and wish to make their pleasure known personally.

The format of the scroll has remained standard over the years, which poses a particular challenge for the artist; the work could easily have become repetitive. Cora has addressed this challenge partly through the development of her own technique, learning some of the different calligraphies along the way: "I'd practice and practice and make them as different as I possibly could. The text could be italic, it could be roundhand, it could be unctial...I have had a certain amount of artistic freedom."

studio throughout her career, since she feels that if the artwork is going out under her name, she must retain total control of the process to retain its quality. The finished work embodies a transparency through which the flaws could be plainly seen and it is therefore imperative that the entire process is carefully managed and made as flawless as possible.

Cora Healy-Tobin's career has been a study in contrasts. Her study of historic art forms led her to produce work for advertising agencies, oil companies, and government bodies. As the design world became more and more reliant on computers, she benefited from the esteem attached to fine hand-drawn work. She may work alone for endless hours to complete a commission, or work to address the endless needs of people at the Foothills Hospital. Her career has involved those living on the margins of society, as well as those who have come from backgrounds of great privilege. "I've worked with the very poor and the very wealthy," she remarks. Through it all, Cora seeks to further her own practice as an artist while she also seeks

to encourage positive change in her community. What is remarkable is that she has been able to integrate her sense of social responsibility into her own artistic practice. As an artist, Cora Healy-Tobin views her calling as one to serve. Although she is highly accomplished and recognized in her field, she does not consider her work to be without a greater social purpose. "I look at it as a gift given to me. And I try to use it," she notes modestly.

The treatise of Edward Johnston on hand-writing articulate the goals to which an artist must aspire: "In so far as tradition fails to bound or guide us we must think for ourselves and practice or make methods and rules for ourselves: endeavours that our work should be effective, rather than having 'a fine effect'—or be, rather than appear, good..." It is an aspiration towards which Cora's artwork—and her life—have always been directed.

Allison Sivak

EDITORIAL NOTE

The information contained in the biographies was taken primarily from the induction ceremony programs and have been edited for consistency. Where more recent information has become available, the biographies have been updated. In those instances where a recipient of the Award is now deceased, this has been noted at the end of the relevant entry.

The Alberta Order of Excellence

The Alberta Order of Excellence Act was accorded Royal Assent in the Alberta Legislature on November 16, 1979 and named The Lieutenant-Governor of Alberta as Chancellor of the Order

Section 2 of the Act states: "There is hereby established a society of honour to be known as The Alberta Order of Excellence consisting of those persons who are members of the Order. The object of the Order is to accord recognition to those persons who have rendered service of the greatest distinction and of singular excellence for or on behalf of the residents of Alberta."

Scribe - Cora Healy Tobin

Chancellors of the Alberta Order of Excellence

The Honourable Frank LynchStaunton — 1980 1985

The Honourable Helen Hunley — 1985 1991

The Honourable Gordon Towers — 1991 1996

The Honourable H.A. "Bud" Olson — 1996 2000

The Honourable Lois E. Hole, — 2000 2004

The Honourable Norman L. Kwong — 2005

Members of the Governing Council

NAME	CITY OR TOWN	APPOINTMENT
		FROM · TO
Dr. Robert Westbury Chairman	Edmonton	January 2004

artist.Cora healy-Toam

MEMBERS OF THE GOVERNING COUNCIL

NAME	CITY OR TOWN	APPOINTMENT FROM	TO
THE HONOURABLE			
Samuel S Lieberman QC LLD Chairman September 1997	**Edmonton**	September 1997	December 2003
A Comm Gordon J Greig Rtd	**Spruce Grove**	September 1997	December 2002
Nels Nelson	**Grimshaw**	September 1997	December 2002
Dr. Harold Storlien	**Medicine Hat**	January 2001	
Jack Gorr	**Three Hills**	January 2001	
Harley Hotchkiss	**Calgary**	January 2003	
Mrs. Bunny Ferguson	**Edmonton**	January 2003	
Walter Paszkowski	**Sexsmith**	January 2003	

Cora Healy-Tobin

Members of the Governing Council

name	city or town	appointment from	to
Dean Bell	Sherwood Park	April 1988	March 1994
Peggy Amatt	Canmore	April 1991	March 1994
Beverly Feldman CHAIRMAN October 1996 July 1997	Edmonton	April 1991	July 1997
Dr. Keith V. Robin	Lethbridge	January 1995	Dec. 2000
The Honourable Mr. Justice Tevie H. Miller CHAIRMAN January 1996 August 1996	Edmonton	April 1993	August 1996
W. Gordon Buchanan	High Prairie	January 1995	July 1997
James Christie	Trochu	May 1995	Dec. 2000
Mrs. Jean Fraser	Calgary	May 1996	Dec. 2002

Cora Healy-Tobin

MEMBERS OF THE GOVERNING COUNCIL

NAME	CITY OR TOWN	APPOINTMENT FROM	TO
THE HONOURABLE Mr. Justice Howard Irving CHAIRMAN March 1983 December 1992	EDMONTON	December 1983	December 1992
Mrs. Islay Arnold	LETHBRIDGE	April 1983	March 1988
Dr. Bernard Snell	EDMONTON	April 1985	March 1991
Dr. Gordon Townsend	CALGARY	April 1985	March 1988
Mr. Roy Watson	EDMONTON	April 1985	March 1988
Mr. Frank Swanson	CALGARY	April 1985	March 1987
Mr. Allan Anderson CHAIRMAN December 1992 1995	CALGARY	April 1988	December 1995
Dr. Walter Mitson	LETHBRIDGE	April 1988	March 1994

Ora Healy-Tobin

The Alberta Order of Excellence

Members of the Governing Council

Name	City or Town	Appointment From	To
Mr. Harry T. Hargrave CHAIRMAN	EDMONTON	March 31, 1980	November 30, 1983
Mr. Peter L.P. Macdonnell VICE-CHAIRMAN	EDMONTON	March 31, 1980	March 31, 1985
Most Reverend Paul J. O'Byrne	CALGARY	March 31, 1980	April 30, 1983
Honourable Mr. Justice Carlton Clement	EDMONTON	March 31, 1980	March 31, 1985
Mrs. Martha Cohen, C.M.	CALGARY	March 31, 1980	March 31, 1985
Mr. Louis A. Desrochers CHAIRMAN December 1, 1983 to March 31, 1985	EDMONTON	March 31, 1980	March 31, 1985

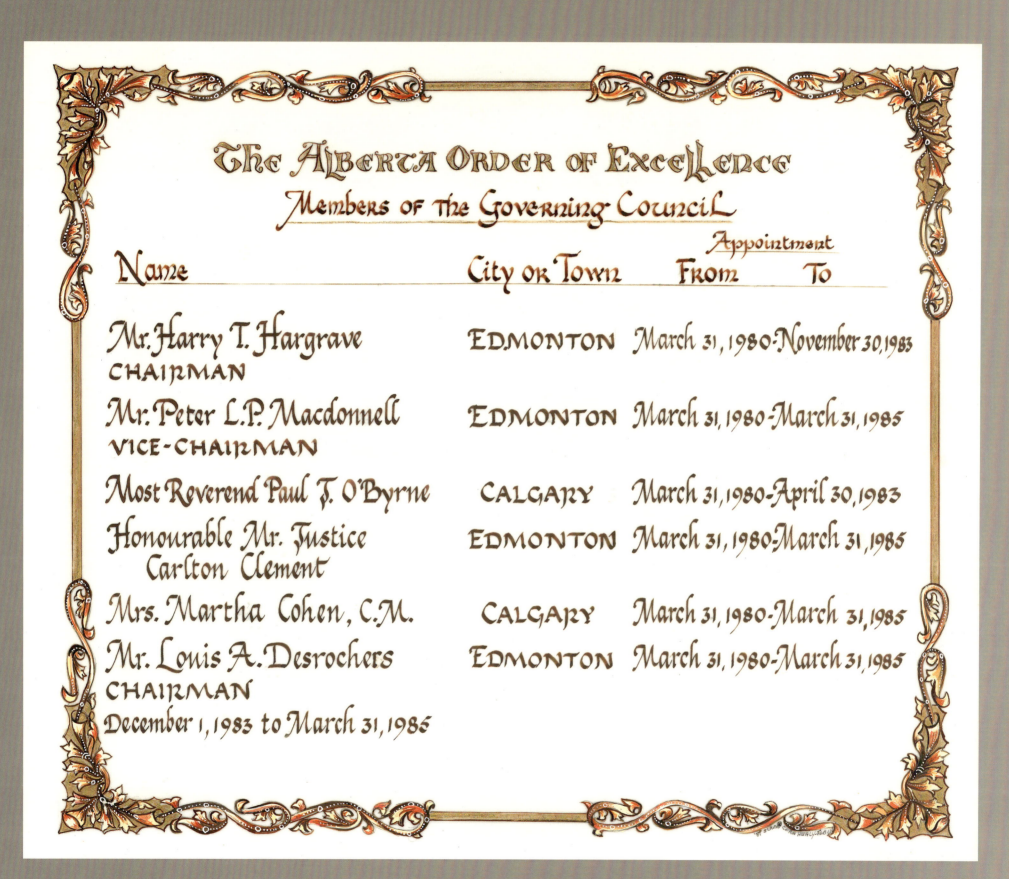

Senator The Honourable Ernest Charles Manning

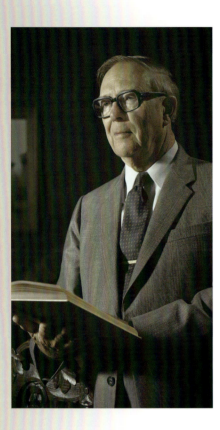

Inducted: 1981

ERNEST CHARLES MANNING WAS BORN at Carncluff, Saskatchewan in 1908 and was raised on a farm in the Rosetown area. He attended William Aberhart's Prophetic Bible Institute in Calgary in 1927 and upon graduation in 1929 became a permanent resident of Alberta.

In 1935, Mr. Manning entered the Alberta Government's cabinet as provincial secretary; at 26, he was the youngest cabinet minister in British parliamentary history since William Pitt the Younger. When he became premier in 1943 at the age of 35, he was the youngest first minister since Pitt.

He served continuously for 33 years as a minister of the Crown, 25 of those years as premier. A consistent advocate of economic, social and political reform, Mr. Manning presided over a generation of social and economic change. This included the formative years of Alberta's Oil and Gas Development Program, which led to the province's role as a major source of natural resources.

Besides serving as premier of Alberta, Mr. Manning also held a number of other positions, such as minister of trade and industry, minister of mines and minerals, provincial treasurer, attorney general and president of the executive council.

In 1967, his views on national politics were published in a book entitled *Political Realignment, a Challenge to Thoughtful Canadians*. His book called for the development of a distinctly new political ideology, combining humanitarian concern with the dynamics of a responsible free enterprise society.

Upon retirement from public office in 1968, Mr. Manning established his own research and consulting firm, Manning Consultants Limited, in Edmonton.

In 1970, he was appointed to the Canadian Senate, where he participated in numerous studies and inquiries on matters of national public policy.

Senator Manning was the chairman of the board of Fluor Canada Limited. He also served as a director of Stelco Inc., Manufacturers Life Insurance Company, McIntyre Mines Limited, Melcor Developments Ltd., Burns Foods Ltd., and OPI Ltd.

He was the recipient of a number of honours and awards including:

Honorary Degree (LLD) Doctor of Laws, University of Alberta, 1948

Honorary Degree (DUC) Doctor of the University of Calgary, University of Calgary 1967

Honorary Degree (LLD) Doctor of Laws, McGill University, 1967

Honorary Degree (LLD) Doctor of Laws, University of Lethbridge, 1972

Member of the Canadian Privy Council (PC), 1967

Companion of the Order of Canada (CC), 1970

In addition to his long and varied political and business career, Mr. Manning was known internationally as an active Christian layman. He directed and was heard weekly on a national religious radio program, the oldest and most far-reaching broadcast of its kind in Canada.

Mr. Manning is now deceased.

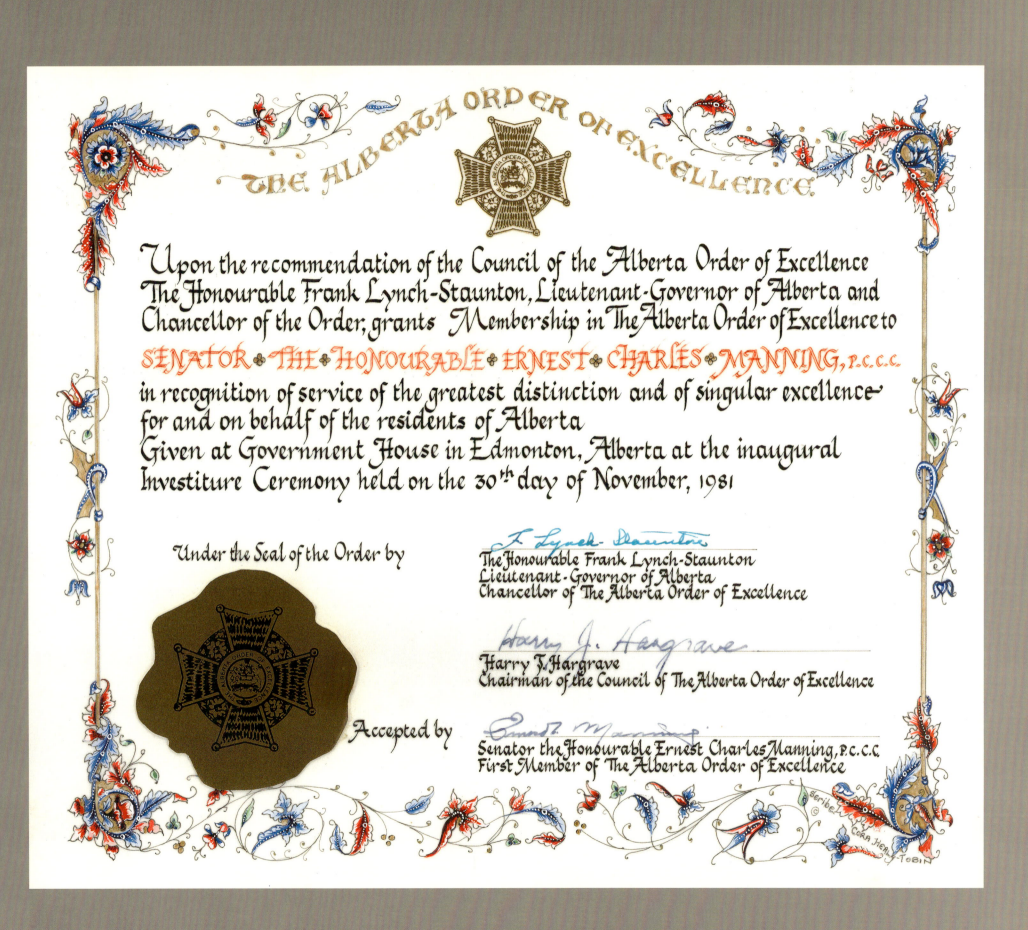

THE ALBERTA ORDER OF EXCELLENCE

Upon the recommendation of the Council of the Alberta Order of Excellence The Honourable Frank Lynch-Staunton, Lieutenant-Governor of Alberta and Chancellor of the Order, grants Membership in The Alberta Order of Excellence to

SENATOR ✦ THE ✦ HONOURABLE ✦ ERNEST ✦ CHARLES ✦ MANNING, P.C.C.C.

in recognition of service of the greatest distinction and of singular excellence for and on behalf of the residents of Alberta

Given at Government House in Edmonton, Alberta at the inaugural Investiture Ceremony held on the 30th day of November, 1981

Under the Seal of the Order by

F. Lynch-Staunton
The Honourable Frank Lynch-Staunton
Lieutenant-Governor of Alberta
Chancellor of The Alberta Order of Excellence

Harry J. Hargrave
Harry J. Hargrave
Chairman of the Council of The Alberta Order of Excellence

Accepted by

Ernest Manning
Senator the Honourable Ernest Charles Manning, P.C.C.C.
First Member of The Alberta Order of Excellence

Scribe © Cora Healy-Tobin

Dr. Walter Hugh Johns

Inducted: 1982

WALTER HUGH JOHNS WAS BORN IN 1908 on a farm near Exeter, Ontario. In 1930, he received a BA honours in Classics from the University of Western Ontario. At Cornell University, he received a PhD in Classics and Ancient History in 1934.

From 1930 to 1938, Dr. Johns served as teaching fellow at Victoria College in Toronto, graduate instructor at Cornell University and professor at Waterloo College. Moving to Alberta in 1938, he taught at the University of Alberta in positions from lecturer to professor until 1973.

At the University of Alberta, he also served in activities such as assistant to the dean of Arts and Sciences, 1945–1947; assistant to the president, 1947–1952; dean of Arts and Sciences, 1952–1957; vice-president, 1957–1959; and president from 1959 to 1969.

As university president, he gave inspired guidance during a period of unprecedented growth, which saw the student population increase two and a half times, the complement of full-time teachers quadruple, and the physical size of the University more than triple.

With typical energetic dedication, Dr. Johns played a major role, over a period of twenty years, in establishing junior colleges at Lethbridge, Red Deer, Medicine Hat, Grande Prairie and official association with Camrose College. He assisted in drafting the new Universities Act of 1966, and was involved in the steady development of programs and faculty in Calgary, which culminated in full autonomy for the University of Calgary.

In 1952, he was sponsored by the Carnegie Foundation for a study tour of British universities and in 1954 he toured universities in British Columbia, Washington, Oregon and California. He attended meetings of Commonwealth universities in Montréal, London, Melbourne and Sydney, as well as meetings of the International Association of Universities in Mexico City and Tokyo.

In great demand as an accomplished speaker, he gave hundreds of speeches throughout Alberta: from Hinton to Wainwright, and from Medicine Hat and Lethbridge in the south to Peace River and Beaverlodge in the north. For the Canadian Club, he embarked on a speaking tour to British Columbia in 1970 and also covered the Prairies for them in 1971.

Dr. Johns wrote articles, book reviews and speeches, which were published in various journals. As his major literary work over a period of eight years, he researched and compiled a comprehensive 544-page illustrated history of the University, entitled *A History of the University of Alberta, 1908–1969*, which was published by the University of Alberta Press in 1981.

Dr. Johns was the recipient of a number of awards and honours including:

Honorary Degree (LLD) University of Western Ontario, 1959
Doctorat ès lettres, Université Laval, 1964
Honorary Degree (LLD) University of Saskatchewan, 1968
Honorary Degree (LLD) Waterloo Lutheran University, 1968
Honorary Degree (LLD) University of Alberta, 1970
Honorary Life Member, University of Alberta Alumni Association
Golden Jubilee Award, University of Alberta Alumni Association
Alberta Achievement Award, 1977
Officer of the Order of Canada, OC, 1978

He was active as a member and executive member of numerous academic, community and cultural associations, such as the Classical Association of Canada; the American Philological Association; the Humanities Association of Canada; the Council of the Association of Universities and Colleges of Canada, of which he was president, 1966–1967; the Senate of St. Stephens' College; the United Way Campaign; University Hospitals Board; the Governor-General's Award Board for Academic Non-Fiction; Alberta Novelists Award Committee; Chairman, Alberta Task Force on Nursing Education; Chairman, Proceedings Committee, Seventh National Northern Development Conference; Chairman, Alberta Press Council; the board of Allen Gray Auxiliary Hospital; and the Fund Raising Advisory Committee of the University of Alberta.

Dr. Johns is now deceased.

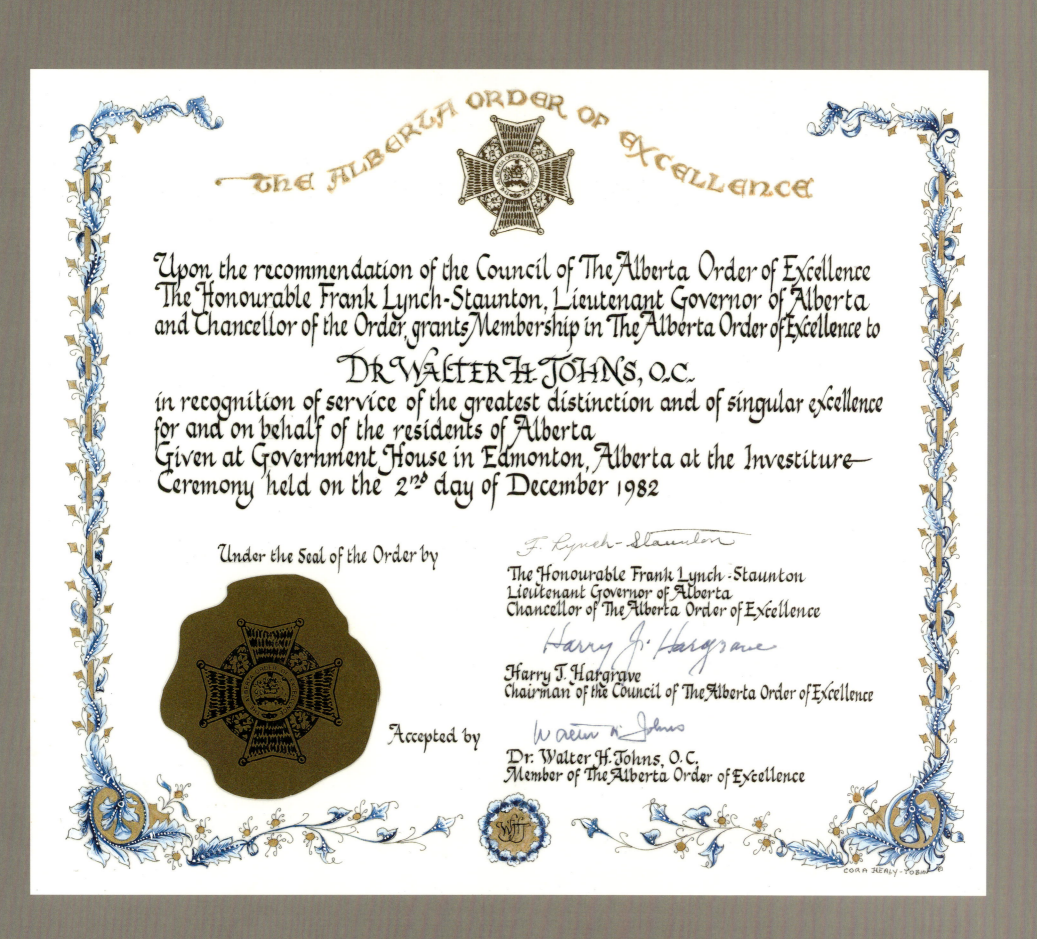

THE ALBERTA ORDER OF EXCELLENCE

Upon the recommendation of the Council of The Alberta Order of Excellence
The Honourable Frank Lynch-Staunton, Lieutenant Governor of Alberta
and Chancellor of the Order grants Membership in The Alberta Order of Excellence to

Dr Walter H. Johns, O.C.

in recognition of service of the greatest distinction and of singular excellence
for and on behalf of the residents of Alberta
Given at Government House in Edmonton, Alberta at the Investiture
Ceremony held on the 2nd day of December 1982

Under the Seal of the Order by

F. Lynch-Staunton

The Honourable Frank Lynch-Staunton
Lieutenant Governor of Alberta
Chancellor of The Alberta Order of Excellence

Harry J. Hargrave

Harry J. Hargrave
Chairman of the Council of The Alberta Order of Excellence

Accepted by

Walter H. Johns

Dr. Walter H. Johns, O.C.
Member of The Alberta Order of Excellence

CORA HEALY-TOBIN

The Honourable Dr. J.W. Grant MacEwan

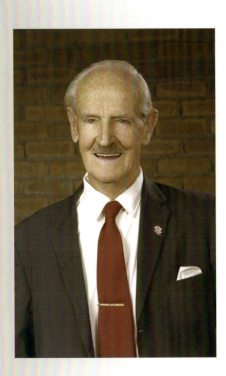

Inducted: 1982

JOHN WALTER GRANT MACEWAN WAS BORN in 1902. His pioneer parents farmed north of Brandon, Manitoba and later at Melfort, Saskatchewan. He attended the Ontario Agricultural College, graduating in 1926. Later he did post-graduate work in agricultural science at Iowa State University. He received a BSA from the University of Toronto and an MS from Iowa State University.

For some years following, Grant MacEwan held senior positions with the University of Saskatchewan and the University of Manitoba. Before taking the post of dean of Agriculture at Manitoba, he was professor of Animal Husbandry and Farm Superintendent at the University of Saskatchewan. Through these years, he became widely known across Western Canada for public service, especially in judging livestock, writing, radio broadcasting, lecturing and the conduct of fairs and exhibitions.

After 23 years of university work, he resigned and moved to Calgary, mainly to write. However, he became involved in political life and served on Calgary Council for 12 years, nine as an alderman and three years as mayor. From 1955 to 1959, he was a member of the provincial legislature, and in the last part of that period was Leader of the Opposition.

Appointed lieutenant-governor of Alberta, he took office on 6 January 1966 and retired on 2 July 1974. During these eight and a half years, he added a new dimension to this high office, preserving its dignity while at the same time softening some of the traditional formal protocol. With down to earth humour and astounding stamina, Dr. MacEwan fulfilled a staggering number of engagements in every corner of the province, reaching out to touch thousands of Albertans, endearing himself to all.

As an author, Dr. MacEwan was a regular contributor to various farm magazines and newspapers, and saw more than 20 books published. Of these, four were technical: *The Science and Practice of Canadian Animal Husbandry, General Agriculture, Breeds of Livestock in Canada*, and *Feeding Farm Animals*. The remainder had to do with the history and development of Western Canada, Western biography and conservation. A partial list of these books includes: *Between the Red and the Rockies, Agriculture on Parade: The Story of the Afairs and Exhibitions of Western Canada, Calgary Calvacade, Hoofprints and Hitching Posts, Tatanga Mani: Walking Buffalo of the Stonies, Harvest of Bread, Sitting Bull—The Years in Canada,* and most recently *The Best of Grant MacEwan* and *Alberta Landscapes* in collaboration with photographer Rusty MacDonald.

Dr. MacEwan was the recipient of a number of awards and honours including:

Honorary Degree (LLD) University of Alberta, 1966
Honorary Degree, (DUC) Doctor of the University of Calgary, 1967
Honorary Degree (LLD) University of Brandon, 1969
Honorary Degree (LLD) University of Guelph, 1972
Honorary Degree (LLD) University of Saskatchewan, 1974
B'Nai Brith Humanitarian Award, 1970
Canadian Brotherhood Council Award, 1972
Officer of the Order of Canada, OC, 1974
Premier's Award for Excellence, 1977
Dr. MacEwan is now deceased.

THE ALBERTA ORDER OF EXCELLENCE

Upon the recommendation of the Council of The Alberta Order of Excellence The Honourable Frank Lynch-Staunton, Lieutenant Governor of Alberta and Chancellor of the Order, grants Membership in The Alberta Order of Excellence to

THE HONOURABLE DR. J. W. GRANT MACEWAN, O.C.

in recognition of service of the greatest distinction and of singular excellence for and on behalf of the residents of Alberta

Given at Government House in Edmonton, Alberta at the Investiture Ceremony held on the 2nd day of December 1982

Under the Seal of the Order by

The Honourable Frank-Lynch-Staunton
Lieutenant Governor of Alberta
Chancellor of The Alberta Order of Excellence

Harry T. Hargrave
Chairman of the Council of The Alberta Order of Excellence

Accepted by

The Honourable Dr. J. W. Grant MacEwan O.C.
Member of The Alberta Order of Excellence

CORA HEALY-TOBIN ©

The Right Honourable Charles Joseph Clark

Inducted: 1983

CHARLES JOSEPH "JOE" CLARK WAS BORN on 5 June 1939 to Grace and Joseph A. Clark of High River. He grew up in High River and graduated from High River High School. Mr. Clark obtained a BA degree in History in 1960 and an MA degree in Political Science in 1973 from the University of Alberta.

An interest in politics has always been a governing force in his life. His early work includes private secretary to then Alberta Progressive Conservative leader W.J.C. Kirby, 1959; national president of the Progressive Conservative Student Federation, 1962–1964; a member of Premier Lougheed's political organization, 1966–1967; special assistant to the Honourable Davie Fulton, 1967; and executive assistant to the Honourable Robert Stanfield, 1967–1970. From 1965 to 1967, he was a lecturer in Political Science at the University of Alberta.

Mr. Clark was first elected to the House of Commons in October 1972, representing the constituency of Rocky Mountain. From 1972 to 1974, he was chairperson of the Progressive Conservative Caucus Committee on Youth. He was re-elected to the House of Commons in 1974, and from 1974 to 1976 he was chairman of the Progressive Conservative Committee on the Environment.

In 1976, he was elected national leader of the Progressive Conservative Party and served as prime minister of Canada from May 1979 to February 1980. At the age of 37, Mr. Clark was the youngest leader ever elected to head the national party, and at 40, he became the youngest prime minister of Canada in history.

The Clark administration adopted a determined stance in four areas: control of government spending and the encouragement of private sector growth; development of an energy self-sufficiency policy; the advancement of freedom of information legislation; and the strengthening of the consultative approach to federal/provincial relations.

Mr. Clark made important breakthroughs in Québec. He learned to speak French, studied Québec culture and went to that province often to seek support and to promote the unity of the country.

During his term as Leader of the Opposition from March 1980 to January 1983, some significant accomplishments were achieved. He successfully led his party in its efforts to ensure that Canada's constitutional changes be more generally acceptable, particularly in Western Canada and in Québec.

In the energy debate, Mr. Clark held the government to account for weakening Parliament and let the division bells ring until the government agreed to split its omnibus energy bill for more effective scrutiny by Parliament. In establishing the Via Rail Task Force, he challenged the government's right to act without the usual form of public consultation on a matter of vital importance to large and small communities throughout Canada.

Through the task force on the budget and the economy, and by determined efforts in the House of Commons, Mr. Clark and his party forced the reversal of over fifty measures in the 1981 MacEachen budget. Mr. Clark demonstrated that on economic matters Parliament and all Canadians must be consulted, and their economic activities understood, if the country is to have a positive economic future.

A strong believer in the populist philosophy, Mr. Clark attempted to make the House of Commons more responsible and credible by stimulating and increasing debate. He sought to forge agreement on the idea of Canada being a community of communities.

Mr. Clark was awarded an Honorary Doctorate of Laws from the University of New Brunswick in May 1976 and has been named a Fellow in the Faculty of Administrative Studies at York University. He was awarded an Honorary Degree (LLD) from the University of Alberta in 1985.

He married Maureen Anne McTeer in 1973, and they have one daughter.

Dr. Mary Percy Jackson

Inducted: 1983

IN HER DAY, DR. MARY PERCY JACKSON was often described as a 'living legend.' She served the people of the Peace River country as a physician for over 45 years.

Born in England in 1905, Dr. Jackson grew up in an urban setting, leading a rather sheltered life. She graduated from the University of Birmingham in 1927 with degrees in surgery and medicine. By the time she was 24 years old, she had accumulated impressive experience. She had been House Physician at Birmingham General Hospital, Casualty House Physician in the children's hospital, and House Surgeon in the maternity hospital.

In 1929, in answer to an advertisement in a medical journal for women doctors to go to Alberta, Dr. Jackson embarked on an adventure that was originally intended to be only a one-year assignment. In an attempt to provide better medical services in outlying areas, the Alberta Government hired Dr. Jackson and three other British doctors. Following an orientation tour with a travelling medical clinic, she was assigned to the territory of Battle River, a vast area covering 250 square miles that soon grew to nearly 400 square miles. The nearest medical aid was the town of Peace River, 120 kilometers to the south. It was connected with her territory by a dirt road, which was impassable in bad weather. She travelled by saddle horse.

Despite extremes in temperature and isolation, the solitary pioneer doctor ministered to her patients, often travelling many miles on horseback on virtually unmarked trails, and fording rivers and streams.

Dr. Jackson was "Doc" to homesteaders who immigrated from Norway, Hungary, Russia, Germany and the Ukraine, in addition to the Aboriginal population. A typical week's caseload might include several fractured limbs or a broken back; a birth; cases of dysentery, pneumonia, smallpox, scarlet fever or tuberculosis; as well as the other illnesses expected in a family practice; and perhaps some tooth extractions, as there were no dentists in the area.

In 1931, she married rancher and fur trader Frank Jackson, a widower with three children, and moved to his homestead at Keg River, 500 miles northwest of Edmonton. No longer under contract with the provincial government, she continued her dedicated service as a general practitioner in the area, much of the time without payment. She treated five generations of patients from all over the Peace region and was universally loved and respected by all who knew her.

During her long career, Dr. Jackson treated hundreds among the Aboriginal and Métis population and developed many long-standing friendships with them. In 1975, she was named "Woman of the Year" by the Voice of Native Women.

In 1976, she was awarded an Honorary Doctor of Laws Degree from the University of Alberta. Also in that year, she and her husband received an Alberta Achievement Award for outstanding service. The couple had previously been recognized for their contributions with a Master Farm Family Award in 1953.

Dr. Jackson received the Alberta Centennial Medal and the Canadian Centennial Medal, and a school at the junction of the MacKenzie Highway and Keg River is named for her. She retired from active practice in 1975 and held senior membership in the Canadian Medical Association, senior life membership in the Alberta Medical Association and a life membership in the College of Family Physicians.

Dr. Jackson is now deceased.

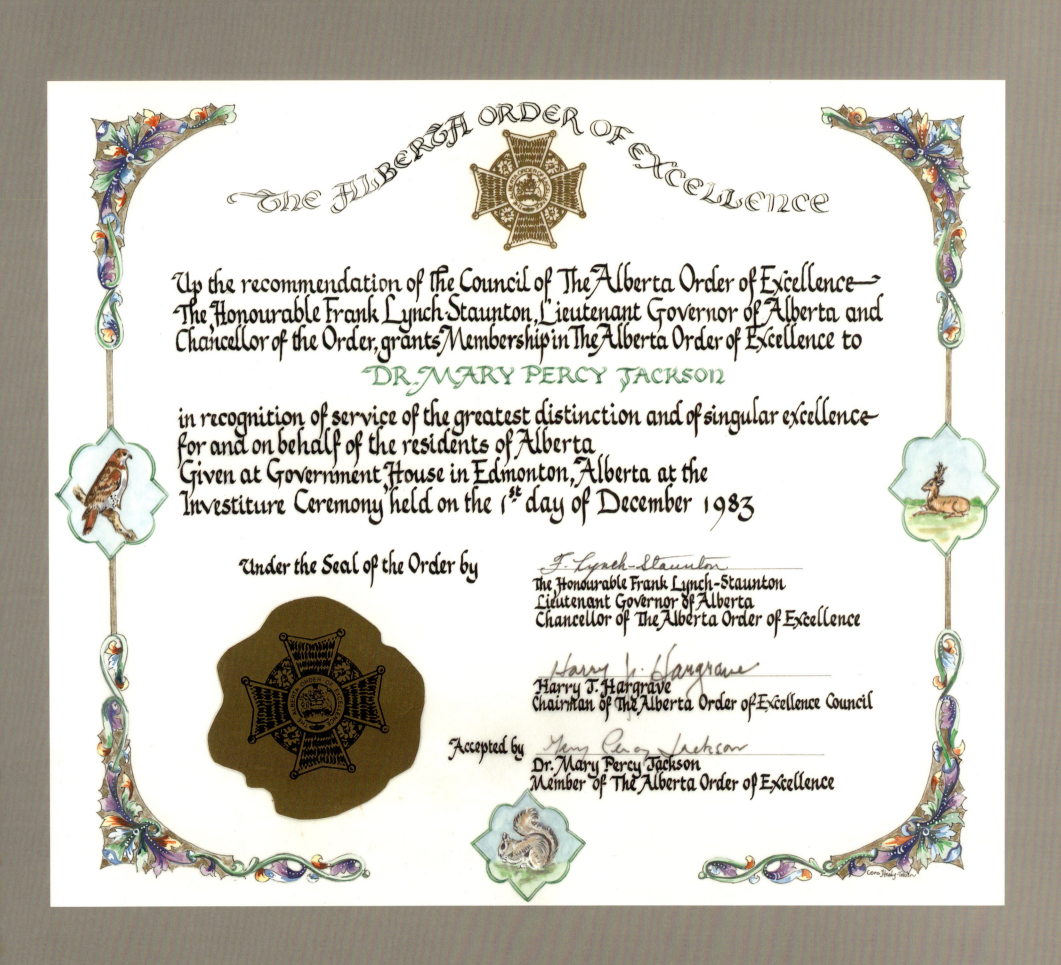

THE ALBERTA ORDER OF EXCELLENCE

Up the recommendation of the Council of The Alberta Order of Excellence—
The Honourable Frank Lynch-Staunton, Lieutenant Governor of Alberta and
Chancellor of the Order, grants Membership in The Alberta Order of Excellence to

DR. MARY PERCY JACKSON

in recognition of service of the greatest distinction and of singular excellence
for and on behalf of the residents of Alberta
Given at Government House in Edmonton, Alberta at the
Investiture Ceremony held on the 1st day of December 1983

Under the Seal of the Order by

F. Lynch-Staunton
The Honourable Frank Lynch-Staunton
Lieutenant Governor of Alberta
Chancellor of The Alberta Order of Excellence

Harry J. Hargrave
Harry J. Hargrave
Chairman of The Alberta Order of Excellence Council

Accepted by *Mary Percy Jackson*
Dr. Mary Percy Jackson
Member of The Alberta Order of Excellence

Dr. Chester A. Ronning

Inducted: 1983

CHESTER ALVIN RONNING WAS BORN IN CHINA in 1894, the second of seven children. His parents were Lutheran missionaries who set up a mission in China and served there for 11 years. Chester Ronning and his brothers and sisters grew up speaking Chinese. The family left China on furlough in 1899, narrowly missing being caught in the Boxer Rebellion.

They spent time in Norway and Iowa, after which they passed through Canada on their way back to China. In Calgary, they met a group of Norwegian settlers who had taken homesteads at a place called Bardo. The Ronnings decided to purchase some land for a future home, and they returned from China to that homestead six years later. After living at Bardo for five years, the family moved to the Peace River country where Chester met Inga Horte whom he married in 1918.

In 1921, Chester Ronning, his wife Inga and their daughter Sylvia set out for China, where he had accepted a position as Principal of a teacher's school in Fracheng, his childhood home. They stayed for six years, returning to Alberta in 1927. Dr. Ronning became principal of Camrose Lutheran College, and the next 15 years were spent there. The Ronnings built their home a few blocks from the College and raised six children. Pursuing his interest in the arts, Chester Ronning took up painting, and sculpting, and also directed several choirs.

During the Second World War, he left his post at the College to become head of the discrimination unit of Royal Canadian Air Force Intelligence. When the war ended, he was asked to go to China to help Canada's Ambassador to Chungking. In 1945, he arrived in China, followed a year and a half later by his wife and four children. His family stayed for two years, but he remained there, serving as Ambassador until his departure in 1951.

He became head of the American and Far Eastern Division in the Department of External Affairs, was then appointed Ambassador to Norway and Iceland, and in 1956, he was sent to India as High Commissioner. He also served as Acting Head of Delegations to the Geneva Conferences on Korea in 1954, on Laos in 1961 and 1962, and as Special Envoy to Hanoi and Saigon in 1966, where he attempted to negotiate an end to the Vietnam War.

In a difficult period covering a quarter of a century, Chester Ronning worked to bridge gaps in communications between North America and China. Because of his involvement with China over the years, he developed a unique comprehension of that country and its people, and constantly strove for better understanding between East and West.

Dr. Ronning graduated from the University of Alberta in 1916 with a BSc degree in education, and worked towards a MA degree during the 1930s. He was awarded Honorary Degrees from the Universities of Alberta, Calgary, Lethbridge, Waterloo, and Simon Fraser, and St. Olaf's College in Minnesota. He was a life member of the Alberta Teachers Association. In Camrose, a school was named for him, and in India, three places commemorated his name.

He was designated an Officer of the Order of Canada in 1967 and became a Companion of the Order of Canada in 1972.

In October of 1983, Dr. Ronning and five of his children visited China where they were honoured at a banquet in the Great Hall of the People, and at his birthplace of Fencheng there was a gala birthday party celebrating his 90th year.

Dr. Ronning is now deceased.

THE ALBERTA ORDER OF EXCELLENCE

Upon the recommendation of the Council of The Alberta Order of Exellence The Honouralbe Frank Lynch-Staunton, Lieutenant Governor of Alberta and Chancellor of the Order, grants Membership in The Alberta Order of Excellence to

DR. CHESTER A. RONNING o.c., c.c.

in recognition of service of the greatest distinction and of singular excellence for and on behalf of the residents of Alberta
Given at Government House in Edmonton, Alberta at the Investiture Ceremony held on the 1st day of December, 1983

Under the Seal of the Order by

F. Lynch-Staunton
The Honourable Frank Lynch-Staunton
Lieutenant Governor of Alberta
Chancellor of The Alberta Order of Excellence

Harry J. Hargrave
Harry J. Hargrave
Chairman of the Council of The Alberta Order of Excellence

Accepted by

Chester Alvin Ronning
Dr. Chester A. Ronning O.C., C.C.
Member of The Alberta Order of Excellence

Dr. Alexander Johnston

Inducted: 1984

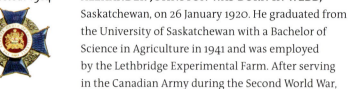

ALEXANDER JOHNSTON WAS BORN IN WEBB, Saskatchewan, on 26 January 1920. He graduated from the University of Saskatchewan with a Bachelor of Science in Agriculture in 1941 and was employed by the Lethbridge Experimental Farm. After serving in the Canadian Army during the Second World War, he completed a Masters of Science at the University of Montana in 1954. Dr. Johnston then returned to Lethbridge to work as a research scientist at the Canada Agriculture Research Station, where he served until his retirement in 1981.

Dr. Johnston's research activity was in the field of range management. His studies of the effects of cattle grazing on the vast natural grasslands of Alberta led to the development of new management techniques, designed to maintain this vital natural resource for the benefit of all Albertans.

Dr. Johnston's research results were published in more than 100 scientific and popular articles. He was highly regarded by cattle producers, land administrators and wildlife supporters for his sound approach to resource management.

His success in interpreting and applying research results gave him an international reputation and recognition as a leading authority on range management in North America. He acted as an advisor on range research across the Canadian Prairies, the Yukon, Newfoundland and Pakistan.

From October 1961 to November 1962, Dr. Johnston fulfilled an assignment as range improvement advisor to the Government of West Pakistan. He travelled extensively in Pakistan, India and Iran and developed an intimate knowledge of the local problems of range livestock production. He classified the grass cover of the country, consolidated the available information on range management, and prepared a *Handbook of Range Research for West Pakistan*. In recognition of his contribution, he was given a special award by the Secretary of Agriculture for West Pakistan.

Dr. Johnston also studied the history of agricultural development in Western Canada. This study contributed greatly to the formulation of recommendations for agricultural practices that would avoid or correct mistakes of the past. His talent for recognizing and relating significant historical events gained him a reputation as one of Alberta's finest amateur historians.

He was actively involved with the Alberta Historical Society and served on the Public Advisory Committee on the Conservation of Historical and Archeological Resources, the Historic Sites Advisory Committee, the Alberta Historical Resources Foundation and the Alberta Museums Association.

Dr. Johnston concentrated his efforts on the history of Southern Alberta. He was able to find traces of the old Whoop-Up Trail, and by following up on this he became an expert in locating the various camps and forts of the American whiskey traders. He wrote about Southern Alberta's whiskey trade, the Indian Battle at the Belly River, the Blackfoot Indian utilization of the flora of the Northwestern Great Plains, the Horses of the Blackfoot, Indian lore, and the history of the rangelands of Western Canada.

He was a recognized authority on the historical use of native plants by Canadian Aboriginals. In acknowledgement of his contribution to the recording of Aboriginal history, he was inducted as an Honorary Indian Chief into the Kainai Chieftainship and given the name of Rainy Chief (Sotaina).

Dr. Johnston was a fellow of the Agricultural Institute of Canada, a fellow of the Society of Range Management, and an honorary life member of the Western Stock Growers Association. In 1976, he was awarded an Honorary Doctorate (LLD) from the University of Lethbridge.

Dr. Johnston is now deceased.

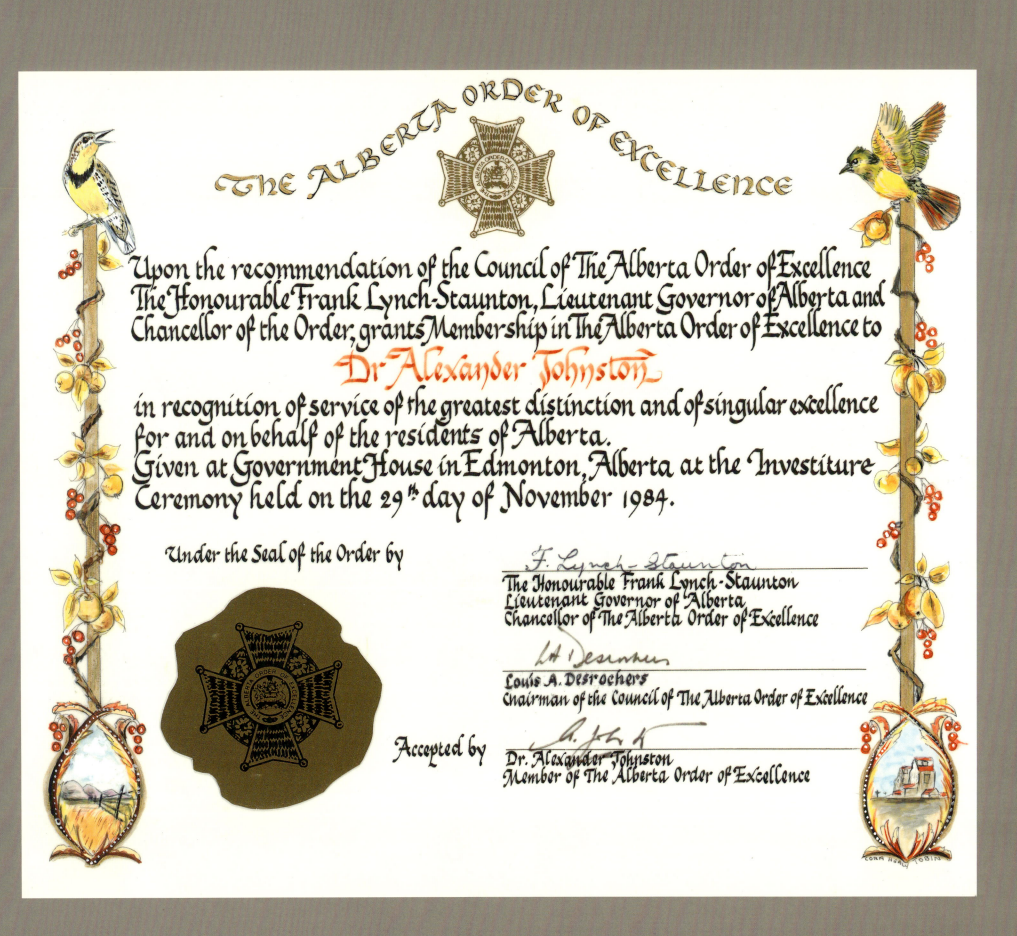

THE ALBERTA ORDER OF EXCELLENCE

Upon the recommendation of the Council of The Alberta Order of Excellence
The Honourable Frank Lynch-Staunton, Lieutenant Governor of Alberta and
Chancellor of the Order, grants Membership in The Alberta Order of Excellence to

Dr Alexander Johnston

in recognition of service of the greatest distinction and of singular excellence
for and on behalf of the residents of Alberta.
Given at Government House in Edmonton, Alberta at the Investiture
Ceremony held on the 29ᵗʰ day of November 1984.

Under the Seal of the Order by

F. Lynch-Staunton
The Honourable Frank Lynch-Staunton
Lieutenant Governor of Alberta
Chancellor of The Alberta Order of Excellence

Louis A. Desrochers
Louis A. Desrochers
Chairman of the Council of The Alberta Order of Excellence

Accepted by

A. Johnston
Dr. Alexander Johnston
Member of The Alberta Order of Excellence

CORA HEALY TOBIN

The Honourable Ronald Martland

Inducted: 1984

RONALD MARTLAND, ONLY THE SECOND Albertan ever to be appointed to the Supreme Court of Canada, served on the court for 24 years prior to his retirement in February 1982 at the mandatory age of 75.

Born in Liverpool, England, in 1909, he came to Edmonton with his parents in 1911. His father was for many years an architect for the City of Edmonton. After attending public and high school in Edmonton, he attended the University of Alberta, where he obtained a BA degree in 1926 and an LLB degree in 1928. During his years in the Faculty of Law, he obtained first class standing every year, won the Carswell Prize for leading his class and on graduation won Chief Justice Harvey's Gold Medal.

In his final year, he was selected as the Rhodes Scholar from Alberta and spent the next three years at Hertford College, Oxford, obtaining a BA degree (first class) in 1930 and a BCL degree (first class) in 1931. At the same time, he became the first Canadian to be awarded the Vinerian Law Prize, the highest academic award granted in the Oxford Faculty of Law. While at Oxford, he also found time to play on the University hockey team.

On returning to Edmonton, he was articled to the late H. R. Milner, QC and was called to the Bar of Alberta in 1932.

During the ensuing years, he became one of the leading counsels in Alberta and participated in a number of the leading cases in the province. These led to appearances before the Supreme Court of Canada and the Privy Council in Britain, which until 1949 was the highest court of appeal for Canada. During his years of practice in Alberta, he took an active part in the affairs of the Law Society of Alberta, serving as a bencher from 1948 to 1958. He was also appointed an honorary bencher.

Mr. Martland was appointed to the Supreme Court of Canada in January 1958, and his length of service matches that of many of the longest-serving Justices. During his term, he participated in more than 1700 cases, wrote the judgement of the court or the majority judgement in some 230 cases, concurring judgements in more than 70 cases and dissenting judgements in more than 40 cases.

Mr. Martland was made a Companion of the Order of Canada in 1982. He received honorary degrees from the University of Alberta and the University of King's College, Nova Scotia.

He was an honorary professor of Law at the Universities of Alberta and Calgary and was an Honorary Fellow of Hertford College, Oxford.

Mr. Martland was an active member of the Anglican Church of Canada and during his days in Edmonton served as chancellor of the Anglican Diocese of Athabasca. Later, while a member of the Supreme Court, he served as chancellor of the Anglican Diocese of Ottawa.

Mr. Martland is now deceased.

THE ALBERTA ORDER OF EXCELLENCE

Upon the recommendation of the Council of The Alberta Order of Excellence The Honourable Frank Lynch-Staunton, Lieutenant Governor of Alberta and Chancellor of the Order, grants Membership in The Alberta Order of Excellence to

Honourable Ronald Martland cc.q.c.

in recognition of service of the greatest distinction and of singular excellence for and on behalf of the residents of Alberta.
Given at Government House in Edmonton, Alberta at the Investiture Ceremony held on the 29ᵗʰ day of November, 1984.

Under the Seal of the Order by

F. Lynch-Staunton
The Honourable Frank Lynch-Staunton
Lieutenant Governor of Alberta
Chancellor of The Alberta Order of Excellence

Louis Desrochers
Louis A. Desrochers Q.C.
Chairman of the Council of The Alberta Order of Excellence

Accepted by

Ronald Martland
Honourable Ronald Martland
Member of The Alberta Order of Excellence

Dr. David S.R. Leighton

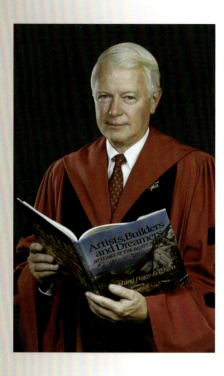

Inducted: 1985

DR. DAVID S.R. LEIGHTON WAS BORN IN REGINA, Saskatchewan, on 20 February 1928 and attended school in Regina, Calgary and Ottawa.

He obtained his BA from Queen's University, and an MBA with High Distinction as well as a DBA from Harvard University.

On 1 July 1970, Dr. Leighton became director of the Banff Centre. Over the next 12 years, he guided the Centre through a period of unprecedented growth. Under his leadership, a master plan was developed and executed in order to enhance the role of this unique institution that encourages the advancement of Canadian cultural and professional life.

Concentrating on intensive residential training of a practical, non-degree nature, the School of Fine Arts, School of Management and Conference Services all seek to meet national and international standards of excellence, while continuing to serve the people of Alberta and beyond in the areas of fine arts, management studies, arts management, environmental studies and educational conferences.

Author of a number of books on marketing and editor of business publications, Dr. Leighton, with his wife Peggy, researched and wrote Artists, Builders, and dreams—50 years at the Banff School, which was published in 1982 to commemorate the Centre's 50th Anniversary. In this book, Dr. Leighton says: "In its fiftieth year, the Banff Centre presents a picture of glowing health. It boasts excellent people at every level and in all departments. Its facilities are first class, and it is financially sound. Standards have risen, and with them our reputation internationally."

"In many respects, the story of the Banff Centre reflects Canada's cultural development. As our nation has matured, so have the arts, and the Banff School has played an important part in that process. The history of the Centre is, above all, the story of individuals, men and women with a common purpose; to create on a mountainside overlooking the Bow Valley in the Rocky Mountains a school to foster the flowering and maturing of the arts and management in Canada and around the world. These individuals comprise a brilliant parade of artists, builders and dreamers who shared a vision and made it come true."

He was awarded an Honorary Doctor of Laws, LLD, in 1972 from the University of Windsor for his contribution to the fields of business and the arts.

Dr. Leighton has served on boards of several national businesses, professional and public interest organizations. He has held teaching appointments at Harvard University, the University of Western Ontario, Stanford University, Emmanuel College, Cambridge, England, the University of Lausanne, University of Tel Aviv and the University of London, England.

THE ALBERTA ORDER OF EXCELLENCE

Upon the recommendation of the Council of the Alberta Order of Excellence
The Honourable W. Helen Hunley, Lieutenant-Governor of Alberta
and Chancellor of the Order, grants Membership in the Order to

Dr. David S. R. Leighton

in recognition of service of the greatest distinction and of singular
excellence for or on behalf of the residents of Alberta

Given at Government House at Edmonton, Alberta
on the 28th day of November 1985

Under the Seal of the Order by

The Honourable W. Helen Hunley
Lieutenant-Governor of Alberta and
Chancellor of the Alberta Order of Excellence

The Honourable Mr. Justice Howard Irving
Chairman, Alberta Order of Excellence Council

Accepted by

Dr. David S.R. Leighton
The Alberta Order of Excellence

Dr. G. Richard A. Rice

Inducted: 1985

DR. GEORGE RICHARD AGAR RICE was born in Teddington, Middlesex, England on 24 January 1901. He came to Canada in 1919 and by 1922 was operating one of Alberta's first radio stations, CJCA Edmonton. His "Hello to the North" radio service in the 1920s is a classic in Canadian Broadcasting.

In 1934, Dr. Rice started Sunwapta Broadcasting Ltd. with the operation of radio station CFRN Edmonton. FM was added in 1951, followed by the launching of CFRN Television in 1954. In 1964, FM licensing was completed for full stereo broadcasting by CKXM.

Dr. Rice was the first Canadian broadcaster to establish yearly scholarships for Canadian journalism students through the Radio Television News Directors Association, and he also established other scholarships for promising young Canadians in the Arts through the Banff School of Fine Arts and the Montréal School of Fine Arts.

His ongoing contributions in the field of broadcasting were formally recognized in 1976 with the presentation of the Ted Rogers/Velma Rogers Graham Award, honouring "the individual making the most significant contribution to the Canadian broadcasting system."

Extremely active in community activities, Dr. Rice served three terms on the University of Alberta Senate and was general chairman in 1969 for the $25 million fundraising campaign for the three Alberta Universities. He was chairman of the Board of Alberta's Government House Foundation and was a founding subscriber and honorary director of Canada's Aviation Hall of Fame. Dr. Rice was also a strong and consistent supporter of the arts, education, health and welfare, and youth organizations in the province.

He received numerous honours, such as Honorary Doctor of Laws (LLD), University of Alberta, 1965; first Premier's Award for Service in 1977; Award for contributions to the Arts from the Financial Post and the Canadian Conference of Arts and Council for Business and the Arts 1980; Canadian Business Leader of the Year Award from the Faculty of Business, University of Alberta, 1982.

In 1984, Dr. Rice was appointed a Member of the Order of Canada, received the Western Broadcaster's Award for Broadcaster of the Half Century and was named to the Canadian Broadcast Hall of Fame.

During his active and dynamic role as president of Sunwapta Broadcasting Ltd., Dr. Rice still found time to pursue his lifetime interest in theatre and entertainment.

Dr. Rice is now deceased.

THE ALBERTA ORDER OF EXCELLENCE

Upon the recommendation of the Council of the Alberta Order of Excellence The Honourable W. Helen Hunley, Lieutenant-Governor of Alberta and Chancellor of the Order, grants Membership in the Order to

Dr. G. Richard A. Rice, C.M.

in recognition of service of the greatest distinction and of singular excellence for or on behalf of the residents of Alberta

Given at Government House at Edmonton, Alberta on the 28th day of November 1985

Under the Seal of the Order by

The Honourable W. Helen Hunley
Lieutenant-Governor of Alberta
Chancellor of the Alberta Order of Excellence

The Honourable Mr. Justice Howard Irving
Chairman, Alberta Order of Excellence Council

Accepted by

Dr. G. Richard A. Rice, C.M.
The Alberta Order of Excellence

Dr. Winnifred M. Stewart

Inducted: 1985

WINNIFRED STEWART WAS BORN on 26 June 1908 in Fernie, British Columbia, and moved to Edmonton in 1911. After high school, she entered nurse's training and graduated from Edmonton General Hospital as a Registered Nurse.

The name Winnifred Stewart is synonymous with helping mentally handicapped children. For thousands of families, she helped turn despair, frustration and social stigma into hope, understanding and community acceptance.

Motivated by a desire to help her son Parker Stewart, who was born with severe disabilities, she devoted 20 years to experimental research work into new teaching methods. Under her methods, Parker Stewart achieved a level of development that was previously considered impossible. Dr. Stewart became convinced that schools for the mentally handicapped were both practical and essential.

In 1953, she met with other parents and formed what is now known as the Winnifred Stewart Association for the Mentally Handicapped. It was the first school of its kind in Canada.

In 1954, Dr. Stewart was the first woman to address the Alberta Legislature from the floor of the House. This resulted in the first recognition by a government in Canada to provide financial aid to schools for mentally handicapped children. The following year she became the driving force in establishing Canada's first association for teachers of the mentally handicapped and was instrumental in founding an Alberta association for mentally handicapped children.

During the period from 1954 to 1970, Winnifred Stewart organized and founded schools in 19 communities across Western Canada. All these schools use the curriculum and teaching methods developed by Dr. Stewart for which she is internationally recognized. She sent information to interested groups as far away as Moscow, Russia.

In 1956, Dr. Stewart was chosen by the Mental Health Association as the one person who had contributed the most to child welfare and health in Alberta, and in 1956 she was named Edmonton's Citizen of the Year.

The year 1968 saw the opening of the Western Industrial Research Training Centre, a multi-million dollar institution serving the mentally handicapped. This centre was unique in North America and was inspired by Winnifred Stewart.

Dr. Stewart worked closely with the University of Alberta, providing a practical workshop for research projects. She also established a working relationship with 45 school divisions within the province with children attending the Winnifred Stewart School. Persevering in urging the Edmonton Association to establish a Vocational Training Sheltered Workshop for the mentally handicapped, Dr. Stewart saw the realization of that dream with the opening of Cerwood Industries in 1979.

In 1972, Winnifred Stewart was named an Officer of the Order of Canada, and in the same year received an Honorary Doctor of Laws (LLD) from the University of Alberta.

Dr. Stewart is now deceased.

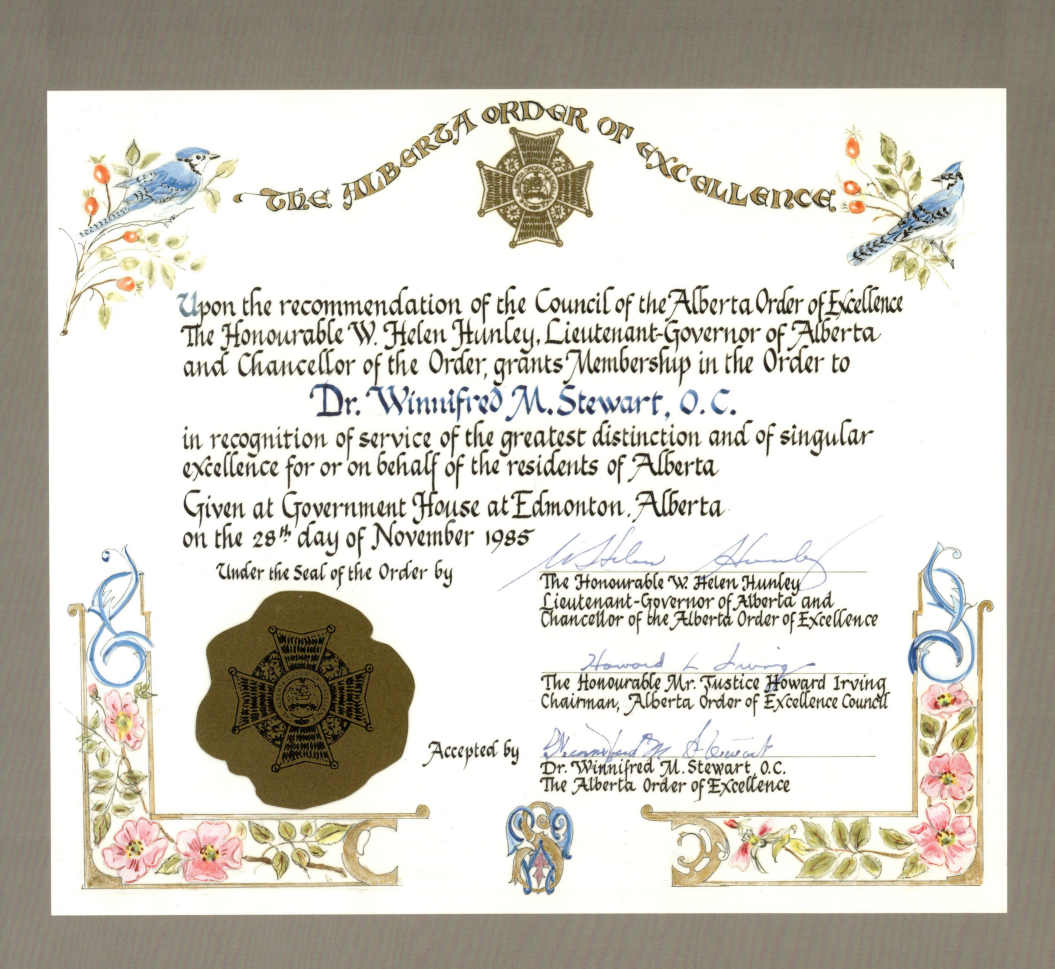

THE ALBERTA ORDER OF EXCELLENCE

Upon the recommendation of the Council of the Alberta Order of Excellence The Honourable W. Helen Hunley, Lieutenant-Governor of Alberta and Chancellor of the Order, grants Membership in the Order to

Dr. Winnifred M. Stewart, O.C.

in recognition of service of the greatest distinction and of singular excellence for or on behalf of the residents of Alberta

Given at Government House at Edmonton, Alberta on the 28th day of November 1985

Under the Seal of the Order by

The Honourable W. Helen Hunley
Lieutenant-Governor of Alberta and
Chancellor of the Alberta Order of Excellence

The Honourable Mr. Justice Howard Irving
Chairman, Alberta Order of Excellence Council

Accepted by

Dr. Winnifred M. Stewart O.C.
The Alberta Order of Excellence

Dr. John Carter Callaghan

Inducted: 1986

JOHN CARTER CALLAGHAN WAS BORN in Hamilton, Ontario, in 1923. As a child, he was fascinated by the structure and function of the human body. One of his most treasured possessions was a copy of *Gray's Anatomy*. At the age of 14, John Callaghan was busily dissecting animal hearts and lungs purchased from the local butcher shop. Predictably, his interest led him to the study of medicine and he graduated from the University of Toronto in 1946 as an MD.

He spent a year as Junior Rotating Intern at Toronto General Hospital before becoming demonstrator in Anatomy at the University and part-time Medical Officer at Lynhurst Lodge, Toronto. From 1948 to 1949, he was Medical Officer for the Department of Indian and Eskimo Affairs at Aklavik, NWT, then became a Research Fellow at the Banting Institute in Toronto. With Dr. W.G. Bigelow, Dr. Callaghan developed a method of hypothermia that is now routinely used in all open-heart surgery.

During 1949 to 1950, Dr. Callaghan was the co-developer of the world's first cardiac pacemaker, an intravenous device that has restored the rhythm of the slow or uneven heartbeat of millions of people all over the world enabling them to lead normal lives.

In 1950, he became senior intern at Sunnybrook Hospital in Toronto. From 1951 to 1954, he was Assistant Resident in Surgery, Assistant Resident, Senior Resident and Fellow in Cardiac Surgery at Toronto General Hospital, after which he went to England as Assistant to Sir Russell Brock at Guy's Hospital in London. In 1955, Dr. Callaghan was appointed Fellow in Surgery by Stanford University and moved to the University of Alberta where he became lecturer in Surgery. In 1958, he was appointed assistant clinical professor of Surgery and head of the Division of Cardiovascular and Thoracic Surgery.

In 1956, Dr. Callaghan performed a number of Canadian firsts in heart surgery, including the first open-heart surgery and the first successful complete repair of the blue baby malformation. He was responsible for developments in open-heart surgery that received international acclaim, and the high level of his abilities in the field of cardiovascular surgery resulted in operations that saved many lives.

Dr. Callaghan was an examiner in the Specialty of Cardiovascular Surgery for the Royal College of Physicians of Canada, and past president of the Canadian Society of Cardiovascular and Thoracic Surgeons. He was also past president of the Western Thoracic Surgical Association, an American society of chest and heart surgeons, and is past president of the prestigious Lyman Brewer III International Surgical Society. As president of this Society in 1981, Dr. Callaghan headed a group of prominent surgeons to inaugurate the first international heart and thoracic meeting ever held in the People's Republic of China.

Among the honours received by Dr. Callaghan include the Lister Prize in Surgery and the Reeve Prize in Surgical Research from the University of Toronto, 1949–1950; the Alberta Achievement Award for Excellence in medical research from the Government of Alberta, 1983; Citizen of the Year, City of Edmonton, 1984; Honorary Chairman, Alberta Heart Foundation, 1984; Distinguished Scientist Award, North American Society of Pacing and Electrophysiology, 1985; Officer of the Order of Canada, 1985.

In September 1986, Dr. Callaghan retired from his position at the University of Alberta Hospital as Head of the Division of Cardiovascular and Thoracic Surgery.

Dr. John Carter Callaghan used his exceptional skill to save lives and improve the quality of life for millions of people. His contribution to mankind is of global significance and the impact of his work will continue to benefit many future generations.

Dr. Callaghan is now deceased.

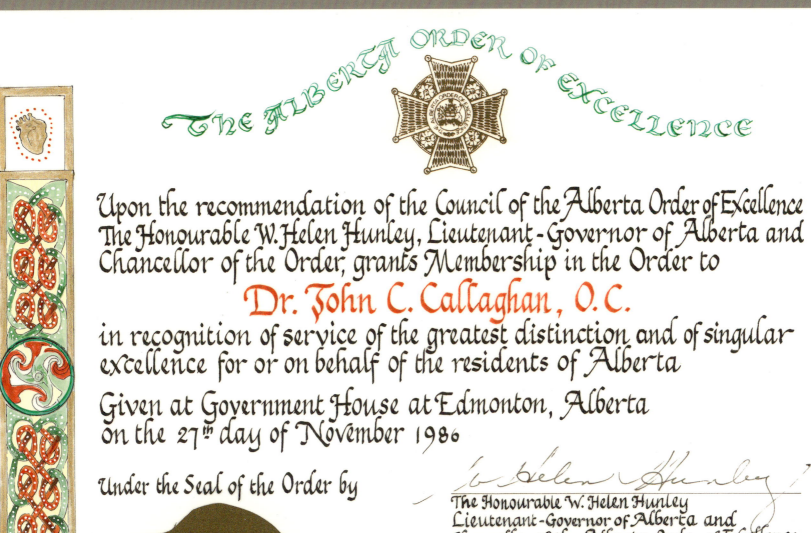

THE ALBERTA ORDER OF EXCELLENCE

Upon the recommendation of the Council of the Alberta Order of Excellence The Honourable W. Helen Hunley, Lieutenant-Governor of Alberta and Chancellor of the Order, grants Membership in the Order to

Dr. John C. Callaghan, O.C.

in recognition of service of the greatest distinction and of singular excellence for or on behalf of the residents of Alberta

Given at Government House at Edmonton, Alberta on the 27th day of November 1986

Under the Seal of the Order by

The Honourable W. Helen Hunley
Lieutenant-Governor of Alberta and
Chancellor of the Alberta Order of Excellence

The Honourable Mr. Justice Howard Irving
Chairman Alberta Order of Excellence Council

Accepted by

Dr. John C. Callaghan, O.C. Member
The Alberta Order of Excellence

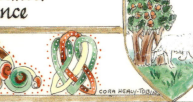

CORA HEALY-TOBIN

Leonard Kane Haney

Inducted: 1986

LEONARD KANE HANEY WAS BORN on 26 August 1915 in Picture Butte. Graduating from the Olds School of Agriculture in 1937, he embarked on his registered seed production business.

A frequent visitor to the Lethbridge Research Station, Mr. Haney was highly regarded for his major role in the exchange of information between scientists and the agriculture industry, and for his assistance in formulating plant breeding objectives. With the successful conclusion of a breeding program and the release of a new crop variety, he was often instrumental in arranging for multiplication of the seed, either through his own commercial enterprise or by other seed growers.

As a leading member of the Canadian Seed Growers Association, Mr. Haney played a prominent role in publicizing the importance of using seed of high physical and genetic purity in commercial crop production. Canadian pedigreed seed supports a commercial grain production system that is based on integrity and has given Canada a worldwide reputation as a supplier of high-quality grains.

Leonard Haney exemplified this integrity that is now taken for granted in the seed industry. He has encouraged other growers to enhance their proficiency by arranging visits to research institutions for field demonstrations and discussions on plant breeding objectives. His home farm has been host to many visiting foreign delegations, often including world political leaders. In 1985, he went to Russia as a representative on a mission to promote Alberta products and technologies.

In 1969, Mr. Haney was made a Robertson Associate of the Canadian Seed Growers Association, the highest honour any seed grower can achieve, and in 1984 he was presented with the Outstanding Service Award by the Alberta Branch of the Canadian Seed Growers Association. In 1974, he became an executive member of the Canadian Seed Growers Association and was national president from 1981 to 1983.

Mr. Haney has been an active member of the community at large, giving of his time and energetic effort in various capacities to Education, Church, Civic and Service organizations. He has served as county councillor, School Board chairman, as well as chairman of the Zone 6 School Trustees Association, and has been a member of the Senate and the Board of Governors of the University of Lethbridge.

He received the Distinguished Service Award from the Council on School Administration of the Alberta Teachers Association in 1969 and was named Life Member of the Alberta School Trustees Association in 1970. He was appointed to the Olds College Hall of Fame in 1974 and accorded a Life Membership in the Alumni Association. In 1985, he was named Businessman of the Year by the Picture Butte and District Chamber of Commerce.

THE ALBERTA ORDER OF EXCELLENCE

Upon the recommendation of the Council of the Alberta Order of Excellence
The Honourable W. Helen Hunley, Lieutenant-Governor of Alberta and
Chancellor of the Order, grants Membership in the Order to

Leonard K. Haney

in recognition of service of the greatest distinction and of singular
excellence for or on behalf of the residents of Alberta

Given at Government House at Edmonton, Alberta
on the 27th day of November 1986.

Under the Seal of the Order by

(signature)

The Honourable W. Helen Hunley
Lieutenant Governor of Alberta and Chancellor
of the Alberta Order of Excellence

(signature)

The Honourable Mr. Justice Howard Irving,
Chairman, Alberta Order of Excellence Council

Accepted by _(signature)_

Mr. Leonard Haney, Member
The Alberta Order of Excellence

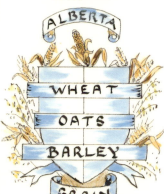

ALBERTA
WHEAT
OATS
BARLEY
GRAIN

PEDIGREE EDUCATION
FEED RESEARCH

HANEY

CORA HEALY-TOBIN

Herbert Thomas Hargrave

Inducted: 1986

HERBERT THOMAS (BERT) HARGRAVE WAS BORN in 1917 in Medicine Hat and grew up on the family ranch at Walsh. After graduating from high school, he worked and saved for two years in order to begin first-year studies in Agriculture at the University of Alberta.

As a result of the summers spent as a student at the Swift Current Experimental Station, he made a decision to transfer to the University of Saskatchewan and graduated with his Bachelor of Science in Agricultural Engineering in 1942.

Mr. Hargrave served his country for four years in the Canadian Army as a captain in command of 250 mechanics in the Royal Canadian Electrical and Mechanical Engineers. In 1944, he was named a Member of the British Empire (MBE) for distinguished service in overseeing the modification of Sherman Tanks into troop-carrying "Kangaroos" used for the breakout from the Normandy beachhead. In 1984, he was invited to Normandy by Canada's Minister of Defense to take part in the 40th Anniversary of D-Day.

In 1945, Mr. Hargrave returned to the ranch at Walsh to help his father who was in failing health and in 1948 took over the entire operation. He spent the rest of his life maintaining and developing the simple facts and philosophies of living in harmony with the environment that were taught to him by his father.

He was a longstanding member of the Western Stock Growers Association, served as president and member of the Board of Governors and in 1984 was named an honorary life director. An active member and executive member of the Alberta Cattle Commission and the Canadian Cattleman's Association, Mr. Hargrave was honoured as the 1982 Canadian Cattleman of the Year. The Northern Institute of Livestock Exhibitions, an international organization centered in Billings, Montana, named Mr. Hargrave Cattleman of the Year for Western Canada in 1975.

In 1972, Bert Hargrave was elected Member of Parliament for Medicine Hat and during the following 12 years served with dedication and distinction the interests of his constituency and Canadian agriculture in general.

He became recognized as the most informed spokesman for Alberta's cattle and beef industry in the House of Commons. He served with great competence on the important Special Commons Committee on Trends in Food Prices and the Standing Committee on Agriculture. As chairman of a Committee on Beef Imports, he was instrumental in bringing into existence the Beef Import Act. Highly respected for his knowledge and gentlemanly approach, Mr. Hargrave's circle of friends in Ottawa included many from all parties. In recognition of his 12 years of service to southeastern Alberta, he was honoured as a Life Member of the Medicine Hat Chamber of Commerce in 1984.

Mr. Hargrave's interest in grass and rangeland care, culture and preservation was legendary, and he had a long association with the Prairie Farm Rehabilitation programs. Having dealt with drought and water supply in one of the driest regions of the prairies, his advice was sought after by farmers, associations and government agencies. In 1985, he received the Distinguished Service Award from the Canadian Water Resource Association for outstanding contributions to the development and management of water in Canada. He also received an Honorary Degree (LLD) from the University of Alberta.

Directing his energies toward the community at large, Mr. Hargrave served as a member of the Board of Governors of the University of Alberta and the University of Calgary and was a strong supporter of the Medicine Hat College. He was a member of the Senate of the University of Lethbridge and also served as a member of the National Farm Debt Review Board.

Bert Hargrave exemplified the highest standards of excellence, as a cattleman, rancher, agriculturist, parliamentarian, and as an Albertan who continually gave of himself for the betterment of society.

Mr. Hargrave is now deceased.

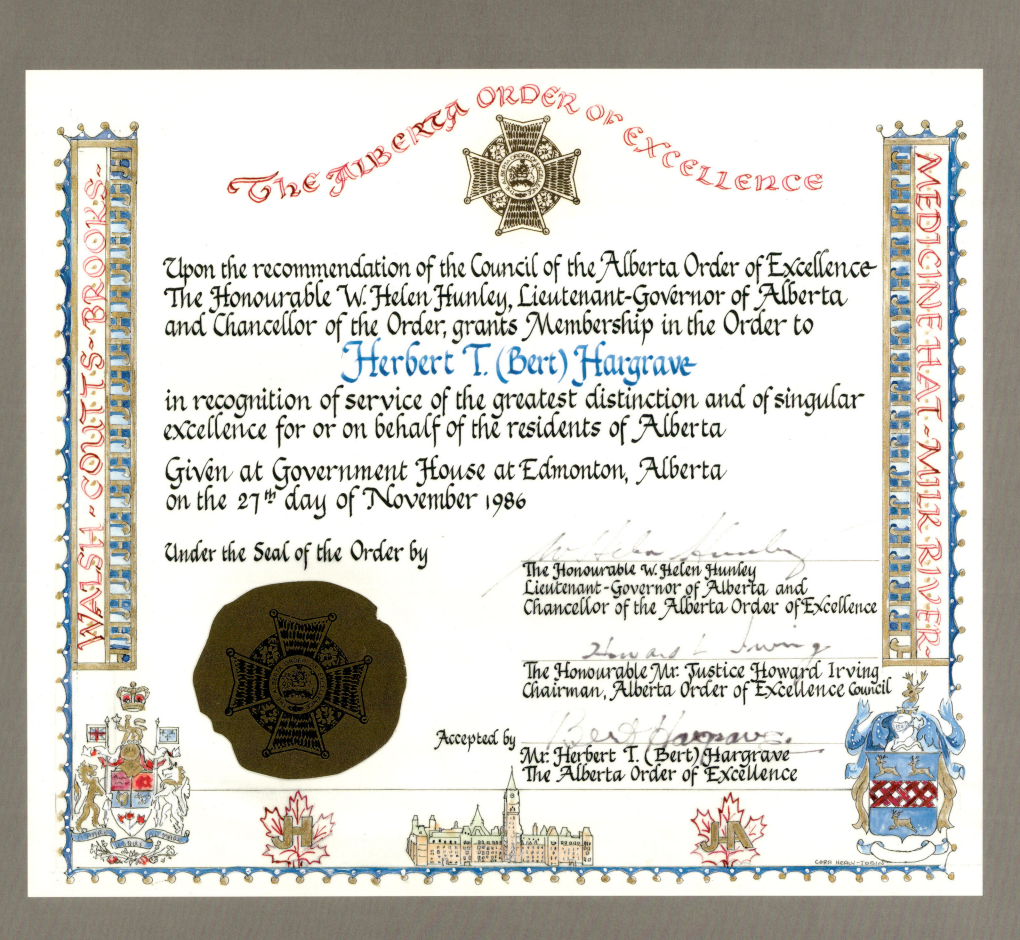

THE ALBERTA ORDER OF EXCELLENCE

WALSH · COUTTS · BROOKS ·

MEDICINE HAT · MILK RIVER ·

Upon the recommendation of the Council of the Alberta Order of Excellence The Honourable W. Helen Hunley, Lieutenant-Governor of Alberta and Chancellor of the Order, grants Membership in the Order to

Herbert T. (Bert) Hargrave

in recognition of service of the greatest distinction and of singular excellence for or on behalf of the residents of Alberta

Given at Government House at Edmonton, Alberta on the 27th day of November 1986

Under the Seal of the Order by

The Honourable W. Helen Hunley
Lieutenant-Governor of Alberta and
Chancellor of the Alberta Order of Excellence

The Honourable Mr. Justice Howard Irving
Chairman, Alberta Order of Excellence Council

Accepted by

Mr. Herbert T. (Bert) Hargrave
The Alberta Order of Excellence

CORA HEALY-TOBIN

Dr. Esther Robins

Inducted: 1986

ESTHER ROBINS WAS BORN ESTHER MANOLSON on 13 September 1933 in Calgary. She was a grand-daughter of pioneers who settled there at the turn of the century. She graduated from the Calgary Holy Cross Hospital Nursing Program with an RN in 1955.

In 1976, Dr. Robins was diagnosed with cancer and experienced numerous recurrences and remissions of the disease. After completing treatment for her second recurrence, she searched for a way to assist cancer patients who needed help in coping with the disease.

She heard of an American program called CanSurmount, a volunteer help program in which a specially trained, cured or controlled cancer patient visits another who is having difficulty in dealing with the disease. Esther Robins travelled to Denver, Colorado, in 1978 to participate in the CanSurmount training course. Returning to Calgary, she began the first Canadian CanSurmount program at the Foothills Hospital. Under her direction the program moved into other local hospitals, then spread throughout Alberta and into eight provinces across Canada.

As Co-ordinator of Alberta and Canada CanSurmount, Esther Robins criss-crossed the country many times explaining the program; training CanSurmount volunteers and their local co-ordinators in new locations; negotiating with hospital administrators and others to set up the necessary institutional support; giving in-service seminars and workshops to inform and gain support from health care professionals and others; helping to solve problems; and providing ongoing support for each fledgling group.

She was an effective leader who worked solely as a volunteer: making presentations to introduce the program, training volunteer visitors and making visits herself. Despite her own recurring illness and despite institutional red tape, her determination and faith in the program created rewarding successes.

In 1984, Esther Robins was responsible for two videotapes produced by the University of Calgary Departments of Medicine and Education and the Canadian Cancer Society.

The first production was a 50-minute training film to help standardize and ensure the quality of training given to volunteers across the country. Health care professionals and other volunteer groups could use the videotapes as a basis for discussion and as a means to better understand the purpose of CanSurmount and other self-help programs for patients and families.

The second production was a shorter videotape designed to effectively introduce CanSurmount to the widest possible audience of patients, professionals, service groups and others.

In recognition of her dedicated contribution to CanSurmount in Canada, Esther Robins was awarded the Canadian Medical Association Medal of Honour in 1982, the first non-physician to received the award. She was co-honoured with her husband for outstanding community service at the 1981 Jewish National Fund Negev Dinner, and in that same year she received an Alberta Achievement Award. In 1984, Dr. Robins was invested as a Member of the Order of Canada, and in 1985 she received an honorary Doctor of Laws degree (LLD) from the University of Calgary.

Descriptions of this remarkable individual invariably include "courageous, caring, sensitive, understanding, dynamic, charismatic, inspiring, decisive, humorous, energetic, persuasive, enthusiastic, visionary, dedicated." All of these qualities, together with a profound faith, enabled Esther Robins to take a difficult personal situation and develop it into an opportunity to help thousands of people across Canada.

Dr. Robins is now deceased.

THE ALBERTA ORDER OF EXCELLENCE

Upon the recommendation of the Council of the Alberta Order of Excellence
The Honourable W. Helen Hunley, Lieutenant-Governor of Alberta and
Chancellor of the Order, grants Membership in the Order to

Esther Robins, C.M.

in recognition of service of the greatest distinction and of singular
excellence for or on behalf of the residents of Alberta

Given at Government House at Edmonton, Alberta
on the 27th day of November 1986

Under the Seal of the Order by

The Honourable W. Helen Hunley
Lieutenant-Governor of Alberta and
Chancellor of the Alberta Order of Excellence

The Honourable Mr. Justice Howard Irving
Chairman, Alberta Order of Excellence Council

Accepted by

Mrs. Esther Robins, C.M. Member
The Alberta Order of Excellence

CORA HEALY-TOBIN.

Dr. C. Fred Bentley

Inducted: 1987

DR. C. FRED BENTLEY IS A SOIL SCIENTIST who has worked internationally in agricultural education, research and extension with an emphasis on the maintenance of agricultural lands and the expansion of food production in developing countries.

Born in 1914 in Cambridge, Massachusetts, Dr. Bentley grew up on a farm near Edmonton and attended Edmonton Normal School. He taught school for three years before entering the University of Alberta and receiving a BSc (Agriculture) and an MSc (Soil Science). His PhD, also in soil science, is from the University of Minnesota.

After serving as an instructor in Soil Science at the University of Minnesota and as an assistant professor of Soil Science at the University of Saskatchewan, Dr. Bentley returned to the University of Alberta as an assistant professor in 1946. He rose to become dean of the Faculty of Agriculture in 1959.

Ten years later, he resigned as dean to serve as the first special advisor in agriculture with the Canadian International Development Agency (CIDA) in Ottawa. On returning to Edmonton, he remained active at the University in teaching and international development assistance. In 1979, he became Professor Emeritus of Soil Science.

While Dr. Bentley has distinguished himself as an outstanding educator, he has also been a "conscience" for agriculture, both in Canada and internationally. He began his overseas work in development assistance in Sri Lanka in 1952. Over the years, he was a Team Leader for CIDA and other teams to India (1967), Sri Lanka (1979–1980), Indonesia (1980), China (1983), the Sudan (1984), sub-Saharan Africa and the Sahel Region, Africa (1985) and Pakistan (1986).

From 1972 to 1982, he was chairman of the governing board of ICRISAT (International Crops Research Institute for the Semi-Arid Tropics) in Hyderabad, India and played a major role in its development as one of the world's major international agricultural research centres.

In 1985, he established the International Board for Soil Research Management with headquarters in Bangkok, Thailand, an undertaking that attracted support from CIDA and other countries.

Dr. Bentley has been involved in establishing an agricultural university and a vocational agricultural college in Northern China; in planning a genetic resources bank for West Africa; and in providing an assessment of national agricultural research capability in the Francophone countries of West Africa. He also led a CIDA team dryland agriculture project in Pakistan and served as a consultant for Canadian government agencies, the United Nations, the World Bank and numerous private organizations.

In addition to his international work, Dr. Bentley has contributed significantly to the national scene, in particular through strong and active support to professional agricultural organizations. He received an Honorary Degree (DSc) from the University of Alberta. He is past president of the International Society of Soil Science, the Canadian Society of Soil Science, the Agricultural Institute of Canada and the Alberta Institute of Agrologists. He is a Fellow of six professional or scientific societies, including the Agricultural Institute of Canada and the Royal Society of Canada. Dr. Bentley has received numerous honorary awards from industry and government in recognition of his far-ranging contributions to agriculture.

THE ALBERTA ORDER OF EXCELLENCE

Upon the recommendation of the Council of the Alberta Order of Excellence
The Honourable W. Helen Hunley, Lieutenant-Governor of Alberta
and Chancellor of the Order, grants Membership in the Order to

Dr. C. Fred Bentley

in recognition of service of the greatest distinction and of singular
excellence for or on behalf of the residents of Alberta

Given at Government House at Edmonton, Alberta
on the 19th day of November 1987

Under the Seal of the Order by

The Honourable W. Helen Hunley
Lieutenant Governor of Alberta and
Chancellor of the Alberta Order of Excellence

The Honourable Mr. Justice Howard Irving
Chairman, Alberta Order of Excellence Council

Accepted by

Dr. C. Fred Bentley, Member
The Alberta Order of Excellence

CORA HEALY-TOBIN

Dr. James H. Gray

Inducted: 1987

DR. JAMES H. GRAY WAS BORN IN WHITEMOUTH, Manitoba, in 1906 and spent his childhood years in Winnipeg. A high school dropout, he began working as an office boy at the Winnipeg Grain Exchange when he was 16. By 1930, he was the manager of a Lethbridge stockbroker's office, but lost his job when the stock market crashed and spent the next few years on relief.

It was during this period that he started writing. By 1935, he had landed a job as a reporter with the *Winnipeg Free Press*, became an editorial writer and was appointed Ottawa correspondent for the newspaper in 1946. A disagreement with his editor on how best to market the prairie wheat crop prompted his departure from the newspaper, and he returned to the West.

Dr. Gray became a freelance correspondent for a string of eastern newspapers and became editor of the Calgary-based *Farm and Ranch Review*, and later of the *Western Oil Examiner*.

From 1958 to 1964, he was manager of public relations for Home Oil, after which he retired permanently in order to write.

In his first book, *The Winter Years*, published in 1966, Dr. Gray wrote of the Depression in Western Canada. The book was an instant success and established the beginning of a market for social history based on the western experience. A second book, a series of childhood recollections called *The Boy From Winnipeg*, was followed by *Men Against the Desert*, which chronicled the Prairie farmer's struggle to overcome wind and drought during the Depression. His book records the triumph of the farmers and scientists who painstakingly discovered how to farm the drylands successfully.

These first three books were published within three years and heralded a subsequent surge of books on Western Canada, and publishers were convinced for the first time of the market for western Canadian history.

In the early 1970s, Dr. Gray wrote *Red Lights on the Prairies*, a history of prostitution in the early years; *Booze: The Impact of Whisky on the Prairie West* an exploration of the myths and realities of the decade of prohibition on the Prairies; *The Roar of the Twenties*; *Troublemaker* (an autobiography); and *Boomtime and Bacchanalia Revisited* (1982).

A Brand of its Own: A History of the Calgary Exhibition and Stampede and *Talk to My Lawyer* followed in the mid 1980s.

Dr. Gray not only pioneered the publishing of Western Canadian social history, but is largely responsible for its more prominent inclusion in Alberta school curriculums. In the early 1980s, he won the support of former Premier Peter Lougheed, who also felt Western history was being neglected, and was one of the founders of the $6-Million Alberta Heritage Resources Education Project. The project funded the publication of 35 western Canadian histories, 11 anthologies, nine additional histories and 12 readers on specially commissioned themes.

These books were distributed to every school library in Alberta, senior citizens' homes and other institutions.

Dr. Gray sponsored Gold Medal Awards for outstanding achievement in the study of western Canadian history at six western universities and contributed privately to the University of Calgary History Department.

His books garnered numerous awards, including the 1967 Canadian Historical Society Award, the 1968 and 1975 Alberta Historical Society Awards, the 1967 Margaret McWilliams Medal and the 1971 University of British Columbia Silver Medal.

Dr. Gray received honorary doctorates from the University of Calgary, the University of Brandon and the University of Manitoba.

Dr. Gray is now deceased.

THE ALBERTA ORDER OF EXCELLENCE

Upon the recommendation of the Council of the Alberta Order of Excellence The Honourable W. Helen Hunley, Lieutenant-Governor of Alberta and Chancellor of the Order, grants Membership in the Order to

Dr. James H. Gray

in recognition of service of the greatest distinction and of singular excellence for or on behalf of the residents of Alberta

Given at Government House at Edmonton, Alberta on the 19ᵗʰ day of November 1987

Under the Seal of the Order by

W. Helen Hunley
The Honourable W. Helen Hunley
Lieutenant-Governor of Alberta and
Chancellor of the Alberta Order of Excellence

Howard Irving
The Honourable Mr. Justice Howard Irving
Chairman, Alberta Order of Excellence Council

Accepted by _James H. Gray_
Dr. James H. Gray, Member
The Alberta Order of Excellence

CORA HEALY-TOBIN

Dr. Arthur T. Jenkyns

Inducted: 1988

ARTHUR JENKYNS WAS CHAIRMAN of the Board of Operation Eyesight Universal, a Calgary-based organization that funds programs devoted to sight restoration and the prevention of blindness in 14 developing countries.

Born and educated in Winnipeg, Mr. Jenkyns was involved in the food industry with Swift Canadian for many years before entering the insurance brokerage business. He took early retirement from Marsh and McLennan Ltd. to become the first executive director of Operation Eyesight.

In 1933, Dr. Ben Gullison, a Canadian medical doctor, started what grew into a small mission hospital in Sompeta on the east coast of India. Over the next decade, the hospital began concentrating on the treatment of eye problems, with an estimated 200,000 curable blind persons within travelling distance of the hospital. In the early 1960s, Dr. Gullison undertook a fund-raising tour across Canada, explaining that thousands of blind persons had cataracts that could be easily removed, and their sight restored, for less than $10 per eye.

His address to the First Baptist Church in Calgary inspired Mr. Jenkyns and several business colleagues, who pledged one another that they would finance cataract surgery in India on an ongoing basis. Others quickly followed suit, and a neophyte Calgary support group was formed. Mr. Jenkyns ran Operation Eyesight in his spare time for 13 years, retiring in 1977 in order to work full time with the organization.

By that time, the group had raised more than $1 million for Operation Eyesight Universal and saw the work extended in India as well as Bangladesh, Nepal, Kenya, Malawi, Peru and Haiti, among other countries.

Since 1963, more than nine million people have received treatment under the program. Operation Eyesight helps finance the building and operation of modern ophthalmic clinics and hospital eye wards. These facilities are largely staffed by nationals working in their own countries, some trained by Operation Eyesight.

Since the majority of people needing eye care in developing countries are located in rural areas with no access to doctors or facilities, Operation Eyesight provides modern Mobile Eye Units, staffed by trained personnel, to examine and treat thousands of people each year in outlying districts. Where population warrants, patients are examined at eye camps, with treatment and surgery carried out in large tents or community buildings.

In addition to his international work, Mr. Jenkyns maintained a life-long affiliation with the Boy Scouts. He was honorary regional commissioner for the Calgary region, Scouts Canada. In 1971, he was decorated by the governor-general with the Silver Wolf. He received an Honorary Doctor of Laws degree from the University of Calgary and an honorary fellowship of the Academy of General Education in Manipal, India. He was made an Officer in the Order of St. John of Jerusalem.

Mr. Jenkyns is now deceased.

Margaret E. Southern

Inducted: 1988

MARGARET SOUTHERN GREW UP IN CALGARY where she excelled in a wide range of sports activities. A growing family interest in equestrian sports, coupled with a lack of facilities for Albertans wishing to compete, resulted in the Southerns building Spruce Meadows.

Spruce Meadows opened in 1975 and is considered as one of the world's finest competitive show jumping complexes.

Mrs. Southern received a degree in physical education from the University of Alberta in 1953 and won the Bakewell Trophy that year as the University's outstanding female athlete. Subsequently, she became the first woman appointed as an instructor in the University of Calgary's physical education department.

She was a founding, eight-year member of Calgary's first Parks and Recreation Board and was instrumental in the formation of Calgary's ambitious land banking program, which ensured lands for future recreational use. Mrs. Southern was influential in the creation and development of Fish Creek Park, the first provincial park within an Alberta city.

She was also a member of the original Downtown Tree Planting Committee, which planted more than 500 trees in 1975 to celebrate Calgary's centennial. She has made important contributions as a volunteer with Skate Canada and the World Skating Championships. In 1981, Alberta Recreation and Parks presented her with the Energize 81 Award in recognition of her outstanding volunteer contributions to municipal recreation development.

In 1984, she and her husband, Ron Southern, received several honours, including the Alberta Light Horse Association's Horseman of the Year Award and the federal government's Canadian Tourism Medallion, in recognition of outstanding service to Canadian and world tourism, furthering and enhancing international understanding. In 1986, they received the Calgary Booster Club's Sportsmen of the Year Award.

Mrs. Southern has held executive positions with the Alberta Equestrian Federation and the Canadian Equestrian Federation. She is former chairperson of the Business Development Committee of the Calgary Chamber of Commerce, a member of the du Maurier Council for the Arts and holds directorships with a number of major Canadian corporations.

THE ALBERTA ORDER OF EXCELLENCE

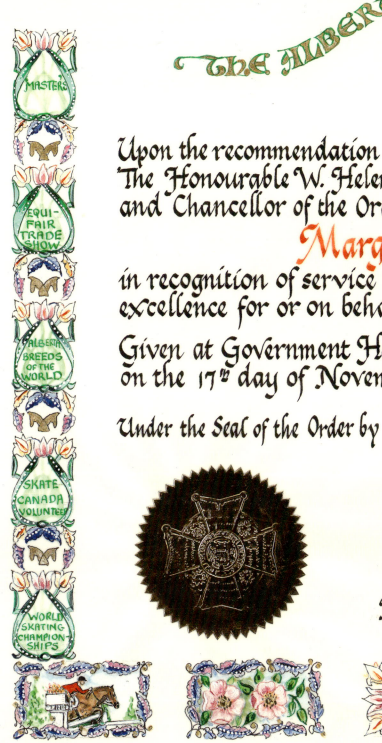

Upon the recommendation of the Council of the Alberta Order of Excellence The Honourable W. Helen Hunley, Lieutenant-Governor of Alberta and Chancellor of the Order, grants Membership in the Order to

Margaret E. Southern

in recognition of service of the greatest distinction and of singular excellence for or on behalf of the residents of Alberta

Given at Government House at Edmonton, Alberta on the 17ᵗʰ day of November 1988

Under the Seal of the Order by

The Honourable W. Helen Hunley
Lieutenant Governor of Alberta and
Chancellor of the Alberta Order of Excellence

The Honourable Mr. Justice Howard Irving
Chairman, Alberta Order of Excellence Council

Accepted by

Margaret E. Southern, Member
The Alberta Order of Excellence

The Honourable Peter Lougheed

Inducted: 1989

FOUR GENERATIONS OF ALBERTANS in the Lougheed family span the entire history of Alberta as a Canadian province. Mr. Lougheed's parents, the late Edgar Donald and Edna (Bauld) Lougheed were well-known residents of Calgary. Mr. Lougheed's grandfather, the late Senator James Lougheed, first came to Calgary when there were only a few hundred people living there. Sir James was the only Albertan ever to be knighted and was the first Conservative from Alberta to serve in a federal cabinet. The senator played a key role in the formation of Alberta as a province.

Peter Lougheed, later to become the Honourable Peter Lougheed PC, CC, QC, was born in Calgary on 26 July 1928. He was educated in Calgary public and secondary schools before attending the University of Alberta, where he received his Bachelor of Arts and Bachelor of Law degrees. Later, he graduated from Harvard University with a Master of Business Administration degree.

In business, Peter Lougheed quickly demonstrated his leadership qualities. In 1956, he joined one of Canada's largest construction firms, and by 1962 he had become General Counsel, Vice-President and an elected director of the Mannix group of companies.

Peter Lougheed's rise in public office was at least as meteoric. In 1965, at the age of 36, he was elected leader of the Progressive Conservative Party of Alberta. The party had no elected members in the provincial legislature at that time.

Less than two years later, he led his party to become the official opposition with six seats. On 30 August 1971, in a stunning upset, Peter Lougheed became premier of Alberta with his party gaining 49 of 75 seats. Alberta had been governed by the Social Credit administration for over 35 years, and the province had never before elected a Progressive Conservative government.

In each of the following elections of 1975, 1979 and 1982, the Honourable Peter Lougheed and his party increased their popular vote and their majority.

There are many accomplishments of significance to Albertans during Peter Lougheed's time in office, including the Heritage Savings Trust Fund; strengthening of small-town and rural Alberta; the Alberta Bill of Rights (his first formal act as premier); establishment of provincial rights during the repatriation of Canada's constitution; a successful defence of Alberta's natural resources; and a back-to-basics junior and senior high school curriculum.

The Honourable Peter Lougheed has been known as a champion of the interests of Western Canada, but at the same time, has clearly supported Canadian unity. His electoral support from Albertans helped him to become one of Canada's most influential leaders.

Her Majesty The Queen appointed Mr. Lougheed as a member of the Privy Council of Canada in 1982. In 1987, Mr. Lougheed was appointed a Companion of the Order of Canada. He has an Honorary Degree (LLD) from the University of Alberta.

Mr. Lougheed retired as premier and as leader of the Progressive Conservative Party of Alberta on 1 November 1985 and subsequently became a senior partner in the Bennett Jones law firm of Calgary. In addition, he became a lecturer at the University of Calgary and the Banff Centre of Management.

Throughout his life, Peter Lougheed has maintained a keen interest in sports. He played professional football with the Edmonton Eskimos, was active in all Calgary efforts to stage the Winter Olympics, was honorary chairman of the XV Olympic Games Organizing Committee and continues to participate in active sports.

In honour of his active support of the Banff Centre, along with that of Mrs. Lougheed, a new building was dedicated as the "Jeanne and Peter Lougheed Building" in 1987.

Mr. Lougheed's public life and private initiatives have had a decided and lasting effect on all Albertans.

THE ALBERTA ORDER OF EXCELLENCE

Upon the recommendation of the Council of the Alberta Order of Excellence
The Honourable W. Helen Hunley, Lieutenant-Governor of Alberta and
Chancellor of the Order grants Membership in the Order to

Honourable Peter Lougheed

in recognition of service of the greatest distinction and of singular
excellence for or on behalf of the residents of Alberta

Given at Government House at Edmonton, Alberta
on the 22nd day of November 1989

Under the Seal of the Order by

W. Helen Hunley

The Honourable W. Helen Hunley
Lieutenant-Governor of Alberta, and
Chancellor of the Alberta Order of Excellence

Howard L. Irving

The Honourable Mr. Justice Howard Irving
Chairman, Alberta Order of Excellence Council

Accepted by

Peter Lougheed

Honourable Peter Lougheed, Member
The Alberta Order of Excellence

Dr. Maxwell William Ward

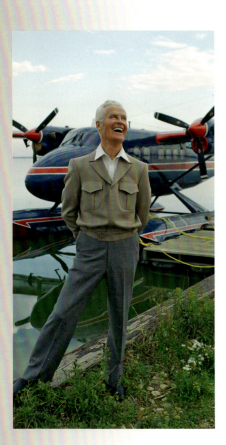

Inducted: 1989

BORN AND EDUCATED IN EDMONTON, Maxwell W. Ward joined the Royal Canadian Air Force in 1940, where he received his pilot's wings and served as a commissioned flight instructor at various Canadian bases during the Second World War.

After discharge from the RCAF in 1945, Mr. Ward flew as a bush pilot in the Northwest Territories. In 1946, he organized his own company, Polaris Charter Co. Ltd., based in Yellowknife, and with one two-passenger, single-engine Fox Moth aircraft, carried supplies and passengers throughout the sub-Arctic.

In 1953, he acquired a 14-passenger, single-engine Otter that operated on wheels, skis or floats and, duly licensed by the Canadian Transport Commission for the first time, launched Wardair Ltd. into commercial service. The Otter revolutionized bush air transport, opening up the Arctic to Wardair, which carried mining prospectors, mine machinery, medical teams, oil exploration crews, musk ox, fish and all people and things needing transportation in Northern Canada. Ward loved the Arctic and the challenges of flying into its many unmapped areas of those earlier years.

Wardair expanded steadily. Its fleet of Otters increased, and Beaver aircraft were added, then the larger Bristol Freighters, capable of carrying tractors, trucks, automobiles, powerplants, mining machinery, small buildings, oil, gasoline, cows, horses, hay, and groceries at six tons per trip. When DeHavilland built the Twin Otter and then the 4-engine Dash 7, Wardair was the first to operate them in Canada.

Wardair stepped up to 4-engine Douglas DC6AB aircraft in 1961, carrying 14-ton payloads to the then-developing airstrips in the high Arctic. The year 1962 saw the beginnings of what Wardair is today, when international passenger charter services were launched between Western Canada and the United Kingdom. A charter market was created, flying war brides and former Europeans back to the UK and Europe for a visit at a price they could afford.

In 1967, Wardair bought the first Boeing aircraft ever sold in Canada with the purchase of a 109-seat Boeing 727. This aircraft achieved the highest utilization of any 727 in the world and flew between Western Canada, Europe and the UK with a refueling stop at Sonderstrom, Greenland. This significantly cutting the DC-6 flying time from 20 to 21 hours per crossing down to 9 to 10 hours. During winter months, the aircraft flew to Hawaii and the Caribbean.

Wardair went on to purchase a 189-seat Boeing 707 in 1968 and another in 1969. In 1972, Wardair purchased its first 456-seat Boeing 747 jumbo jet.

By 1988, Wardair operated an international wide-bodied fleet of three Boeing 747–100 aircraft, three McDonnell Douglas DC-10–30 aircraft, and 12 Airbus A310–300 aircraft.

Recognized as Canada's largest international charter air carrier, Wardair offered departures to and from a variety of holiday destinations, along with scheduled flights between Canada and the UK, and within Canada.

Mr. Ward's pioneering of air transportation in the Northwest Territories has been of immeasurable value to Alberta and has maintained for this province its standing as the supply base for the western Arctic and the Yukon Territory. On the national scene, Mr. Ward was in the forefront of those urging deregulation of the airline industry.

Among the honours Max Ward has received are the following:

The Billy Mitchell Award, 1971

Companion in the Order of Icarus, 1963

The Trans-Canada McKee Trophy, considered Canada's highest award in the field of aviation, 1973

Canada's Aviation Hall of Fame, 1974

Officer in the Order of Canada, 1975

Royal Canadian Air Force Association's Gordon R. McGregor Trophy "in recognition of outstanding and meritorious achievement by Canadians in the field of air transportation," 1979

The George Orsaki "Marketing Executive of the Year" Award by Sales and Marketing Executives of Toronto, 1981

The "International Marketing Award" by the Sales and Marketing Executives International, 1986

Mr. Ward holds Honorary Doctor of Law degrees from the University of Alberta, York University, Trent University and Carleton University, and honorary doctorate degrees from Athabasca University and Lakeland University.

Dr. Raymond Lemieux

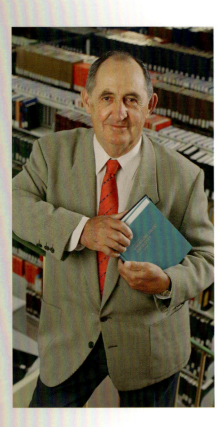

Inducted: 1990

DR. RAYMOND LEMIEUX ENJOYED a brilliant career in carbohydrate science research. He was president and research director of Raylo Chemicals, which developed ways to produce substances such as semisynthetic antibiotics, rubber-related compounds and heavy water. Chembiomed was formed to exploit Dr. Lemieux's carbohydrate chemistry research for the medical care industry, particularly in bloodbanking.

Raymond Lemieux was born in Lac La Biche in 1920. His parents homesteaded there but moved to Edmonton when he was six to enable their children to have the schooling advantages that the larger centre offered.

Chemistry was Dr. Lemieux's favourite subject in high school; he was encouraged by John Convey, a graduate student in physics, who was then courting his sister Annette. He recalls: "After examining a text book on physical chemistry at the public library...I asked John if he knew that the product of the specific heat and the atomic weight of an element is 6.4. It was a bit discouraging to learn that I had rediscovered the Dulong-Petit law, which dates back to 1819. Nevertheless, the seed for my career as a chemist was really planted then."

He entered the University of Alberta in 1939 and led his class in the freshman chemistry courses. After graduating with a BSc in Honours Chemistry in 1943, he began graduate studies at McGill University, where he obtained his PhD in Organic Chemistry in 1946.

At this time, the discovery that the antibiotic streptomycin was a carbohydrate promised a surge of activity concerned with the role of carbohydrate structures in living organisms. Dr. Lemieux won a postdoctoral scholarship at Ohio State University, where he undertook research on the structure of streptomycin, sponsored by Bristol Laboratories Inc.

"There can be no argument that this move, more than any other, set the pattern for my life as a research chemist," Dr. Lemieux commented.

He met his future wife, Virginia, at Ohio State (she was studying for a PhD degree in high-resolution infrared spectroscopy), and they were married in New York City in 1948.

Following the Ohio State work, Dr. Lemieux returned to Canada to continue what was to be a brilliant career in carbohydrate science research. He joined the University of Saskatchewan as an assistant professor for two years, then accepted a position as senior research officer with the National Research Council's Prairie Regional Laboratory in Saskatoon. There he initially investigated the use of wheat starch (because of the large wheat surplus that existed). About a year after his arrival, the NRC suggested he pursue whatever research area he desired.

"This simple vote of trust opened my way to fundamental studies of the physical and chemical properties of carbohydrates and paved my return to academia," Dr. Lemieux said.

In 1953, prior to leaving the NRC, he and a postdoctoral fellow, George Huber, announced the synthesis of sucrose to wide acclaim, and he was invited to speak at an influential seminar on the chemistry of natural products in New Brunswick, an opportunity he regards as seminal to his career.

He moved to Ottawa in 1954 to establish the Department of Chemistry and to help build the newly founded Faculty of Pure and Applied Sciences. In addition to building an exceptionally strong department "in an atmosphere of research," he established an international standing in chemistry through major contributions to the improvement of the understanding of chemical bonding and to the determination of molecular structures and shapes.

In 1961, Dr. Lemieux and his family came home to Alberta, where Harry Gunning was building a strong Department of Chemistry with world-class research facilities. Dr. Lemieux became professor and chairman of the Division of Organic Chemistry. He was appointed University Professor in 1981 and named Professor Emeritus in 1985.

While Dr. Lemieux's life work was basic research, there have been extremely significant applications of this work that are largely responsible for the nucleus of high technology industry in Alberta.

A year after his arrival in Edmonton, Dr. Lemieux founded R&L Molecular Research Ltd., which focussed on the development of semisynthetic antibiotics. This led to the establishment of Raylo Chemicals Ltd. (which subsequently purchased R&L) where Dr. Lemieux was president and research director. Raylo's main activity was the development of processes for the production of a wide range of substances, including semisynthetic antibiotics, rubber-related compounds, and heavy water for customers worldwide. In the 1960s, Raylo was the largest private sector employer of PhDs in Alberta and later spun-off founders of other high technology enterprises in Edmonton.

In 1977, the initially university-owned corporation, Chembiomed Ltd., was formed to exploit the growing potential of Dr. Lemieux's research in carbohydrate chemistry to the medical care industry, particularly the bloodbanking area. The company also led in other areas of diagnostic technology, including techniques to achieve successful organ transplants when tissues are not compatible.

Dr. Lemieux was widely acknowledged for his accomplishments and captured many prestigious awards for chemistry in the world. The American Chemical Society published his memoirs, *Explorations with Sugars: How Sweet it Was*, as part of a series of 22 books by some of the world's most eminent organic chemists.

His major awards include: the King Faisal International Award for Science, 1990; an Honorary Doctor of Philosophy from the University of Stockholm, 1988; an Honorary Doctor of Science from the University of Alberta; the Tishler Award, Harvard University, 1983; the Haworth Medal of The Royal Chemical Society, England, 1978; and the C.S. Hudson Award of the American Chemical Society, 1966. He was elected a Fellow of The Royal Society of London in 1967, a great distinction shared by few living Canadian scientists.

Canadian awards include the Gairdner Foundation International Award, 1985; the Medal of Honour, Canadian Medical Association, 1985; the Sir Frederick Haultain Prize, Alberta, 1982; the Izaak Walton Killam Prize of The Canada Council, 1981; Officer of the Order of Canada, 1968; the Palladium Medal, Chemical Institute of Canada, 1964.

Dr. Lemieux is now deceased.

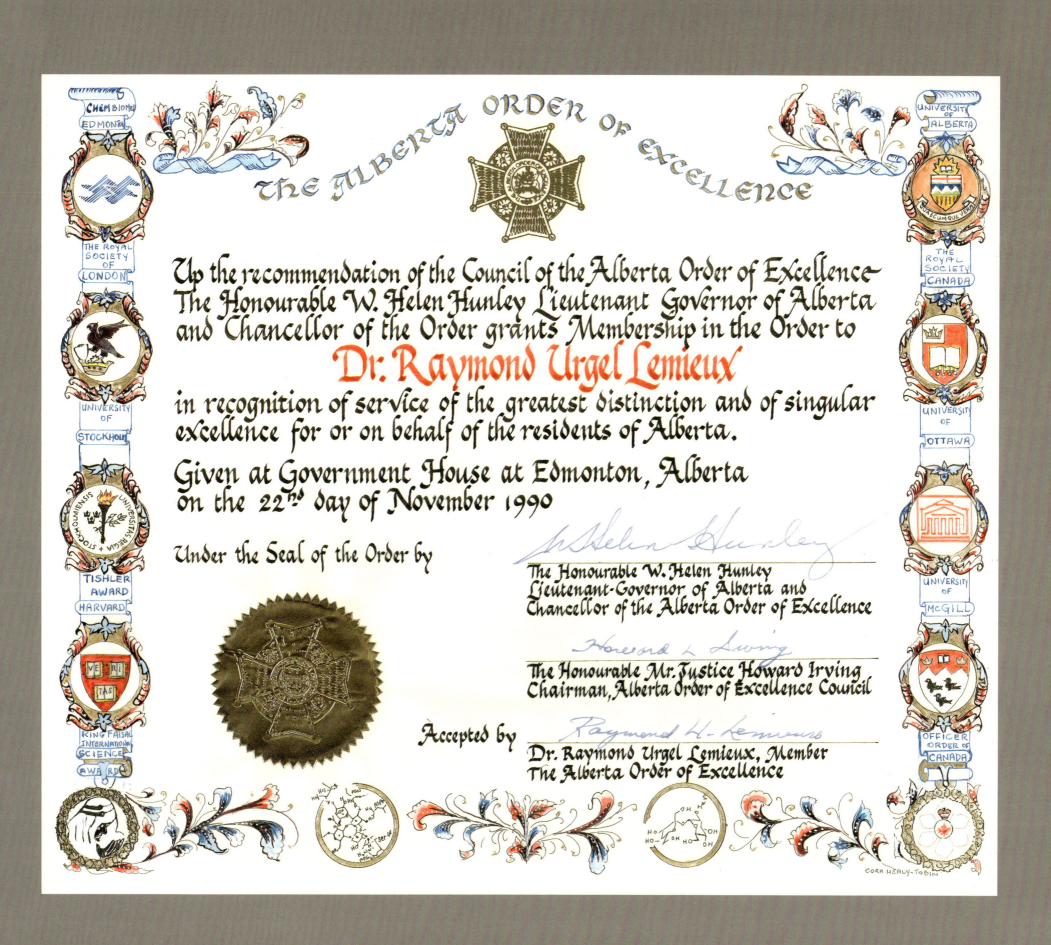

THE ALBERTA ORDER OF EXCELLENCE

Up the recommendation of the Council of the Alberta Order of Excellence
The Honourable W. Helen Hunley Lieutenant Governor of Alberta
and Chancellor of the Order grants Membership in the Order to

Dr. Raymond Urgel Lemieux

in recognition of service of the greatest distinction and of singular
excellence for or on behalf of the residents of Alberta.

Given at Government House at Edmonton, Alberta
on the 22ⁿᵈ day of November 1990

Under the Seal of the Order by

The Honourable W. Helen Hunley
Lieutenant-Governor of Alberta and
Chancellor of the Alberta Order of Excellence

The Honourable Mr. Justice Howard Irving
Chairman, Alberta Order of Excellence Council

Accepted by

Dr. Raymond Urgel Lemieux, Member
The Alberta Order of Excellence

CORA HEALY-TOBIN

Dr. Joseph H. Shoctor

Inducted: 1990

DR. JOE SHOCTOR'S INFLUENCE on Canadian theatre development is legendary. He introduced Edmonton to professional theatre in the old Salvation Army. Dr. Shoctor was also an original founder of the Edmonton Eskimo football club, involved with the United Way and appointed Queen's Counsel.

Joe Shoctor was born in Edmonton, an "east end kid" who grew up in the inner city. His immigrant father had a junk business where the Edmonton Art Gallery once stood.

"My childhood was rich," Dr. Shoctor says. "My parents taught me by example to be a survivor, to conquer adversity, and to do so with spirit and zest."

Downtown remained a focus for Joe Shoctor's life and his creation of professional theatre in Edmonton. His influence on Canadian theatre development is legendary.

His theatrical bent was evident early in life. As a teenager, he originated, produced and directed Victoria High School Varieties.

While studying law at the University of Alberta, he originated the Varsity Show, served on Student Council, was president of the Literary Association, and won a Literary "A" ring, the Inter-Collegiate Debating Trophy (the McGowan Cup) and a football "A"-and-Bar with the University of Alberta Golden Bears.

He introduced Edmonton to professional theatre in the 60s with a controversial performance of *Who's Afraid of Virginia Woolf?* The opening night performance to an audience of 300 people won rave reviews, and by the end of the first year, 1,300 Edmontonians were Citadel subscribers. Audiences continued to grow, along with The Citadel's national reputation.

The Edmonton facility became internationally renowned with developers of new art centers across North America frequently requesting site visits.

One national magazine said: "When the Citadel opened its 25th season in September 1989, with Robin Phillips' production of Shakespeare's *A Midsummer Nights' Dream*, it marked a cultural milestone not just for Edmonton but, indeed, the entire nation."

The Citadel on Wheels and Wings, founded in 1968, has toured thousands of miles to schools and communities as far north as the Arctic Circle. drama classes at the Citadel have been offered to countless students.

Dr. Shoctor was governor of the National Theatre School of Canada and Honorary Patron of the National Screen Institute. While he was often associated with theatre, he was a multidimensional man.

He was one of the original founders of the Edmonton Eskimo football club and served as its first secretary-manager.

Beginning in 1968, he worked with United Way and in 1972 served as general campaign chairman, spearheading a campaign that put Edmonton over its goal, the first city in Canada to do so that year and surpassing the city's fundraising objective for the first time in three years.

Dr. Shoctor was chairman of the Mayor's Task Force on the Heart of the City in 1984 and served as chairman of the Edmonton Downtown Development Corporation (EDDC) from 1986 to this year.

His work toward downtown revitalization has been widely recognized, and he was credited with convincing Toronto-based corporations operating in Edmonton to finance EDDC projects. Dr. Shoctor provided the leadership for establishment of the Edmonton Concert Hall Foundation and has been instrumental in bringing about Jasper Avenue improvements, as well as moving plans forward for the Old Towne Market Project.

His awards include: Performing Arts Publicists Association Award for Outstanding Contribution to the Performing Arts (the Sterling Award), 1989; Induction to the Edmonton Cultural Hall of Fame as a Builder, 1987; Officer of the Order of Canada, 1986; Honorary Diploma in Theatre Administration, Grant MacEwan College, 1986; City of Edmonton, Silver Ribbon Award, 1985; Honorary Doctor of Laws, University of Alberta, 1981; State of Israel Prime Minister's Medal, 1978; The Queen's Silver Jubilee Medal, 1978; Province of Alberta Achievement Award for Outstanding Service in the Theatre Arts, 1975.

Dr. Shoctor is now deceased.

טוב חול

THE ALBERTA ORDER OF EXCELLENCE

Up the recommendation of the Council of the Alberta Order of Excellence The Honourable W. Helen Hunley Lieutenant Governor of Alberta and Chancellor of the Order grants Membership in the Order to

Joseph H. Shoctor

in recognition of service of the greatest distinction and of singular excellence for or on behalf of the residents of Alberta.

Given at Government House at Edmonton, Alberta on the 22ⁿᵈ day of November 1990

Under the Seal of the Order by

The Honourable W. Helen Hunley
Lieutenant-Governor of Alberta and
Chancellor of the Alberta Order of Excellence

The Honourable Mr. Justice Howard Irving
Chairman, Alberta Order of Excellence Council

Accepted by

Mr. Joseph H. Shoctor, Member
The Alberta Order of Excellence

UNIVERSITY OF ALBERTA

THE CANADIAN ZIONIST FEDERATION

KEREN HAYESOD
UNITED JEWISH APPEAL

STATE OF ISRAEL MEDAL

QUEENS COUNSEL

PRESIDENT

UNITED WAY CANADA

ORDER OF CANADA

CITADEL THEATRE

CORA HEALY-TOBIN

Dr. Norbert R. Morgenstern

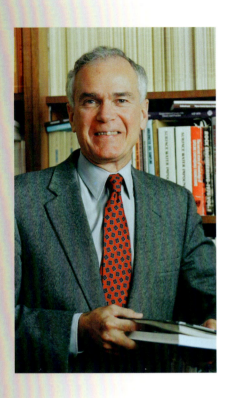

Inducted: 1991

NORBERT RUBIN MORGENSTERN is a University Professor of Civil Engineering and an internationally recognized authority in the field of Geotechnical Engineering.

Professor Morgenstern was born in Toronto on 25 May 1935 and graduated from the University of Toronto in 1956 with a Bachelor of Applied Science in Civil Engineering. He was awarded the Athlone Fellowship for post-graduate studies in the United Kingdom, and after a short period in professional practice, Norbert Morgenstern departed for London to study Soil Mechanics at the Imperial College of Science and Technology at the University of London.

The distinguished leader of the group at Imperial College, Prof. A.W. Skempton, FRS, notes, "Here he so distinguished himself that we gladly took the opportunity of converting him into a research assistant, and in 1960 he came on staff as a Lecturer. Certainly to the advantage of the college, and I think to his own benefit, he then stayed with us for a further eight years."

During this period, Professor Morgenstern was awarded the Diploma of Imperial College and the Doctor of Philosophy (University of London) while he taught, conducted research and established a reputation as a consultant in applied earth sciences. It was at that time Dr. Morgenstern made the first of his many lasting contributions to his subject.

The field of Geotechnical Engineering was started in Western Canada by the late Dean R.M. Hardy, dean of Engineering at the University of Alberta for many years. He and the late Professor S.R. Sinclair encouraged Dr. Morgenstern to return to Canada and join the University of Alberta, which he did in 1968 as professor of Civil Engineering. He was named professor of Civil Engineering in 1983 in recognition of his teaching, research and service accomplishments.

Professor Morgenstern's first research was into the mechanics of slope stability as it applies to the evaluation of landslides and the design of dams. This early research received recognition by the award on two occasions of the British Geotechnical Society Prize. The fruits of this research quickly passed into professional practice.

Following his return to Canada, he systematically began to build the University of Alberta into one of the leading geotechnical schools. Key colleagues were attracted to join him and outstanding graduate students were recruited both from across Canada and elsewhere. The 1970s brought with them expanded engineering challenges in the development of both the arctic and the Alberta oil sands.

Dr. Morgenstern and his colleagues and his students laid the framework for modern permafrost engineering, which has influenced all aspects of geotechnical design in the arctic. At the same time, studies into the geotechnical aspects of the Alberta oil sands contributed significantly to the enhanced safety and economy of developing the resource while research into tailings dams and other waste facilities contributed to improved environmental integrity within the mining industry.

Recognition followed with the Walter Huber Engineering Research Prize from the American Society of Civil Engineers in 1971; the Canadian Geotechnical Society Prize; election to Fellow of the Royal Society of Canada in 1975; and the Legget Award in 1979, which is the highest award of the Canadian Geotechnical Society.

In 1981, Professor Morgenstern was invited to deliver the Rankine Lecture, which is the highest recognition of the British Geotechnical Society. In proposing a vote of thanks, Dr. A.C. Meigh said: "What is also impressive is that Morgenstern and his colleagues have focussed their attention and their research efforts on the major problems confronting the community within which they live, to the benefit not only of that community but others elsewhere. Surely this is the hallmark of a centre of engineering excellence."

In the 1980s, Professor Morgenstern broadened his range of active interests to include offshore engineering, foundation engineering and environmental matters.

He has received honorary degrees from the University of Toronto and Queen's University. He has been elected a Fellow of the Engineering Institute of Canada and the Canadian Academy of Engineering. Other major awards include the Centennial Award of the Association of Professional Engineers, Geologists and Geophysicists of Alberta and the Sir Frederick Haultain Prize in Science from the Government of Alberta.

Professor Morgenstern has not only made outstanding contributions through his teaching and research but also as a consulting engineer. His work as a consultant on water development projects, landslide studies and other resource development projects carried him to over twenty countries on six continents. He has assisted in technology transfer to developing countries through the United Nations and other agencies. Closer to home he has advised on numerous challenging foundation problems, he has been a consultant to many of the arctic development projects of the past two decades and has been closely associated with both operating oil sand mines.

Dr. Morgenstern has served his professional community through numerous committees and task forces that have assisted government and professional societies at all levels. These include: Chairman, Earth Science Grout Selection Committee, National Research Council of Canada (1975–1976); President, Canadian Geoscience Council (1983); President, Canadian Geotechnical Society (1987–1991); and President, International Society for Soil Mechanics and Foundation Engineering (1989–1994). Community involvement has also included the Edmonton Symphony Society and other organizations. In 1988–1989, Dr. Morgenstern assisted the United Nations in the organization of the International Decade for Natural Disaster Reduction which was initiated in 1991.

Professor Morgenstern has been dedicated to excellence in engineering combining teaching, research and practice. But above all Professor Morgenstern has been a much-admired teacher, always accessible to his students, present and past, and an equally admired colleague, always ready to listen and to help. He takes great pride in the achievements of his students, many of whom achieved early recognition. His work has been centered in Alberta, but has been of benefit to his profession throughout Canada and the world at large.

THE ALBERTA ORDER OF EXCELLENCE

Upon the recommendation of the Council of The Alberta Order of Excellence The Honourable Gordon Towers, Lieutenant Governor of Alberta and Chancellor of the Order grants Membership in the Order of Excellence to

Dr. Norbert R Morgenstern

in recognition of service of the greatest distinction and of singular excellence for or on behalf of the residents of Alberta.

Given at Government House at Edmonton, on the 28th day of November 1991.

Under the Seal of the Order by

The Honourable Gordon Towers,
Lieutenant Governor of Alberta and
Chancellor of The Alberta Order of Excellence

The Honourable Mr. Justice Howard Irving
Chairman Alberta Order of Excellence Council

Accepted by

Dr. Norbert R Morgenstern
Member The Alberta Order of Excellence

Dr. Howard V. Gimbel

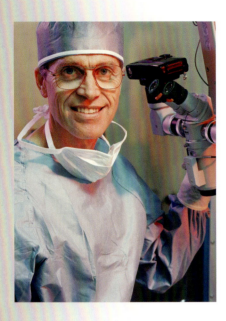

Inducted: 1992

DR. HOWARD GIMBEL IS AN OPHTHALMOLOGIST and pioneer in out-patient cataract and refractive eye surgery.

Born in Calgary in 1934, Dr. Gimbel grew up on a farm near Beiseker, about 100 kilometres northeast of Calgary. He earned a BA in Physics from Walla Walla College, College Place, Washington, and received his doctorate in medicine and a Masters in Public Health from Loma Linda University, Loma Linda, California. He completed his internship and ophthalmology residency at the White Memorial Medical Centre in Los Angeles and began his private practice in Alberta in 1964. Dr. Gimbel began outpatient surgery in 1980 with the opening of the Gimbel Eye Centre and subsequently the Gimbel Eye Surgical Centre was opened in 1984.

Dr. Gimbel was the first ophthalmologist in Canada to use phaco-emulsification for the removal of cataracts. He is the developer of the Continuous-Tear Capsulotomy technique and the Divide and Conquer phacoemulsification technique, which are accepted as international standards of excellence for their safety and effectiveness. The Centre attracts a large number of Canadian and international ophthalmologists to observe his surgical skills and advanced methods of care delivery.

The Centre, in conjunction with the Gimbel Eye Foundation, supports and promotes education, service and medical research. Clinical research by the Centre's ophthalmologists, research physicians and assistants has resulted in numerous scientific publications.

The Foundation has produced award-winning patient education videos and surgical teaching tapes. Dr. Gimbel has also served as a guest lecturer at medical associations and schools around the world.

Dr. Gimbel has served as a member of many associations and societies, which include the Alberta Medical Association; the Canadian Medical Association; the Canadian Ophthalmological Society; the American Academy of Ophthalmology; the American Society of Cataract and Refractive Surgeons; and the International Intraocular Implant Club.

He is a Fellow of the Royal College of Physicians and Surgeons (Canada) and the American Academy of Ophthalmology. He is a clinical assistant professor at the University of Calgary and associate clinical professor at Loma Linda University.

Committed to providing the best medical care and education with the finest available equipment, Dr. Gimbel has combined technical excellence with the art of caring in an atmosphere of open co-operative communication. His dedication to the service of mankind has raised the standard of care in this province, and his innovative techniques have placed him clearly at the forefront of modern cataract surgery in the world. Dr. Gimbel has distinguished himself as a caring physician, a skilled surgeon and an effective teacher.

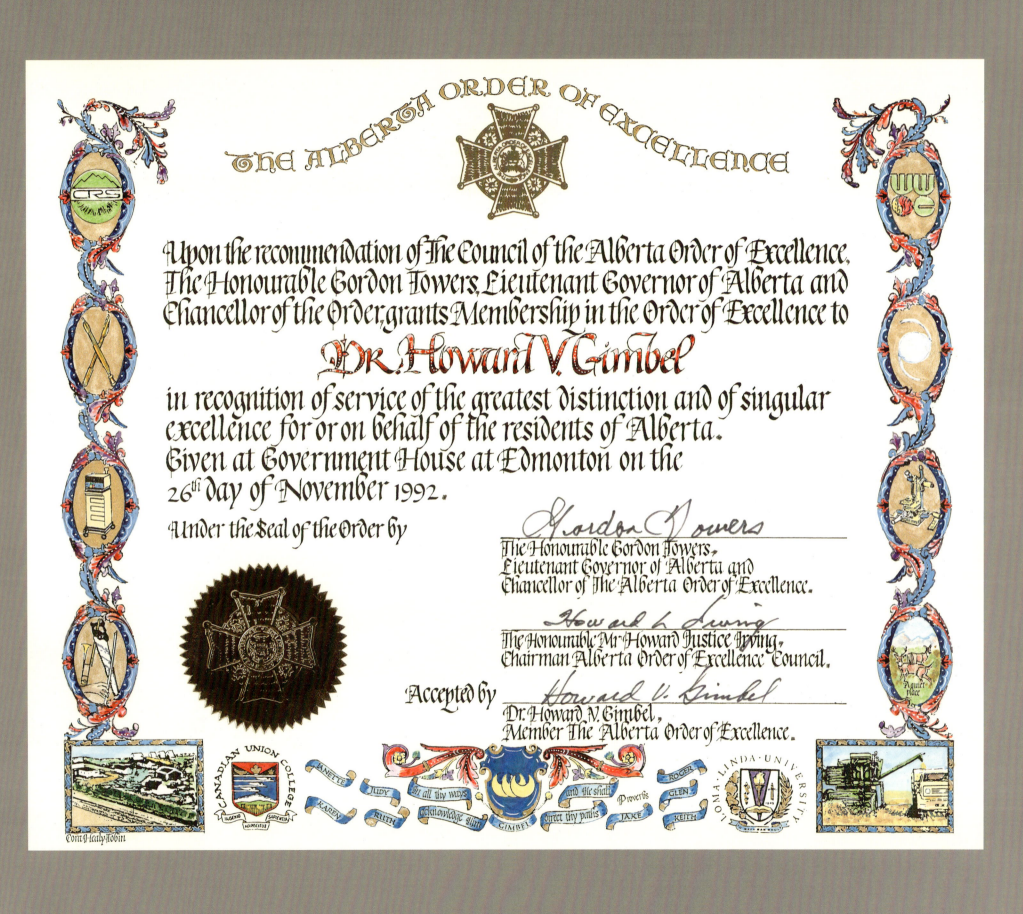

THE ALBERTA ORDER OF EXCELLENCE

Upon the recommendation of The Council of the Alberta Order of Excellence, The Honourable Gordon Towers, Lieutenant Governor of Alberta and Chancellor of the Order, grants Membership in the Order of Excellence to

Dr. Howard V. Gimbel

in recognition of service of the greatest distinction and of singular excellence for or on behalf of the residents of Alberta. Given at Government House at Edmonton on the 26th day of November 1992.

Under the Seal of the Order by

Gordon Towers

The Honourable Gordon Towers,
Lieutenant Governor of Alberta and
Chancellor of The Alberta Order of Excellence.

Howard L. Irving

The Honourable Mr. Howard Justice Irving,
Chairman Alberta Order of Excellence Council.

Accepted by

Howard V. Gimbel

Dr. Howard V. Gimbel,
Member The Alberta Order of Excellence.

Dr. Thomas Benjamin Banks

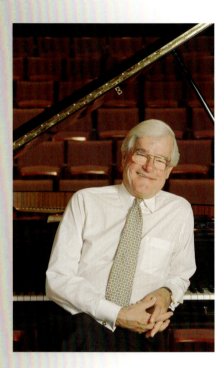

Inducted: 1993

DR. THOMAS (TOMMY) BANKS is recognized for his musical leadership and his contributions to Canada's cultural scene. His talents, expertise and efforts have helped attract major world artists to Alberta stages in major festivals and in television and recording.

His extraordinary musical ability and experience are reflected in his distinguished career. He has conducted almost every major professional orchestra in Canada and has been an accompanist for literally hundreds of well-known performers. His musical direction credits include the 1978 Commonwealth Games, the 1983 World University Games, Expo '86 and the 1988 XV Olympic Winter Games. He has been involved in over 70 internationally syndicated television specials in various roles: executive producer, conductor, composer, arranger and pianist. Through *The Tommy Banks Show* on CBC-TV, then on ITV, then in international syndication, he became known first nationally and then internationally on television.

The double album recorded by his 17-member jazz band at Switzerland's Montreaux International Festival resulted in the 1979 Juno Award. In 1984, his jazz band was the first to tour China in 35 years.

The musical endeavours of Dr. Banks have launched many Albertans on to full-time careers in music here and internationally. His contributions and credibility have resulted in industry-related opportunities in Alberta, and in the process, scores of Alberta artists, studio and technical personnel have become recognized. His efforts and high level of activity over forty years have resulted directly in employment for Alberta musicians and performers and in the construction of related facilities. He has invested personally in various arts businesses.

He was a part of the pioneering efforts that have resulted in our flourishing recording arts industry and in a healthy level of active financial assistance programs for artists and arts projects. Dr. Banks was a founding member of the Alberta Recording Arts Foundation, now the Alberta Recording Industry Association (ARIA). His role as founding chairman of the Alberta Foundation for the Performing Arts was vital in guiding the early development of that organization, which has become one of the most important funding avenues for the arts in Alberta.

Dr. Banks has devoted part of his astonishing energy and talent to the service of our community in the field of music education. He has served in a number of roles including adjudicator, clinician, speaker, musician and administrator. He has served as a member of the Board of Governors and as chairman of the Music Committee of Alberta College, and as chairman of the music program of Grant MacEwan Community College. He has been musical director for Edmonton Musical Theatre, the Citadel Theatre, and for hundreds of television series programs. He was chairman of the Edmonton Concert Hall Foundation and is currently a member of the Canada Council. He is an honorary member of Cosmopolitan International.

In recognition of his role as its founding chairman, the Alberta Foundation for the Performing Arts has established an endowment fund of $25,000, from the proceeds of which the annual Tommy Banks Award is given to recognize the achievements of music directors and young musicians at music festival competitions.

Dr. Banks was a member of the Board of the Alberta Heart Foundation and served as honorary campaign chairman of the Alberta Heart Fund.

He received an Honorary Doctor of Laws degree from the University of Alberta in 1987. He was named an Officer of the Order of Canada in 1991.

THE ALBERTA ORDER OF EXCELLENCE

Upon the recommendation of the Council of The Alberta Order of Excellence
The Honourable Gordon Towers Lieutenant Governor of Alberta and
Chancellor of the Order grants Membership in the Order of Excellence to

Dr. Thomas B. Banks

in recognition of service of the greatest distinction and of singular
excellence for or on behalf of the residents of Alberta
Given at Government House at Edmonton on the
25th day of November 1993

Under the Seal of the Order by

The Honourable Gordon Towers
Lieutenant Governor of Alberta and
Chancellor of The Alberta Order of Excellence

The Honourable Mr Allan H. Anderson
Chairman The Alberta Order of Excellence Council

Accepted by

Dr Thomas B (Tommy) Banks
Member, Alberta Order of Excellence

Dr. Robert Bertram Church

Inducted: 1993

DR. ROBERT (BOB) B. CHURCH IS A PIONEER of molecular genetics and embryo transfer technology in cattle. During his 25-year career at the University of Calgary, he became an internationally known leader and expert in transferring the technologies of genetics, reproductive physiology and molecular biology to the agricultural and biotechnology industries.

Dr. Church was a founding member of the Faculty of Medicine at the University of Calgary and associate dean of Research from 1981 to 1988. He was the first head of the department of Medical Biochemistry, a position he held for 14 years. The department established an endowed lectureship in biotechnology to honour Professor Church. This lectureship will enable the university to promote technology transfer and bioengineering.

Serving in a scientific advisory capacity to numerous biotechnology projects, he has been personally involved in the establishment of 11 new high technology companies in Alberta, the United States, New Zealand and Australia. Dr. Church is a former director of Calgary-based Alberta Livestock Transplants and Alta Genetics Inc.; Connaught Laboratories Ltd. of Willowdale, Ontario; Veterinary Infectious Disease Organization, Saskatoon; and current director of Biostar Inc., Saskatoon; Continental Pharma Cryosan Ltd., Montréal; CIBA Canada and Vencap Equities Ltd., Edmonton.

In 1967, he founded Church Livestock Consultants, which specializes in technical advice and program design in animal breeding, embryo transfer, livestock management and the development of food products worldwide.

Dr. Church has been active in the livestock industry through involvement on various committees in the development of breed organizations, sire and dam evaluation, genetic defect testing and breed development.

While a director of Highfield Stock Farms, he assisted in the development of one of the world's outstanding Simmental and Charolais herds and the establishment of showplace facilities at Aldersyde, Alberta.

In 1974, Dr. Church began operating the Lochend Luing Ranches, northwest of Airdrie. The Lochend Luing Ranch operation is an example of "back to the future" range management in operation. His operation initiated the first verified production protocol for producing, processing, quality control and marketing of a retail-ready product, branded "natural choice." This resulted in his appointment to the Board of Directors of Canada's newly established Agri-Food Competitiveness Council, helping Canada remain competitive in the global marketplace.

In addition to his contributions as a scientist and administrator, Dr. Church has authored over 100 scientific publications in animal genetics and biotechnology. He is also an acclaimed teacher and lecturer, and has been cited for excellence in teaching biology to undergraduate university students. Dr. Church has been an inspiring teacher and supervisor of 17 graduate students and eight postdoctoral fellows. Professor Church was honoured as the Klinck Lecturer of the Agricultural Institute of Canada in 1989.

Dr. Church's contributions to the community are also noteworthy and include 20 years with the Calgary Exhibition and Stampede as director. He was a founding member of the Natural Sciences and Engineering Research Council, a board member for the Alberta Children's Hospital Research Centre, and director of the Canadian Institute for Advanced Research for nearly ten years. He served as a member of the Alberta Research Council, the Medical Research Council of Canada and trustee of the Western Heritage Centre. Dr. Church was appointed as vice-chairman of the Premier's Council on Science and Technology and as a member of the National Advisory Board of the Banff Centre of Management. A recipient of many awards and honours, Dr. Church was inducted in the Canadian Agricultural Hall of Fame in 1991 for his work in the area of cattle genetics. In 1992, he received the Outstanding Contribution to Alberta Science and Technology Community Award from the ASTech Foundation.

A third-generation Albertan, his grandparents homesteaded in the Yankee Valley and Nose Creek districts. Raised on the family farm and ranch at Balzac, Alberta, Dr. Church continues to help his brother Gordon during the busy seeding and harvest seasons.

Described as an outstanding scientist, administrator, teacher and friend, Dr. Robert Church has been credited with bringing modern-day science to the Canadian agricultural community.

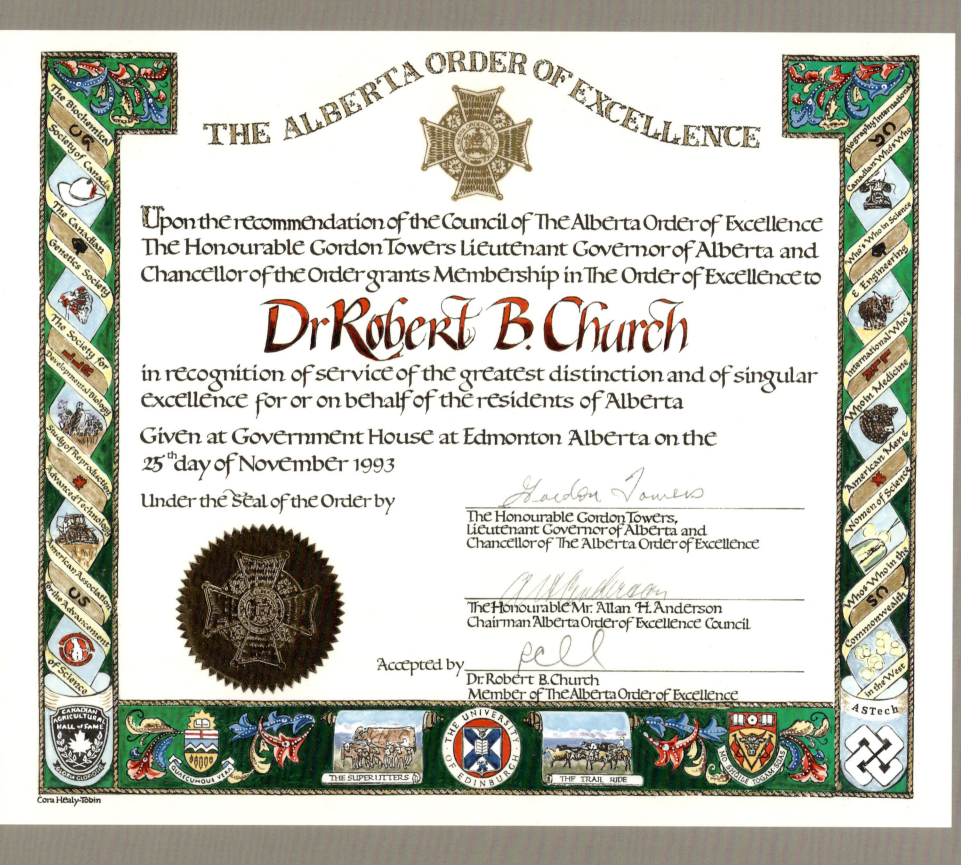

THE ALBERTA ORDER OF EXCELLENCE

Upon the recommendation of the Council of The Alberta Order of Excellence The Honourable Gordon Towers Lieutenant Governor of Alberta and Chancellor of the Order grants Membership in The Order of Excellence to

Dr Robert B. Church

in recognition of service of the greatest distinction and of singular excellence for or on behalf of the residents of Alberta

Given at Government House at Edmonton Alberta on the 25th day of November 1993

Under the Seal of the Order by

Gordon Towers

The Honourable Gordon Towers,
Lieutenant Governor of Alberta and
Chancellor of The Alberta Order of Excellence

The Honourable Mr. Allan H. Anderson
Chairman Alberta Order of Excellence Council

Accepted by

Dr. Robert B. Church
Member of The Alberta Order of Excellence

Cora Healy-Tobin

Dr. Helen Isabel Huston

Inducted: 1994

DR. HELEN I. HUSTON IS AN INSPIRING Canadian who has received international recognition as a medical missionary. Her story is one of fortitude and faith. Dr. Huston devoted 39 years of her life to the people of India and Nepal. For 32 of those years, she served with the United Mission to Nepal (UMN), an interdenominational organization supported by 36 mission boards from 16 countries.

Dr. Huston was born in Innisfail, Alberta, and grew up in many other small Alberta towns. Dr. Huston graduated from the University of Alberta in Medicine in 1951. She interned a year at the Royal Alexandra Hospital in Edmonton and another at Vancouver General Hospital before leaving for India in 1953. She served there with the United Church of Canada for five and a half years.

Soon after Hindi language school, Dr. Helen, as she was called, was loaned to work for three months with the UMN in Kathmandu. Dr. Bethel Fleming, one of the founding members of the United Mission to Nepal and the first Western physician allowed to work in Nepal, had opened a 15-bed hospital for women and children in half of an empty cholera hospital. Soon after, Dr. Fleming was called home urgently to the USA, and the young and inexperienced Dr. Helen was asked to fill in. At that time, there was no road connecting India and Kathmandu, and it was very difficult to get supplies.

Amidst the lush, tropical growth and spectacular beauty of the land, Dr. Helen worked under difficult circumstances. During the 50s, Nepal was just beginning to open its borders to the rest of the world, ending several centuries of isolation. While there, she felt an intense desire to return in the future.

To her great joy, the United Church became a member of the UMN, and she was sent to work under them in Nepal in 1960. Apart from home leave, she spent most of the next 32 years in the village of Amp Pipal, about 140 km northwest of Kathmandu in the sprawling, mountainous Gorkha District. An UMN community service project had been started in Amp Pipal to work in agriculture, education and health.

Pioneering as the first and only doctor for a number of years, she performed emergency operations and all manner of medical services under the most primitive conditions.

In 1965, work began on Amp Pipal hospital. Building the hospital from mud and stone on two terraces of the slopes of the Lig Lig Mountain was a formidable challenge. The move to the partially completed hospital was made in March of 1969. The majority of the donations to build and equip this hospital came from Alberta, some from the rest of Canada and some from other countries.

Dr. Helen's work in Nepal was sponsored in UMN and Canada by the international, interdenominational mission known as "Interserve." Her mission and outreach to the needs of the less fortunate people of the world is an inspiration to Albertans. Encouraged by her example, a number of others have gone abroad to share their talents and their faith in "the two-thirds" world.

In 1980, Dr. Huston was given an honorary life membership in the Nepal Medical Association at Kathmandu, never before granted to a doctor from a foreign country. Awarded the Outstanding Achievement Award by the University of Alberta Medical Alumni Association in 1978, she was recently inducted to their Alumni Wall of Recognition. The University of Alberta also honoured her in 1984 with an Honorary Doctor of Laws degree. Dr. Huston is the first recipient of Sir Edmund Hillary Foundation Award for Humanitarian Services, presented by Sir Edmund in Toronto in 1991. In 1994, she was named to the Order of Canada.

She retired in October 1992, and returned to Alberta in February 1993. Her story is told in the book *A Heart for Nepal: The Dr. Helen Huston Story*, written by Calgary writer, Dr. Gerald Hankins, a classmate of Helen's, fellow medical missionary and member of the Alberta Order of Excellence.

THE ALBERTA ORDER OF EXCELLENCE

Upon the recommendation of the Council of The Alberta Order of Excellence, the Honourable Gordon Towers, Lieutenant Governor of Alberta and Chancellor of the Order, grants Membership in the Order of Excellence to

Dr. Helen I. Huston

in recognition of service of the greatest distinction and of singular excellence for or on behalf of the residents of Alberta.

Given at Government House at Edmonton on the 24th day of November 1994.

Under the Seal of the Order by

Gordon Towers

The Honourable Gordon Towers,
Lieutenant Governor of Alberta,
Chancellor of The Alberta Order of Excellence.

W. Anderson

Dr. Allan Anderson, Chairman,
Alberta Order of Excellence Council.

Accepted by *Helen I. Huston*
Dr. Helen Isabel Huston,
Member, Alberta Order of Excellence.

Dr. Stanley A. Milner

Inducted: 1995

DR. STANLEY A. MILNER IS RECOGNIZED on the international scene as one of the most successful Canadian business leaders in the petroleum industry. It was perhaps prophetic that Stan Milner was born in Calgary, home to most of Canada's oil companies, and that he spent his early years in Turner Valley, birthplace of Alberta's oil industry.

Dr. Milner attended school in Turner Valley, Saskatoon, Gimli and Winnipeg. A graduate of the University of Alberta with a Bachelor of Science degree, he began his career in the wake of the Leduc oil discovery.

His fascination with and aptitude for finance brought him to the investment business. Later, Dr. Milner participated in the development of the first natural gas utility service in the British Columbia interior. This background, combined with field experience and a quiet, firm, farseeing intensity, helped shape his effective oilman's business philosophy.

In the late 50s, three of the Milner brothers formed two small independent exploration companies, financed and built through hard work and persistence: Canadian Chieftain Petroleums Corporation. In 1964, Stan Milner founded Chieftain Development Co. Ltd. and guided its growth until its acquisition in 1988 by Alberta Energy Company Ltd. He is currently president, chief executive officer and a director of Chieftain International, Inc., founded in 1988.

Dr. Milner is also a director of several corporations including Alberta Energy Company Ltd., Canadian Imperial Bank of Commerce, Canadian Pacific Limited and Chieftain International, Inc. He has held several directorships in Canadian and U.S. companies, including Banister Continental Ltd., Canadian Surety Company, CP Air Limited, Delhi International Oil Corporation, Guaranty Trust Company of Canada, Pan-Alberta Gas Ltd., Southern Union Company, Supron Energy Corporation, Wardair, Inc., and Woodward Stores Limited.

Throughout his esteemed career, Stan Milner has taken a keen interest and active part in civic and charitable activities. His commitment to the community and strong belief in being involved has kept the man and Chieftain in Edmonton. Dr. Milner served as an alderman for the City of Edmonton and as chairman of the Edmonton Public Library Board. He has held senior leadership positions on the Board of Governors of the Royal Alexandra Hospital and the University of Alberta Hospital; the Boards of the Edmonton Community Foundation, Junior Achievement, Edmonton Northlands, Edmonton Symphony Orchestra and the Edmonton Eskimo Football Club; and chairman of the Salvation Army Appeal and the Corporate Division of the United Way.

Dr. Milner's continuing interest in the military stems from his service in his early years, serving in the cadet corp, the reserve army and in the Canadian Officer Training Corp. His belief in the military's importance in the province of Alberta led to his appointment as an Honorary Lieutenant Colonel in the South Alberta Light Horse (RCAC) and Honorary Member of the Loyal Edmonton Regiment. He is the Founder and current President of the South Alberta Light Horse Regiment Foundation.

Stan Milner has served in a number of organizations, including president of the Independent Petroleum Association of Canada and the Alberta Chamber of Resources; member of the Listed Company Advisory Committee of the American Stock Exchange, the Board of the Edmonton Chamber of Commerce, the Board of Governors of the Olympic Trust of Canada and the Young Presidents' Organization; and a director of the Conference Board of Canada. Dr. Milner is a member of the World Business Council.

Dr. Milner's interest in business and education prompted his participation on the University of Alberta's Business Advisory Council. He served a three-year term as chair of the University's Board of Governors. In 1991, in conjunction with the Faculty of Business, he established the Stanley A. Milner Chair in Leadership, which is intended to further the understanding and development of effective leadership. In 1994, cited for his competence, wisdom and foresight, he was awarded an Honorary Degree of Doctor of Laws from the University of Alberta.

Stan Milner has been the recipient of numerous honours over the years, including the City of Edmonton's Certificate of Meritorious Service; the Wall Street Transcript Bronze and Gold Awards for the Top Chief Executive Officer in the Canadian Oil Industry; the University of Alberta's Canadian Business Leader Award; the 125th Anniversary of Confederation Commemorative Medal; and induction into the Business Hall of Fame of Junior Achievement of Northern Alberta. In 2003, Dr. Milner was appointed Officer of the Order of Canada.

THE ALBERTA ORDER OF EXCELLENCE

Upon the recommendation of the Council of The Alberta Order of Excellence The Honourable Gordon Towers, Lieutenant Governor of Alberta and Chancellor of the Order grants Membership in The Order of Excellence to

Stanley A Milner

in recognition of service of the greatest distinction and of singular excellence for or on behalf of the residents of Alberta.

Given at Government House at Edmonton Alberta on the 23rd day of November 1995.

Under the Seal of the Order by

The Honourable Gordon Towers,
Lieutenant Governor of Alberta and
Chancellor of The Alberta Order of Excellence to

Mr. Allan H. Anderson Chairman
Alberta Order of Excellence Council

Accepted by

Dr. Stanley A. Milner
Member of The Alberta Order of Excellence

C.H.T.

Dr. Francis G. Winspear

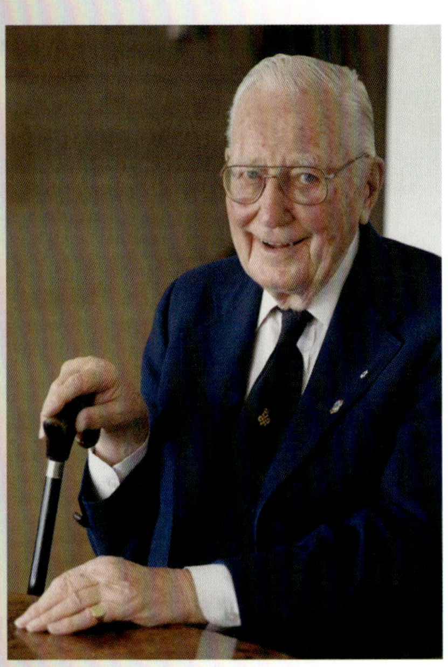

Inducted: 1995

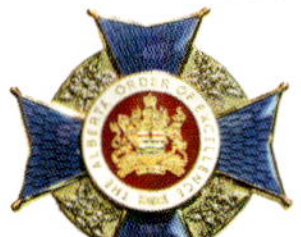

DR. FRANCIS G. WINSPEAR WAS THE PRESIDENT and CEO of at least 19 businesses. There was hardly a major industry that he did not manage or develop over his 60-year career, all of which were important to Alberta's development. Dr. Winspear had a special genius to inspire and lead others, and was a major factor in building the strongest university accounting program in Canada. Dr. Winspear's gift, the single biggest by an individual to a Canadian arts organization, resulted in the successful construction of Edmonton's Winspear Centre concert hall.

Dr. Francis G. Winspear, was commander-in-chief of an international empire of 40 companies. Through his actions, he directly improved the quality of life for many through quality education, increased employment opportunities, the alleviation of hardships, a stronger artistic community and stronger arts organizations. His primary focus was the development of human resources, in particular by supporting universities and talented individuals in order to better realize human potential.

Coming to Canada from England with his family as a young child, Dr. Winspear grew up in a prairie hamlet south of Strathmore. He attended high school in Calgary and graduated at the age of 14. Too young for university, he opted to work four years at the Calgary branch of the Bank of Toronto, take correspondence courses from Queen's University and eventually article with Touche and Co. In 1928, Dr. Winspear was hired by Peat, Marwick and Mitchel to run their sub-office in Edmonton. His ability to encourage and train leaders and the unique hiring practice of surrounding himself with brilliant future accountants resulted in the launch of his own business, Winspear, Higgins, Stevenson and Doan, which became a national firm in 1964.

With a special genius to inspire and lead others, Dr. Winspear was fully engaged in all aspects of life. He was the president and CEO of at least 19 businesses and served on the Board of Directors of 14 other public companies. With a flair for resuscitating failing businesses, there was hardly a major industry that he did not manage or develop over his 60-year career, all of which were important to the development of Alberta from the 1930s through to the 1960s. Among the 40-odd companies he owned, some include Premier Steel, which opened the first basic steel plant in Alberta; the aviation repair giant Northwest Industries; Gold Standard Oils, which was a shareholder in the Great Canadian Oils Sands venture; controlled Echo Bay Mining, one of Canada's largest silver producers; BC Airlines, Swanson Lumber, Consolidated Finance and companies dealing in products as diverse as furniture and oxygen.

Dr. Winspear was associated with the University of Alberta from the late 1920s—as a professor of Accounting for 20 years, dean of the Business School, and Professor Emeritus. He was a major factor in building the strongest university accounting program in Canada, as an instructor for many years, and as a major donor to several faculties at the University of Alberta, as well as a renowned library. Professors in accounting, international business, labour economics and music at the University of Alberta are due to Dr. Winspear's support. The Francis G. Winspear Chair in Professional Accounting was the first chair at the University to be funded by a private donation.

He was astonishingly generous to an array of culture, education and social service groups and an exceptional patron of the arts. Dr. Winspear felt strongly that music is part of an educated man's well-being. Dr. Winspear's gift, the single biggest by an individual to a Canadian arts organization, resulted in the successful construction of Edmonton's newest concert hall, which opened in 1997 and is named in his honour.

He was not a passive financial supporter but was knowledgeable and often contributed needed expertise to strengthen the boards of many organizations. He was one of the founders of the Edmonton Opera Company and, through the Winspear Foundation, established several decades ago and now the Winspear Fund, substantially supports the Edmonton Art Gallery and was the main source of funds for many Alberta and Western Canadian charities.

He was named an Officer in the Order of Canada and received an Honorary Doctor of Laws degree and an Honorary Doctor of Science degree from the University of Alberta.

Dr. Winspear was also past president of the United Way, the Edmonton and Canadian Chambers of Commerce, as well as honorary chairman of Edmonton Opera and the Edmonton Community Foundation.

Dr. Winspear's analytical mind, memory for detail and capacity for working long hours laid the foundation of his fortune. He strongly believed that people should be interested in their communities and do what they can to make them satisfactory in every respect, as beautiful as possible, and as receptive as possible to the good things in life.

Through his uncommon vision, business acumen, leadership, philanthropic activity and care for his community, Dr. Francis Winspear provided a role model for individuals who have known him and known of his accomplishments. His leadership by example will be lasting.

Dr. Francis Winspear is now deceased.

THE ALBERTA ORDER OF EXCELLENCE

University of Alberta
Edmonton
HONORARY DOCTOR OF LAWS

QUAECUMQUE VERA

UVic
UNIVERSITY OF VICTORIA
HONORARY DOCTOR OF SCIENCE

Upon the recommendation of the Council of The Alberta Order of Excellence The Honourable Gordon Towers, Lieutenant Governor of Alberta and Chancellor of the Order grants Membership in the Order of Excellence to

Francis G. Winspear

in recognition of service of the greatest distinction and of singular excellence for or on behalf of the residents of Alberta.
Given at Government House at Edmonton on the 23rd day of November 1995.

Under the Seal of the Order by

Gordon Towers
The Honourable Gordon Towers
Lieutenant Governor of Alberta and
Chancellor of The Alberta Order of Excellence

A H Anderson
Mr. Allan H. Anderson Chairman
The Alberta Order of Excellence Council

Accepted by F. G. Winspear
Dr. Francis G Winspear
Member, Alberta Order of Excellence

VIOLA CHAIR U OF A

ICA

Chartered Accountants of Alberta

"ONE CAN'T LOVE THIS UNIVERSITY BECAUSE OF ITS BUILDINGS. WHAT YOU DO LOVE IT FOR ARE THE PEOPLE WHO HAVE SERVED IT"

CHAIR IN PROFESSIONAL ACCOUNTING

FACULTY OF BUSINESS University of Alberta

CHAIR OF PUBLIC POLICY

EDMUND C. BOVEY AWARD

ORDER OF CANADA

MY MAIN PHILOSOPHY IN LIFE IS TO LEAVE CIVILIZATION A LITTLE MORE ADVANCED THAN WHEN I CAME

UNIVERSITY OF ALBERTA PROFESSOR EMERITUS

ENTREPRENEUR OF THE YEAR

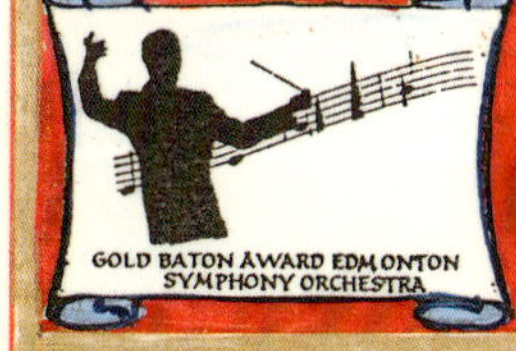
GOLD BATON AWARD EDMONTON SYMPHONY ORCHESTRA

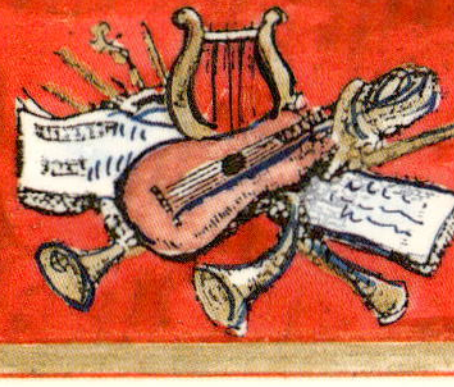

FRANCIS WINSPEAR CENTRE FOR MUSIC

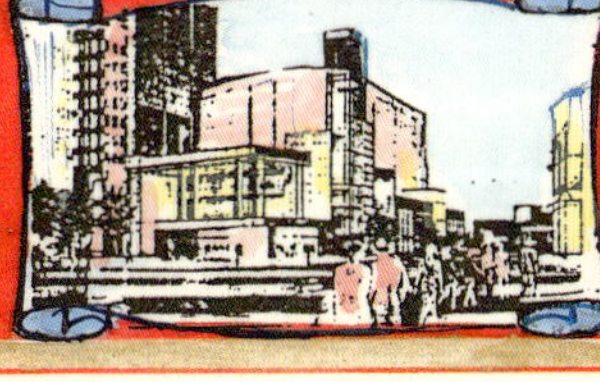

EDMONTON CONCERT HALL FOUNDATION

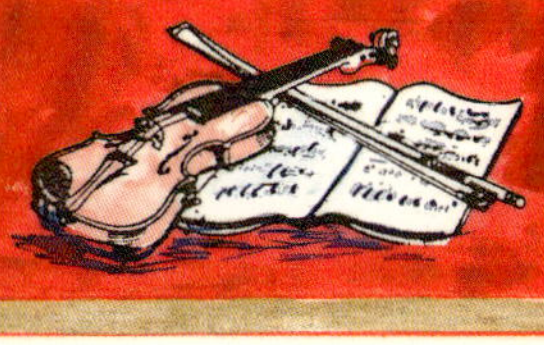

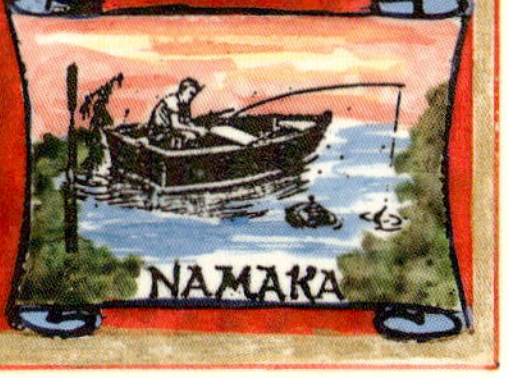
NAMAKA

C.H.T.

Dr. A. Ernest Pallister

Inducted: 1996

DR. A. ERNEST PALLISTER HAS HELPED Albertans and Canadians appreciate and seize this country's enormous potential. He has shown extraordinary foresight not only in recognizing the changing needs of industry, government and society, but also in meeting them.

Born in Edmonton in 1927, Dr. Pallister received his BSc in 1948 from the University of Alberta and a diploma from the Banff School of Advanced Management in 1962.

Dr. Pallister was one of the first Canadians to have conceived of the idea of consortia among government, industry and academia as a superior means of conducting exploration and research. He initiated interdisciplinary exploration for petroleum in Alberta, the Northwest Territories and the Arctic Ocean in the early 1950s. He continued his interest in the Canadian North by serving as chairman of the Arctic Institute of North America, and the Science Institute of the Northwest Territories and as vice-chairman of the Inuvialut Arbitration Board.

Dr. Pallister was the founding chairman of three centres for collaborative research and development: the Centre for Cold Ocean Resources Engineering (C-CORE), established in St. John's in 1975; the Veterinary Infectious Disease Organization (VIDO), established in Saskatoon in 1975; and the Centre for Frontier Engineering Research (C-FER), established in Edmonton in 1984. During this period he was an associate of the Devonian Foundation.

Due to Dr. Pallister's prodigious intellect and leadership abilities, these organizations have become pre-eminent in their fields and are all multi-million dollar, high-technology organizations serving Canadians. Their impact on the economy has been enormous. They have attracted leading scientists and engineers, enabled universities to have a much greater impact on industry and made important contributions to the growth and prosperity of the national economy.

President of Pallister Resource Management Ltd., Dr. Pallister also served as director of major companies such as NOVA, Husky Oil, CanOcean Resources and other Alberta companies. Dr. Pallister has been the principal architect of integrating research and technology with business strategy, thereby enhancing competitiveness and growth. He has promoted Canadian technology and industry at home and abroad and has helped make Canada a significant force in the global arena.

Dr. Pallister has shown how the formidable challenges posed by climate, geography and society can be turned to advantage. He has been able to identify and implement novel, practical solutions to overcoming barriers. While research and development consortia are now commonplace, Dr. Pallister was one of the first to recognize that progress and development are best achieved through multi-sectoral partnerships.

Dr. Pallister has served on numerous boards, committees and councils, providing leadership across a broad spectrum of professional and community organizations. He has served as vice-chairman of the Science Council of Canada and the Banff School of Advanced Management; a designer of the Petroleum Resources Communication Foundation; a director of the Calgary Philharmonic Society; a member of the Federal Task Force on the Canadian Ocean Industry; committee chairman for the Royal Commission on the Ocean Ranger; and President of Casa Higuera Inc. in Mexico.

Dr. Pallister was awarded an Honorary Doctor of Laws degree from the University of Alberta and an Honorary Doctor of Science from Memorial University of Newfoundland. He was given Honorary Life Membership in the Canadian Society of Exploration Geophysicists and the Canadian Society of Petroleum Geologists. He is a Life Member of the Association of Professional Engineers, Geologists and Geophysicists of Alberta. He was made an Officer of the Order of Canada in 1990.

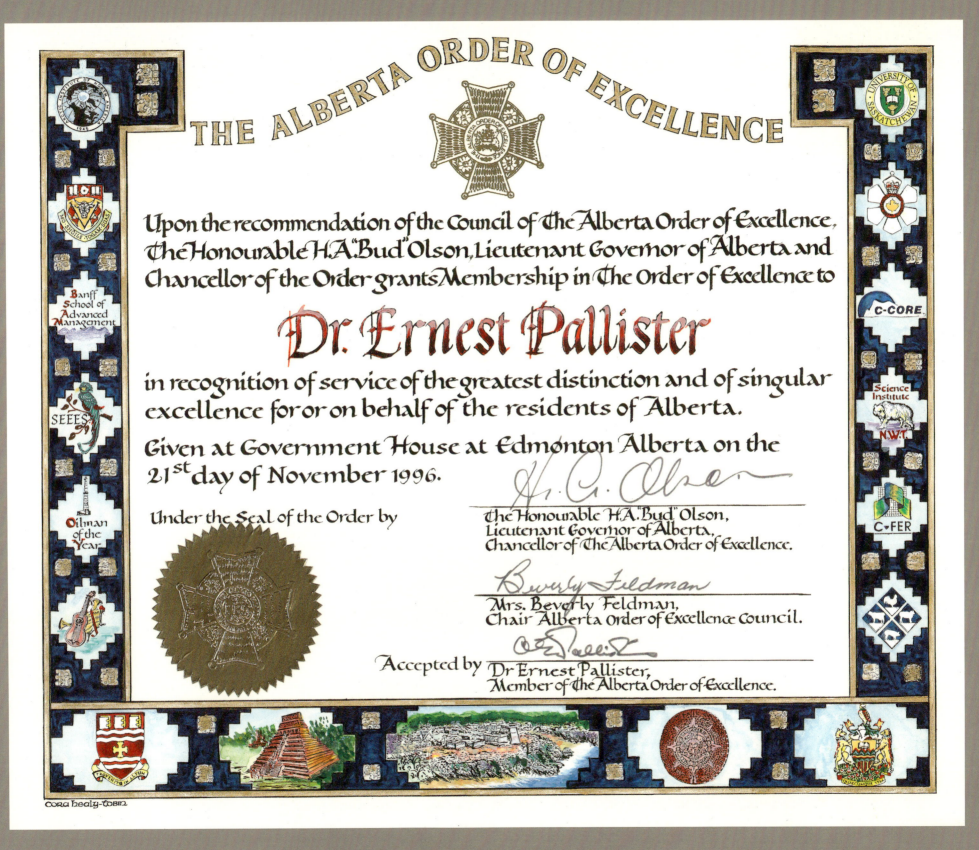

Dr. John Snow

Inducted: 1996

DR. JOHN HAROLD THOMAS SNOW was a man of rare accomplishment. He excelled in not one but two entirely different occupations: fine art and finance.

The artist-banker was born in Vancouver, British Columbia, in 1911. As a young boy, his family moved to England, where they remained during the First World War. Under the influence of his artistic relatives, Dr. Snow developed an enduring interest in art and music.

In 1919, Dr. Snow returned to Canada and settled in Olds. On 3 August 1928, he joined the Royal Bank of Canada and began a distinguished banking career that would last 43 years. The only interruption was to serve as a navigator in the Royal Canadian Air Force and the Royal Air Force during World War II. Tours of duty in Great Britain, India and Northern Africa provided opportunities for him to visit some of the world's great museums, which would profoundly influence his art and his life.

After the war, Dr. Snow returned to Calgary, where he resumed his careers in banking and art. Influenced by the modernist European approaches he was exposed to during the war, Dr. Snow evoked the Prairie experience in a startlingly new, contemporary way in his art.

His desire to make art accessible to persons of all means drew Dr. Snow to printmaking. Encouraged by Glen Alps, a printmaker with the University of Washington in Seattle, Dr. Snow and a friend, architect Maxwell Bates, bought two presses and began to explore fine-art lithography. No one in Alberta was producing fine art lithography at the time, so the two men essentially taught themselves. Not only did they become proficient, but they soon mastered the art form. Alberta is now regarded internationally as a printmaking centre, in large part due to the pioneering work of Dr. Snow.

Dr. Snow's prints have been described as "moody and rich-hued," and "varied and venturesome." He himself has said of his work that "colouring is of primary importance." Dr. Snow has been called "a central figure in Canadian art" who helped usher Alberta into the modernist period—not by imitating foreign styles but by inventing a vocabulary unique to the province. He is praised for his generosity, approachability, and gentleness, qualities that have made him a mentor to new generations of artists.

Dr. Snow retired from the banking world in 1971, as assistant manager of Calgary's main branch. Some of his works are proudly displayed in the bank's head office in Montréal.

A man with wide-ranging interests and talents, he has been an active member of artistic communities throughout Western Canada. Besides maintaining a prolific career in the visual arts, he organized the Calgary Film Society in the late 1940s and served as its president. He is also an accomplished musician and has designed many sets for television and theatre. Dr. Snow was instrumental in creating the New Works Calgary Society, which is dedicated to presenting new composition and has premiered 80 pieces of music, many commissioned by the Society.

Dr. Snow's work has been the subject of numerous exhibitions throughout Canada. His work has also been shown in the U.S., Japan, France, England, Chile, Mexico, Italy, Scotland and Australia. It has also been commissioned by such agencies as the Royal Canadian Academy, Parks Canada, the City of Calgary and Grant MacEwan Community College in Edmonton. His work can be found in the National Gallery of Canada, the residence of the governor-general of Canada and Alberta's Government House in Edmonton.

Dr. Snow is now deceased.

THE ALBERTA ORDER OF EXCELLENCE

Upon the recommendation of the Council of The Alberta Order of Excellence, The Honourable H.A. "Bud" Olson, Lieutenant Governor of Alberta and Chancellor of the Order grants Membership in The Order of Excellence to

Dr John Snow

in recognition of service of the greatest distinction and of singular excellence for or on behalf of the residents of Alberta.

Given at Government House at Edmonton Alberta on the 21st day of November 1996.

Under the Seal of the Order by

The Honourable H.A. "Bud" Olson,
Lieutenant Governor of Alberta and
Chancellor of The Alberta Order of Excellence.

Mrs. Beverly Feldman,
Chair, Alberta Order of Excellence Council.

Accepted by

Dr. John Snow,
Member of The Alberta Order of Excellence.

Cora Healy-Tobin

Ian Malcolm Macdonald

Inducted: 1997

IAN MACDONALD'S INTEGRITY and leadership made Fairview College a pioneer in Alberta's college system. Under his leadership, the college successfully navigated a change in its governance structure and enjoyed exponential growth while remaining on a solid financial footing. He also helped the Alberta cattle industry earn its international reputation for high-quality beef.

Ian Malcolm Macdonald was born in 1932 in Fairview, Alberta, where he grew up on his family's farm. In 1953, he graduated with honours from the first class of the Alberta School of Agriculture, now Fairview College. He went on to earn certificates in Business Administration (1968) and Personnel Management (1969) from the Western Co-operative College in Saskatoon, and in computers for farm management (1991) from Fairview College.

In 1978, Mr. Macdonald was appointed to a six-year term as the chair of Fairview College's first Board of Governors. He returned for a second term in 1987 at the request of the Minister of Advanced Education, becoming the longest-serving board chair in the history of Alberta's college system.

With Mr. Macdonald at the helm, Fairview College successfully navigated the transition from provincial administration to board governance. The college went through a $14 million expansion, growing from an enrollment base of 200 students on a single campus to more than 1,000 students on 12 satellite campuses located throughout northwestern Alberta. The college's programming expanded from agricultural studies to include trades and full apprenticeship programs. Specialty programs, such as beekeeping and motorcycle mechanics, were also introduced.

Fairview College awarded Mr. Macdonald an honorary diploma in 1997 for outstanding service to the college and the community of Fairview. He also received the Canada 125 Confederation Medal in recognition of his work on the College's Board of Governors.

Ian Macdonald has also had a great impact on the development of Alberta's beef industry. He was a member of the Alberta Schools of Agriculture Provincial Advisory Committee in 1962; a founding member and Vice-Chair of the Alberta Cattle Commission from 1969 to 1975; President of the Alberta Livestock Cooperative Ltd. from 1971 to 1978; and President of the Western Cooperative Livestock Markets from 1972 to 1975.

He managed the Peace River Livestock Co-op from 1961 to 1979, overseeing its growth from $500,000 in annual turnover to $7 million. The co-op's businesses included a feed-processing plant and a livestock market, which shipped livestock throughout northwestern Alberta.

Ian Macdonald raised the profile of Aberdeen Angus cattle both in Alberta and internationally. He served as president of the Alberta Aberdeen Angus Association from 1978 to 1979 and as a member of the Canadian Aberdeen Angus Board of Directors from 1978 to 1983, when the "Quality Angus Beef" program was initiated. Now many high-end Canadian restaurants serve only Angus beef under strict quality controls. Aberdeen Angus cattle and bull semen from Mr. Macdonald's Fairmac Farm have been shipped throughout Canada and exported into the United States, Japan and Australia.

Mr. Macdonald also has a distinguished record of service to his community and his country. He received the Queen's Commission in the Royal Canadian Air Force Primary Reserve in 1954. In 1969, Mr. Macdonald was instrumental in establishing a much needed veterinary clinic in Fairview. He served as a member of the Alberta Treasury Branches Agricultural Producers Advisory Committee in 1991 and was appointed to the Board of Directors in 1996. He has also served with the Royal Canadian Legion, the Masonic Lodge and the Rotary Club of Fairview.

Throughout the 42 years of their marriage, Ian Macdonald and his late wife Mary worked side by side to develop their Aberdeen Angus cattle herd and serve their community.

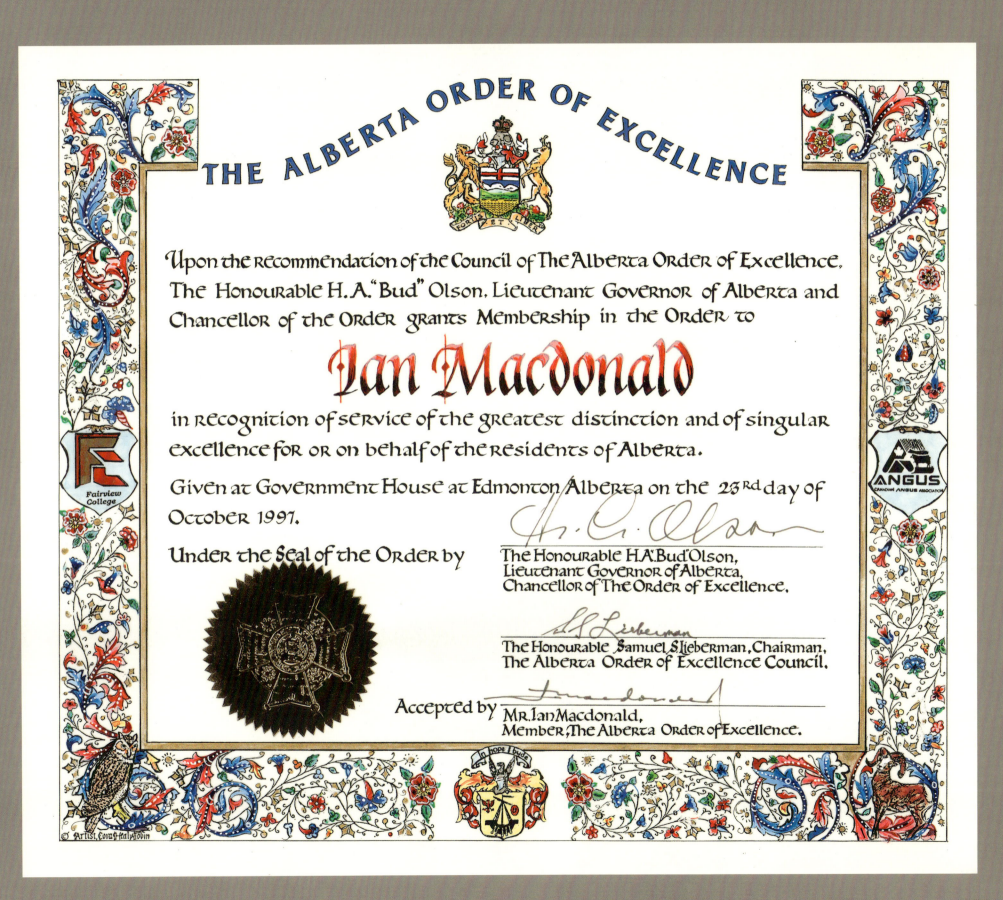

THE ALBERTA ORDER OF EXCELLENCE

Upon the recommendation of the Council of The Alberta Order of Excellence, The Honourable H.A. "Bud" Olson, Lieutenant Governor of Alberta and Chancellor of the Order grants Membership in the Order to

Ian Macdonald

in recognition of service of the greatest distinction and of singular excellence for or on behalf of the residents of Alberta.

Given at Government House at Edmonton, Alberta on the 23rd day of October 1997.

Under the Seal of the Order by

The Honourable H.A. "Bud" Olson,
Lieutenant Governor of Alberta,
Chancellor of The Order of Excellence.

The Honourable Samuel S. Lieberman, Chairman,
The Alberta Order of Excellence Council.

Accepted by

Mr. Ian Macdonald,
Member, The Alberta Order of Excellence.

Arthur Ryan Smith

Inducted: 1997

ARTHUR RYAN SMITH'S QUIET CONFIDENCE has earned him the respect of his peers and accolades from fellow Albertans. His exceptional record of lifelong public service, demonstrated through his terms as a Calgary alderman, a Member of the Legislative Assembly of Alberta, a Member of Parliament and a business advisor, confirm the commitment Mr. Smith has to the betterment of his community.

Born in Calgary in 1919, Mr. Smith first took on the challenge of public service by enlisting with the military in 1939. Serving as a Royal Air Force Bomber Pathfinder Captain until 1944, he received his first award of merit with the Distinguished Flying Cross in 1943.

Following his wartime service, Mr. Smith began a new career in Alberta's oil and gas sector, participating in the early development of this province's valuable resource-based industry.

Continuing to build on his public service career, he ran for and was elected to Calgary city council in 1952, the Alberta Legislature in 1954 and the House of Commons, where he served from 1957 until 1962. While serving as a Member of Parliament, Mr. Smith participated in sessions at the United Nations, representing Canada on issues such as the Middle East and apartheid.

Following his public service career, Mr. Smith resumed his business career. Through the years, he has worked for various corporations. For 18 years, Mr. Smith was the president and Chief Executive Officer for the predecessor company to SNC-Lavolin Inc. He has received international awards for marketing.

Mr. Smith has also shared his business experience with many students. He has lectured on various business subjects at the Banff School of Fine Arts, the Southern Alberta Institute of Technology and Mount Royal College. At the University of Calgary, he lectured for the Political Science Department. In addition to his academic work at these educational institutions, Mr. Smith has assisted in fundraising efforts.

In 1981, his business acumen was noticed by the past mayor of Calgary, Ralph Klein, who asked Mr. Smith to assist in the formation of the Calgary Economic Development Authority. Then, in 1994, Mr. Smith's expertise was required once again when the Alberta Economic Development Authority was created from the model developed in Calgary.

Mr. Smith continues to work as a business consultant and advisor to senior management at SNC-Lavolin Inc., as well as to other clients.

In 1988, Mr. Smith served as the Chief of Protocol at the Calgary Winter Olympics. He has also offered his services in the founding of the Calgary Booster Club, the Olympic Development Association and the University of Calgary's International School of Business.

In 1997, Mr. Smith received yet another honour: the title of Honorary Colonel of the 416 Fighter Squadron. In 1961 and 1962, Mr. Smith was the president of the Air Cadet League.

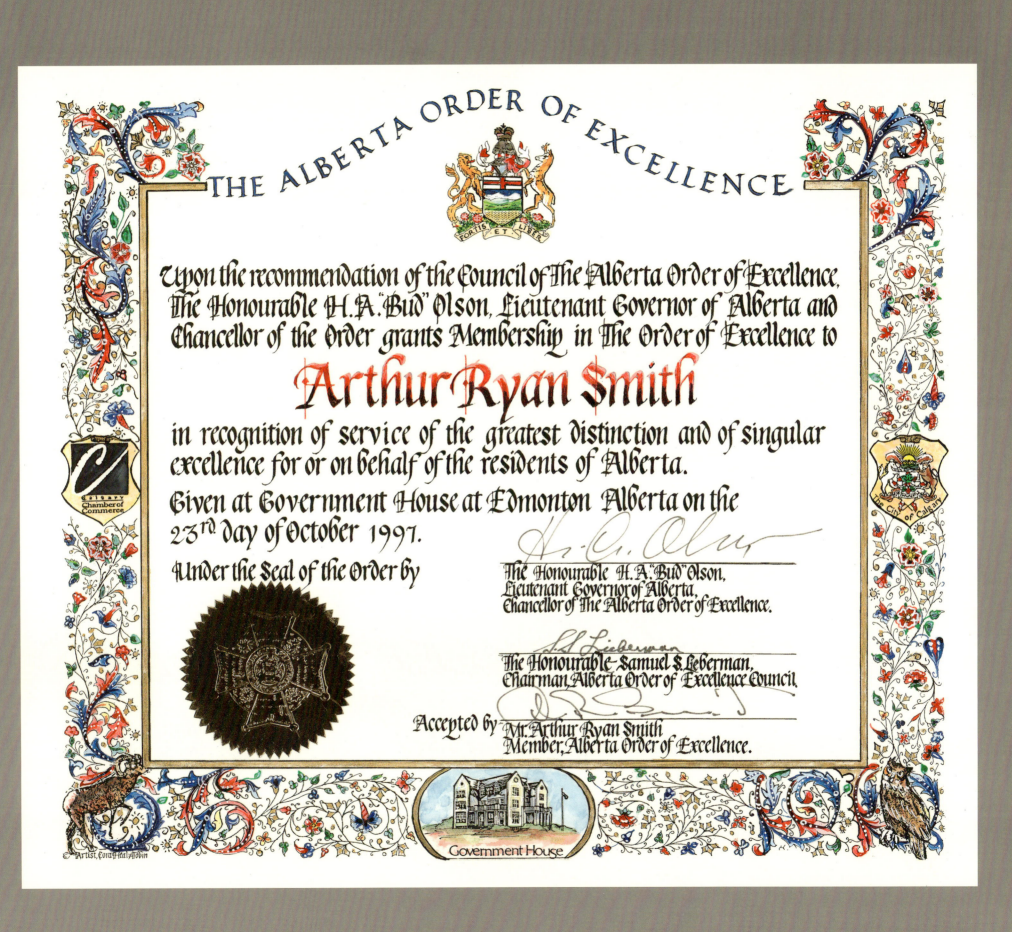

THE ALBERTA ORDER OF EXCELLENCE

FORTIS ET LIBER

Upon the recommendation of the Council of The Alberta Order of Excellence, The Honourable H.A."Bud" Olson, Lieutenant Governor of Alberta and Chancellor of the Order grants Membership in The Order of Excellence to

Arthur Ryan Smith

in recognition of service of the greatest distinction and of singular excellence for or on behalf of the residents of Alberta.

Given at Government House at Edmonton Alberta on the 23rd day of October 1997.

Under the Seal of the Order by

The Honourable H.A."Bud" Olson, Lieutenant Governor of Alberta, Chancellor of The Alberta Order of Excellence.

The Honourable Samuel S. Lieberman, Chairman, Alberta Order of Excellence Council.

Accepted by Mr. Arthur Ryan Smith Member, Alberta Order of Excellence.

Calgary Chamber of Commerce

The City of Calgary

Government House

© Artist, Cora Healy Tobin

Harley Norman Hotchkiss

Inducted: 1998

HARLEY HOTCHKISS IS A BUSINESS and community leader who has made great contributions to health and sports development in Canada.

Harley Norman Hotchkiss was born in Tillsonburg, Ontario, in 1927. After World War II service in the Canadian Merchant Marine from 1944 to 1945, he graduated from Michigan State University in 1951 with high honours, having received a Bachelor of Science in geology. The same institution awarded him an Outstanding Alumni Award in 1989 and a Distinguished Hockey Alumnus Award in 1992. He received an Honorary Doctor of Laws degree from the University of Calgary and was appointed an Officer of the Order of Canada in 1998.

Mr. Hotchkiss has worked as a geologist, manager, and president for several petroleum companies. He has also pursued business interests in oil and gas, real estate, agriculture and professional sports.

Harley Hotchkiss has played a major role in the development of professional and amateur sport in Canada. In 1980, he participated in purchasing the National Hockey League franchise that became the Calgary Flames Hockey Club. This led to the development of the International Hockey Centre for Excellence in Calgary through a commitment of $5 million by the Flames' owners. In conjunction with Hockey Canada and the Canadian Olympic Team, the Centre for Excellence offers coaching clinics and videos, research in hockey development and sports injuries and athletic scholarships to Canadian universities. His long-standing services as chair of the National Hockey League's Board of Governors has made him a strong supporter of Canadian NHL teams in smaller market cities.

Mr. Hotchkiss has also made great contributions to the health sector as a volunteer. At a time when Alberta's health system was undergoing tremendous change, his leadership and dedication helped raise awareness of the many exciting health initiatives occurring in Calgary, and focussed attention on positive outcomes.

From 1994–1997, he co-chaired the Partners in Health Campaign, a $50-million fundraising project to support health-related initiatives in the Calgary area. There were numerous challenges during the campaign, including the reorganization of the health system into regional health authorities, an initially slow economy, and competition from many other fundraising initiatives. Despite these obstacles, the campaign reached its target in less than three years. Funding from Partners in Health supported the development of the first intraoperative magnetic resonance imaging centre in Canada; helped attract world-class researchers and clinicians to Alberta; and bought state-of-the-art medical equipment that has enhanced health care for Albertans.

He is a member of the Foothills Hospital Development Council and a former chair of the Foothills Provincial General Hospital Board of Management.

Harley Hotchkiss is also a member of the Association of Professional Engineers, Geologists and Geophysicists of Alberta, the Canadian Institute of Mining and Metallurgy and Petroleum, the Canadian Society of Petroleum Geologists, the American Association of Geologists, the Geological Association of Canada, the Society of Petroleum Engineers of the American Institute of Metallurgical Engineers, the Calgary Petroleum Club, the Ranchmen's Club and the Griffiths Island Club.

His volunteer commitments have included the United Way, Calgary Family Service Bureau, the Alberta Paraplegic Association, the Independent Petroleum Association of Canada and the Michigan State University Foundation Board. He served as governor and vice-chair of the Banff Centre, chair of the Manning Awards Selection Committee and as a governor and chair of the Alberta Governors of the Olympic Trust of Canada.

THE ALBERTA ORDER OF EXCELLENCE

Upon the recommendation of the Council of The Alberta Order of Excellence The Honourable H.A."Bud" Olson Lieutenant Governor of Alberta and Chancellor of the Order grants Membership in The Order of Excellence to

Harley Norman Hotchkiss

in recognition of service of the greatest distinction and of singular excellence for or on behalf of the residents of Alberta.

Given at Government House at Edmonton Alberta on the 22nd day of October 1998

Under the Seal of the Order by

The Honourable H.A."Bud" Olson,
Lieutenant Governor of Alberta,
Chancellor, The Alberta Order of Excellence.

The Honourable Samuel S. Lieberman, Chairman
The Alberta Order of Excellence Council.

Accepted by

Harley Norman Hotchkiss,
Member, The Alberta Order of Excellence.

UNIVERSITY OF CALGARY

MICHIGAN STATE UNIVERSITY

CALGARY FLAMES

Artist, Cora Healy Tobin

June Louise Lore

Inducted: 1998

JUNE LORE'S INTEREST IN EDUCATION, history and agriculture combined with her limitless energy have left an indelible mark on her community and the province of Alberta.

June Louise Oel was born in Acme, Alberta, in 1930. She attended public school there until her family moved to Calgary. In 1949, she graduated from Crescent Heights High School. Mrs. Lore credits her parents for teaching her the importance of public service and the value of hard work. From an early age, she demonstrated concern for others and an interest in her community.

In 1953, she married Jim Lore, a fellow student at the University of Alberta, and received a Bachelor of Science degree in Nursing the following year. Mr. and Mrs. Lore settled on a farm east of Carstairs where they raised their family.

Mrs. Lore's interest in education led to her involvement with the Home and School Association. In 1968, she became an area director for the Alberta Federation of Home and School Associations and in 1970 was elected president. In that capacity, Mrs. Lore worked closely with Alberta Education, serving on several committees including the modified school year, language arts and the Alberta school evaluation project. In 1976, Mrs. Lore was named president of the Canadian Home and School and Parent-Teacher Federation and became chair of the association's International Committee. Under her leadership, the committee successfully applied for and received funding from the Canadian International Development Agency (CIDA) for their "Friendship for Peace Project."

The "Friendship for Peace Project" encouraged teachers and students across Canada to learn more about developing nations. The project promoted an exchange of friendship, ideas and experiences between classrooms around the world. The CIDA grant assisted in the printing of a brochure that listed many organizations whose work helps to make a difference in the Third World. This brochure was distributed in English and French to every school in Canada and was an excellent resource for educators and students.

In recognition of her many years of dedicated service, Mrs. Lore received life memberships in the Alberta Home and School Association and the Canadian Federation of Home and School and Parent-Teacher Federation.

June Lore is a founding member of the Stockmen's Memorial Foundation, an organization dedicated to honour and remember the builders of the livestock industry. Mrs. Lore has served this organization in the positions of Secretary-Treasurer, President and Chair of the Board of Governors. During her term as president, she negotiated with the Canadian Rodeo Historical Association to jointly build the Western Heritage Centre. This interactive museum situated north of Cochrane, Alberta houses a library with materials covering the history of the livestock industry, works of art by renowned Western and Native artists and historical artifacts of Alberta's ranching and rodeo history.

In 1986, Mrs. Lore received a Woman of Distinction Award from the Calgary YWCA in recognition of the positive contribution she has made to her community through her numerous volunteer efforts.

THE ALBERTA ORDER OF EXCELLENCE

Upon the recommendation of the Council of The Alberta Order of Excellence The Honourable H.A. "Bud" Olson Lieutenant Governor of Alberta and Chancellor of the Order grants Membership in the Order to

June Louise Lore

in recognition of service of the greatest distinction and of singular Excellence for or on behalf of the residents of Alberta.

Given at Government House at Edmonton Alberta on the 22nd day of October 1998

Under the Seal of the Order by

The Honourable H.A. "Bud" Olson,
Lieutenant Governor of Alberta, Chancellor
of The Alberta Order of Excellence.

The Honourable Samuel S Lieberman,
Chairman, Alberta Order of Excellence Council.

Accepted by

June Louise Lore,
Member The Alberta Order of Excellence.

Artist, Cora Healy Tobin

THE WESTERN HERITAGE CENTRE

STOCKMEN'S MEMORIAL FOUNDATION

Sandy Auld Mactaggart

Inducted: 1998

SANDY MACTAGGART IS AN ENTREPRENEUR and philanthropist with provincial, national and international achievements in business, the arts and education.

Sandy Auld Mactaggart was born in Glasgow, Scotland, in 1928. He was evacuated to Canada at the age of 11 during World War II. After schooling in Ontario at Lakefield College School and in New England at the Choate School, he graduated cum laude from Harvard College in 1950 with a Bachelor of Arts degree in Architecture. In 1952, he received his Master of Business Administration degree from the Harvard Business School. He was awarded an Honorary Doctor of Laws degree from the University of Alberta in 1990.

He came to Edmonton in 1952 and two years later incorporated Maclab Enterprises Ltd. with the late Jean de La Bruyère. These companies engaged in property development and venture capital activities in Western Canada, the United States and other parts of the world.

Sandy Mactaggart's interest and support have been extended to many of the major cultural and artistic facilities in Alberta's capital city. He was one of four founders of the Citadel, Edmonton's first professional regional theatre. He continues to support the Citadel as a governor and through the sponsorship of one theatre production each year on the Maclab stage, named in recognition of his company's contributions to its construction.

Mr. Mactaggart's service to post-secondary schools includes duties as a trustee emeritus and former treasurer of the American University of Beirut; member of Harvard Resources Committee; and director and vice-president of the Harvard Alumni Association. In 1995–1996, he served the association as director of the Harvard Clubs in Canada.

From 1983 to 1994, Sandy Mactaggart served on the University of Alberta Board of Governors and chaired the University's Real Estate Advisory Committee. During this time, together with the province, he donated the 257-acre Mactaggart Nature Sanctuary to the University and the City of Edmonton. He chaired the University of Alberta Foundation for the first five years of its existence until 1994. On 1 July 1990, he became the University's 14th chancellor, a position he held for four years. In 1993, he was also appointed interim chair of the University's Board of Governors, and served in that capacity for six months.

In his twin roles of chancellor and chair of the Board of Governors, Mr. Mactaggart helped the University negotiate a transition in leadership and changes in government funding. He took steps to strengthen the bond between the University and the public to create a larger base of community support for post-secondary education. He introduced visiting committees, modeled after a successful program at Harvard, in which community leaders are invited to tour university faculties and meet academic staff. The visiting committees have become a permanent and effective tool to facilitate dialogue between the community and the University.

In 1995, Sandy Mactaggart received the James L. Fisher Award for Distinguished Service to Education from the Washington, DC-based Council for Advancement and Support of Education.

Mr. Mactaggart served in the Calgary Fleet Air Arm Reserve Squadron and on the founding boards of the present Edmonton Art Gallery, the Boys' and Girls' Clubs of Alberta and Tempo School. He is, or has been, a director of several organizations, including the C.D. Howe Institute, the Chief Executives Organization, the Lakefield College School and the Choate Fund in Ontario. In 1993, he was appointed to the Advisory Board of the Royal Society of Canada and the Donner Canadian Foundation, which he served until 1998. In 1997, he was appointed Alberta nominee to the national roster of panelists who adjudicate disputes under the Agreement on Internal Trade.

He received an Honorary Doctor of Laws degree from the University of Alberta in 1990. In 1997, Sandy Mactaggart was appointed an Officer of the Order of Canada.

Mr. Mactaggart's interests have included boating, scuba diving, flying, shooting, car racing, and collecting books, oriental textiles and Chinese paintings. He was married in 1959 to author Cécile Erickson.

THE ALBERTA ORDER OF EXCELLENCE

Upon the recommendation of the Council of The Alberta Order of Excellence The Honourable H.A. "Bud" Olson Lieutenant Governor of Alberta and Chancellor of the Order grants Membership in the Order of Excellence to

Sandy Auld Mactaggart

in recognition of service of the greatest distinction and of singular excellence for or on behalf of the residents of Alberta

Given at Government House at Edmonton Alberta on the 22nd day of October 1998.

Under the Seal of the Order by

The Honourable H.A. "Bud" Olson,
Lieutenant Governor of Alberta, Chancellor
of The Alberta Order of Excellence.

The Honourable Samuel S. Lieberman,
Chairman Alberta Order of Excellence Council

Accepted by

Sandy Auld Mactaggart,
Member The Alberta Order of Excellence.

University of Alberta

QUAECUMQUE VERA

Mactaggart

Artist. Cora Healy Tobin

The Citadel Theatre

Dr. Donald Russell Stanley

Inducted: 1998

DONALD STANLEY HAS BEEN A LEADER in the field of environmental engineering and has also achieved recognition of his numerous community, athletic and business endeavours.

Born on 18 October 1917 in Edmonton, Donald Russell Stanley attended Eastwood High School and graduated with distinction from the University of Alberta with a Bachelor of Science degree in Engineering in 1940. In 1988, the University of Alberta recognized Dr. Stanley's contributions by conferring an Honorary Degree of Doctor of Science on him.

Although he participated in many sports throughout high school and university, including basketball, football and soccer, his major accomplishments were as a hockey player. Like his father, Barney, a member of the Hockey Hall of Fame, Donald Stanley was an exceptional hockey player. He played with two Canadian teams, the Sudbury Wolves and the Edmonton Mercurys, at the World Hockey Championships in Sweden in 1949 and England in 1950, where Canada won the gold cup.

Following his service in the Royal Canadian Air Force as an engineering officer from 1942 to 1945, Donald Stanley returned to Edmonton to begin his engineering career. He was the director of Environmental Engineering for the Government of Alberta, and his responsibilities covered the entire province. During this period he received a Rockefeller Foundation Fellowship, allowing him to attend Harvard University where he received his Master of Science degree in 1948, followed by his Doctorate in environmental engineering in 1953.

In 1954, Dr. Stanley founded Stanley Associates Engineering, a one-man operation that grew into Stanley Technology Group Inc., an international, multi-disciplinary organization with locations in over 40 countries worldwide. The group's recent projects include the Confederation Bridge linking Prince Edward Island with mainland Canada, the rehabilitation of Edmonton's High Level Bridge, as well as numerous water and transportation projects throughout the world. Dr. Stanley continues to serve the group as honorary chair of the board.

Throughout his professional career, Dr. Stanley served as an innovator in developing techniques for the construction and operation of environmental installations. Malaysia, Philippines, Tanzania and Canada have benefited from his methods. His business acumen and engineering abilities have resulted in numerous awards and honours. The Association of Consulting Engineers of Canada has twice honoured him, first in 1984 with the Carson F. Morrison Award for his accomplishments in technical design, leadership in business, ethics and service to the engineering profession and again in 1996 with the Beaubien Award, which is the highest mark of distinction for a Canadian consulting engineer. He also received an Honorary Doctor of Science degree from the University of Alberta in 1988.

In 1997, the Canadian Society for Civil Engineering awarded him the Albert E. Berry Medal for lifelong achievement in the field of engineering. Induction into the University of Alberta's Sports Wall of Fame in 1988 saluted his academic excellence and outstanding performance in athletics.

Dr. Stanley has been active in numerous community organizations. He served as president of both the Alberta and Edmonton Chambers of Commerce, as a member of the University of Alberta Senate and Board of Governors and as president of the Alumni Association. The Commonwealth Games in Edmonton in 1978 benefited from his effort as chair of the Facilities Committee. In 1993, he served as a member of the Alberta Round Table on Environment and Economy and the Legislative Review Panel on the Environment. Taking on wider-reaching responsibilities, he served as a member of the Expert Advisory Committee on Environmental Health for the World Health Organization and was a founding member and fellow of the Canadian Academy of Engineering.

A lifelong resident of Edmonton, Donald Stanley married Joan Bibby in 1960 and raised three children, Mary Louise, Russell and Donald.

Dr. Stanley is now deceased.

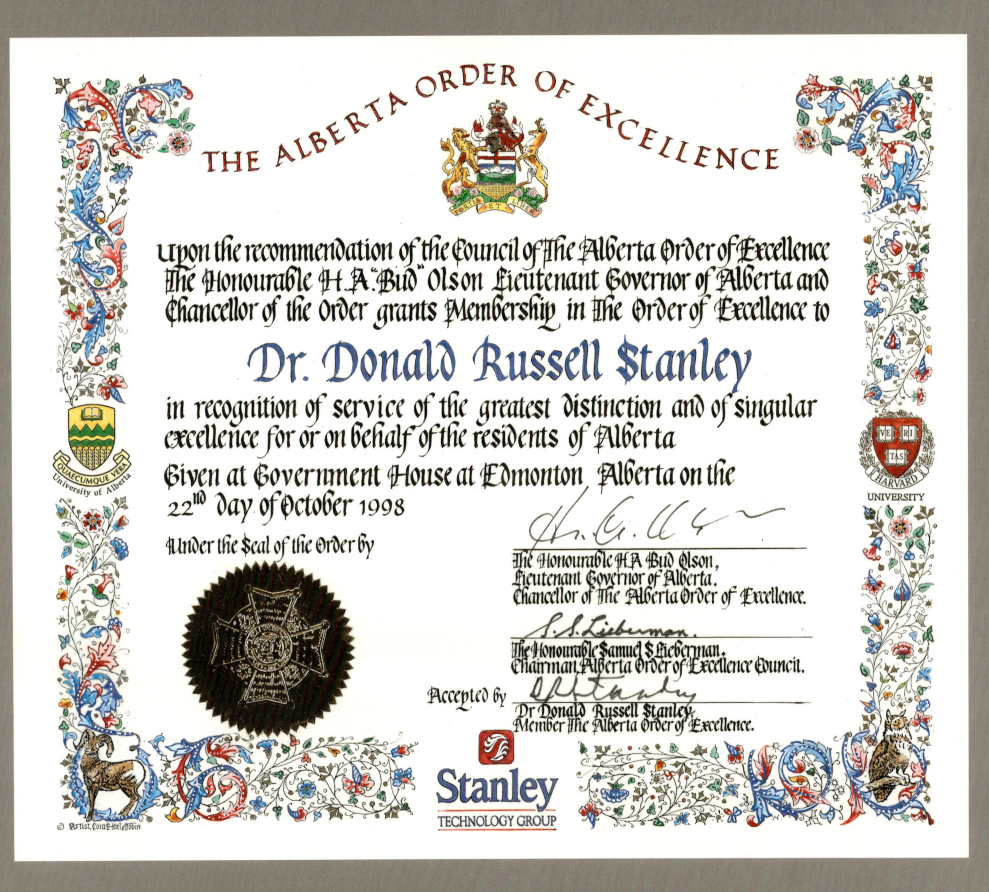

Donald Ross Getty

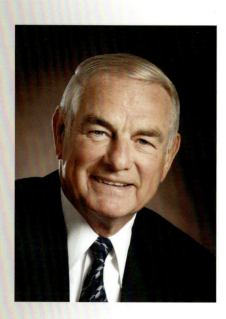

Inducted: 1999

DON GETTY WAS THE 11TH PREMIER of Alberta and has made tremendous contributions to business, politics and athletics in Canada.

Donald Ross Getty was born in Westmount, Québec, in 1933. He graduated from the University of Western Ontario in 1955 with an honours degree in Business Administration. Mr. Getty played on the University's championship football and basketball teams and in 1980 was named to the institution's athletic hall of fame.

In 1955, Mr. Getty made his first trip to Alberta to play football for the Edmonton Eskimos of the Canadian Football League. During his 10-year career, he distinguished himself as the first Canadian quarterback to lead his team to a Grey Cup championship since the import system was introduced. He is also a member of the Edmonton Eskimos Wall of Honour.

Mr. Getty began his business career with Imperial Oil and later became Canada's youngest independent oil company president when he formed Baldonnel Oil and Gas Ltd.

Having achieved a great deal of success in Alberta, Don Getty became interested in public service as a way to give something back to the province he had grown to love. In 1967, he was elected to the Legislature as a Progressive Conservative and helped form the official opposition. After his party won the election in 1971, Mr. Getty was appointed Alberta's first Minister of Federal and Intergovernmental Affairs and worked to ensure that Alberta was an equal partner in making national decisions that affected the province.

Mr. Getty's next cabinet post was as Minister of Energy and Natural Resources. He established Alberta's constitutional right to ownership of its natural resources, began the process of economic diversification by promoting the forestry and petrochemical industries, and helped to negotiate the Syncrude oil sands project. He started the Alberta Energy Company, which played a vital role in the development of Alberta's petrochemical industry, and he was also part of a small core group that conceived the Heritage Savings Trust Fund. The fund is an ongoing legacy of saving for the future: strengthening and diversifying Alberta's economy, and improving the quality of life for current and future generations of Albertans.

In 1979, after 12 years in the legislature, Don Getty left politics to spend more time with his family and return to his business career. His business acumen gained him positions on the boards of Canada's leading companies, including Interprovincial Pipe and Steel Corporation, Genstar Corporation, Nova Corporation and the Royal Bank of Canada.

Remaining interested in provincial politics, Mr. Getty resumed his political career in 1985 when he was elected leader of the Alberta Progressive Conservative Party and sworn in as premier. He led the Government of Alberta through an accelerated diversification of the provincial economy, signed the first agreement in Canada to establish self-government for Métis people and began the process of fiscal restraint in difficult economic times. He also emphasized the importance of families and created Canada's first Family Day holiday.

As premier, Mr. Getty made important contributions that affected all of Canada. Under his direction, Alberta held the country's first senate election, which resulted in Canada's first and only appointment of an elected senator. He also played a leadership role among the premiers during negotiations for the Free Trade Agreement, Triple E Senate, Meech Lake Accord and Charlottetown Accord. In 1992, Don Getty resigned as premier and left the political arena.

Mr. Getty has received several honours for his contributions to Alberta's Aboriginal Peoples. The Whitefish Lake Band made him an Honorary Chief in 1990 and the Métis Nation of Alberta awarded him the Order of the Sash in 1991.

In 1998, Mr. Getty was appointed an Officer of the Order of Canada.

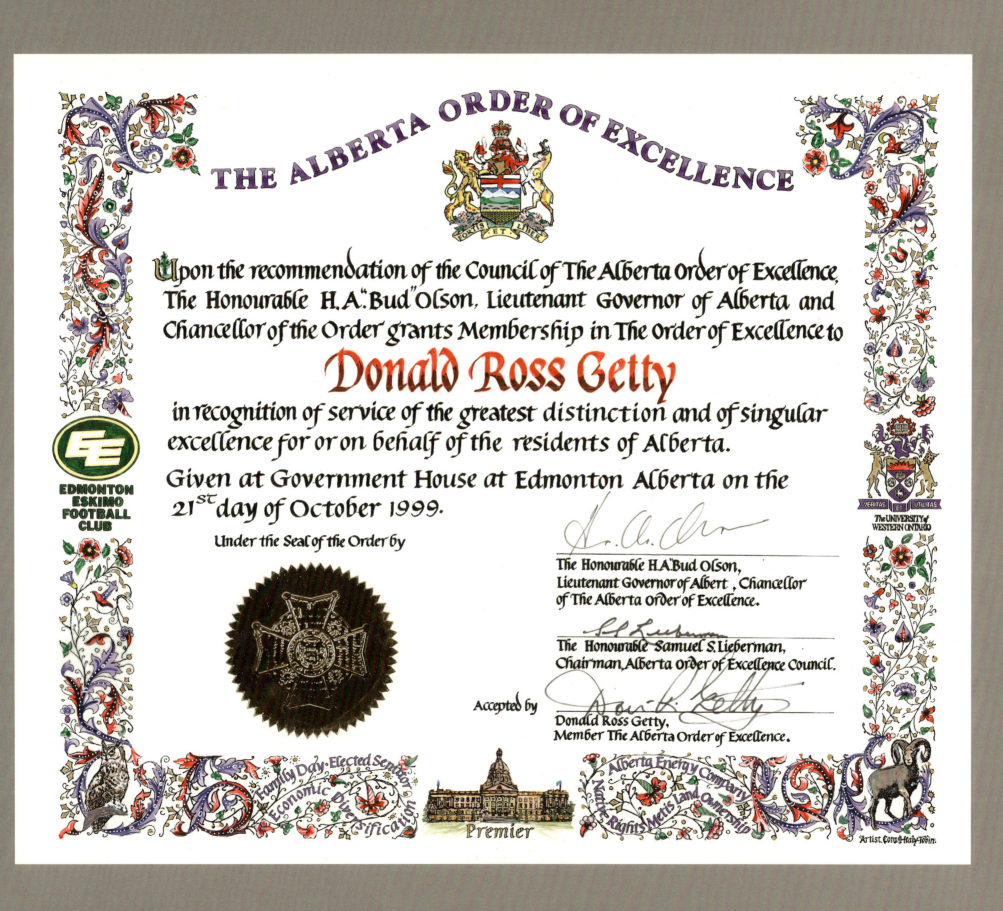

THE ALBERTA ORDER OF EXCELLENCE

Upon the recommendation of the Council of The Alberta Order of Excellence, The Honourable H.A."Bud" Olson, Lieutenant Governor of Alberta and Chancellor of the Order grants Membership in The Order of Excellence to

Donald Ross Getty

in recognition of service of the greatest distinction and of singular excellence for or on behalf of the residents of Alberta.

Given at Government House at Edmonton Alberta on the 21st day of October 1999.

Under the Seal of the Order by

The Honourable H.A"Bud Olson,
Lieutenant Governor of Albert , Chancellor
of The Alberta Order of Excellence.

The Honourable Samuel S. Lieberman,
Chairman, Alberta Order of Excellence Council.

Accepted by

Donald Ross Getty,
Member The Alberta Order of Excellence.

EDMONTON ESKIMO FOOTBALL CLUB

VERITAS ET UTILITAS
The UNIVERSITY of WESTERN ONTARIO

Family Day · Elected Senator · Economic Diversification

Premier

Alberta Energy Company · Native Rights Metis Land Ownership

Artist. Cora Heah Tobin.

Stanley George Reynolds

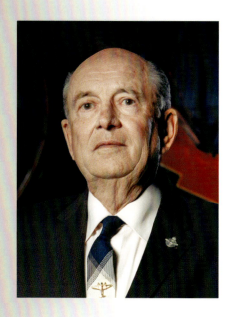

Inducted: 1999

STAN REYNOLDS IS A SUCCESSFUL BUSINESSMAN and dedicated collector whose generous contributions to the province have helped to preserve Alberta's aviation, transportation, industrial and agricultural heritage.

Stanley George Reynolds was born in Wetaskiwin, Alberta, in 1923. He inherited his love of collecting from his father, Ted Reynolds, a pilot and collector.

As a youth, Stan Reynolds worked in his father's garage after school hours. In 1942, his desire to fly aircraft led him to join the Royal Canadian Air Force, where he hoped to become a pilot. After earning his wings, he was stationed in Great Britain as part of a night-fighter squadron.

In 1945, Mr. Reynolds was discharged from the air force and returned to Wetaskiwin, where he started his own business selling used cars. He built this business into one of the most successful automotive dealerships in Alberta and led the development of Wetaskiwin into a major automotive sales centre.

With a rapidly growing business, Stan Reynolds expanded his operations and began selling new and used cars, trucks, farm machinery, industrial equipment, house trailers and airplanes.

Recognizing the growing importance of air transportation, he built the Wetaskiwin Airport and operated the facility until he transferred it to the City and County of Wetaskiwin in 1969. The airport attracted a number of aviation companies that continue to operate in the city. Stan Reynolds also served the people of Wetaskiwin as an alderman from 1952 to 1960.

During the late 1940s, after his business had grown, Mr. Reynolds was able to pursue his interest in collecting antique cars. His first acquisition was a 1911 Overland touring car, which he accepted as a trade-in and decided not to sell. Becoming concerned that Alberta was losing a vital part of its heritage, Mr. Reynolds extended his collection to include tractors, steam engines and airplanes.

By 1955, he had acquired enough items to open the private Reynolds Museum to display some of the extraordinary items he had collected. Stan Reynolds knew that his collection represented an important part of Alberta's social history as well as the technological evolution of the machines that helped develop the province. Rather than remain in his private museum, he felt the collection should be permanently displayed in a public museum where it could better educate and entertain the people of Alberta.

In 1981, Mr. Reynolds made a substantial donation to the province that included 850 important artifacts. This generous gift was the foundation for a new public facility operated by the Government of Alberta that opened in 1992. It was named the Reynolds-Alberta Museum to recognize the Reynolds family.

Mr. Reynolds has given additional gifts to the museum over the years and in 1999 made a second major donation of 60 historic aircraft, the largest and most significant collection in Canada outside of the National Aviation Museum.

Mr. Reynolds has received many honours, including a Heritage Canada Foundation Community Service Award in 1980 for heritage preservation and a Reilly Award from the Alberta Aviation Council in 1987 for his remarkable contributions to aviation in the province. The Wetaskiwin Chamber of Commerce named him Citizen of the Year in 1986, and in 1999 he was appointed a Member of the Order of Canada.

THE ALBERTA ORDER OF EXCELLENCE

FORTIS ET LIBER

Upon the recommendation of the Council of The Alberta Order of Excellence The Honourable H.A. "Bud" Olson, Lieutenant Governor of Alberta and Chancellor of the Order grants Membership in The Order of Excellence to

Stanley George Reynolds

in recognition of service of the greatest distinction and of singular excellence for or on behalf of the residents of Alberta.

Given at Government House at Edmonton Alberta on the 21st day of October 1999.

Under the Seal of the Order by

The Honourable H.A. Bud Olson,
Lieutenant Governor of Alberta, Chancellor
of The Alberta Order of Excellence.

The Honourable Samuel S. Lieberman, Chairman,
The Alberta Order of Excellence Council.

Accepted by

Stanley George Reynolds,
Member, The Alberta Order of Excellence.

CANADA'S AVIATION HALL OF FAME

REYNOLDS-ALBERTA MUSEUM

Artist, Cora Helly Tobin.

Dr. Shirley M. Stinson

Inducted: 1999

DR. SHIRLEY STINSON IS A VISIONARY leader, teacher, administrator, researcher and consultant, whose contributions have changed the face of nursing in Canada.

Born in Arlee, Saskatchewan, in 1929, Shirley Marie Stinson moved to Alberta with her parents as a young child in the mid-1930s. In 1953, her distinguished nursing career began when she graduated from the University of Alberta with a Bachelor of Science degree in Nursing and numerous awards, including the University's Gold Key Award.

In 1958, Shirley Stinson earned her Master's degree in Nursing Administration from the University of Minnesota and received a Doctor of Education degree in 1969 from Teacher's College, Columbia University. She was the first Albertan nurse to complete a doctoral program. She also holds two honorary degrees: a Doctor of Laws from the University of Calgary and a Doctor of Science from Memorial University in Newfoundland.

With the exception of four years as associate director of nursing services at Toronto's Hospital for Sick Children, Shirley Stinson chose to advance her professional career in Alberta. She spent her early career as a public health staff nurse and has been on the University of Alberta faculty since 1969. She was joint professor of the Faculties of Nursing and the Department of Public Health Sciences, Faculty of Medicine, in which she now holds Professor Emerita status. From 1985 to 1991, she served as an adjunct professor, University of Calgary Faculty of Nursing, before becoming an adjunct professor for life.

Her vision and belief that graduate nursing students require knowledge of advanced clinical nursing practice, theory, research and history were the basis for Dr. Stinson's work in the establishment of Western Canada's first Masters in Nursing program in 1975 at the University of Alberta. In concert with colleagues from both the Universities of Alberta and Calgary, she designed what became the first Canadian PhD in Nursing program, which was instituted in 1991.

Shirley Stinson, considered to be the architect of nursing research, played key roles in convincing the Government of Alberta to support nursing research, making Alberta the first province or state in the Western world to earmark funds for nursing research. Through that support, the Alberta Foundation for Nursing Research was established in 1982, with Dr. Stinson as the founding chair. This affirmed the importance of nursing research in health care and further raised the credibility of nursing as a professional discipline.

Dr. Stinson's goal to improve patient care through nursing research profoundly influenced nursing policy and extends beyond Canadian boundaries, where she is held in high esteem by her international colleagues. She has published more than 100 articles, chapters, books and reports. She has lectured and advised professional organizations and institutions worldwide; served on advisory and development committees for international nursing conferences; and has been a consultant to organizations, such as the Pan American World Health Organization, World Health Organization in Geneva and Colombian Nurses Association in Bogota.

Shirley Stinson's distinguished contributions to higher education in nursing and nursing research—provincially, nationally, and internationally—have earned her many awards. These include the Senior National Health Scientist Research Award, the first nurse and woman to receive that award; Canada's highest two nursing awards, the Ross Award in Nursing Leadership from the Canadian Nurses Foundation and the Canadian Nurses Association's Jeanne Mance Award; and the Sir Frederick Haultain Prize in Humanities from the Government of Alberta. Dr. Stinson is honoured by several lifetime memberships and has received the University of Minnesota Board of Regents' Outstanding Achievement Award as well as a Distinguished Alumni Award from Columbia University.

Though she officially retired since 1993, Dr. Stinson continued to share her ideas and experience to benefit the growth of knowledge in all its forms.

She is grateful to God for her family members, friends and other associates and believes anything she is given credit for accomplishing has entailed the collaboration and contributions of others.

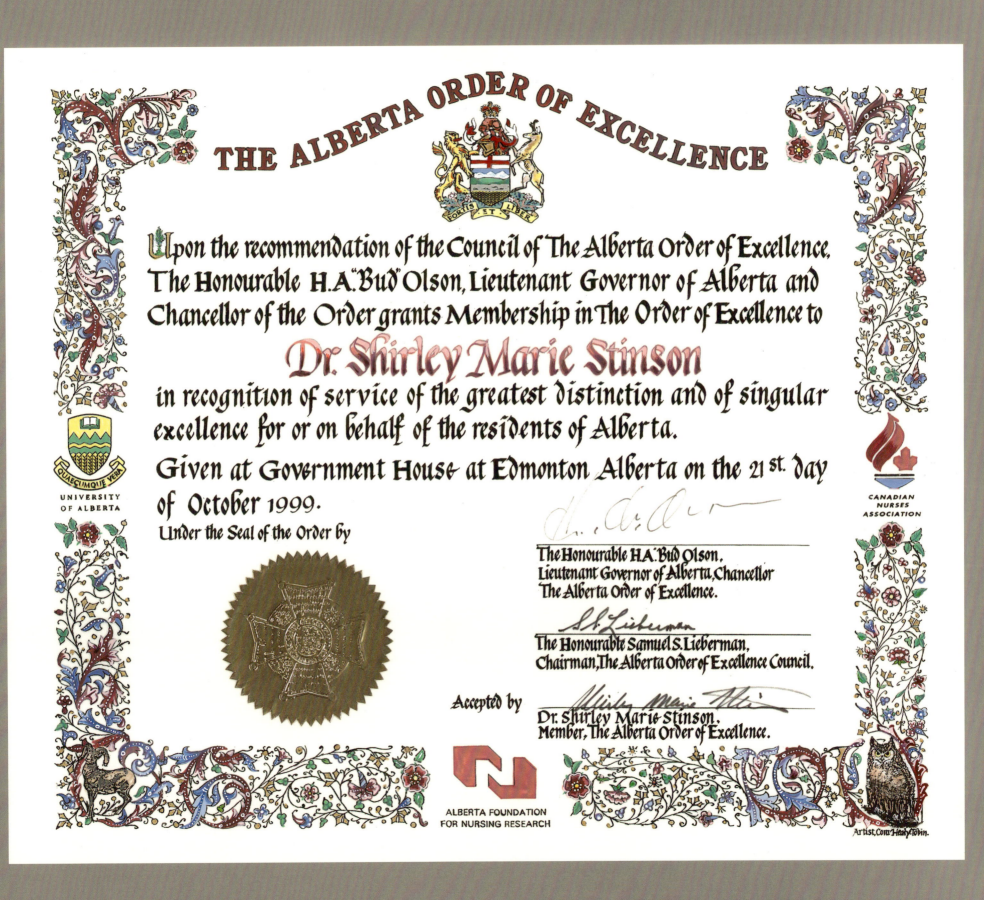

THE ALBERTA ORDER OF EXCELLENCE

FORTIS ET LIBER

Upon the recommendation of the Council of The Alberta Order of Excellence, The Honourable H.A. "Bud" Olson, Lieutenant Governor of Alberta and Chancellor of the Order grants Membership in The Order of Excellence to

Dr. Shirley Marie Stinson

in recognition of service of the greatest distinction and of singular excellence for or on behalf of the residents of Alberta.

Given at Government House at Edmonton Alberta on the 21st day of October 1999.

Under the Seal of the Order by

The Honourable H.A. "Bud" Olson,
Lieutenant Governor of Alberta, Chancellor
The Alberta Order of Excellence.

The Honourable Samuel S. Lieberman,
Chairman, The Alberta Order of Excellence Council.

Accepted by

Dr. Shirley Marie Stinson,
Member, The Alberta Order of Excellence.

QUAECUMQUE VERA
UNIVERSITY OF ALBERTA

CANADIAN NURSES ASSOCIATION

ALBERTA FOUNDATION FOR NURSING RESEARCH

Artist, Cora Healy Tobin.

Jenny Belzberg

Inducted: 2000

JENNY BELZBERG'S PHILANTHROPIC WORK resonates throughout Calgary and beyond. Born in 1928, the lifelong Calgarian has been an agent of change, a mentor and a faithful volunteer. Her leadership abilities have brought success and credibility to a variety of community efforts in the realm of social action and the arts, and enhanced the quality of life for many.

Jenny's initial volunteer work began with local Jewish groups that supported women and families. With organizations such as Beth Israel Sisterhood, Calgary Jewish Community Council, Israel Bonds, Jewish National Fund and the National Council of Jewish Women, she engaged in a range of activities from chairing a review committee for Jewish day schools to honouring Holocaust survivors. With her growing experience and leadership training, her responsibilities expanded. She quickly emerged as a natural leader and rose to executive level positions on both national and international fronts.

Throughout Jenny Belzberg's far-reaching networks, her work could often be linked to her home town. She added civic duties to her list of volunteer activities, including projects with the Calgary Chamber of Commerce and Calgary's City Hall restoration, and served a four-year appointment with the Judicial Council for Provincial Court judges.

As a proponent of community participation, she has had many opportunities to see her ideas take flight. She was the founder of the Canadian Cancer Society's Daffodil Gala and raised significant funds through a joint benefit for the Banff Centre and Calgary Philharmonic Orchestra.

In the late 1980s, her volunteer career gradually shifted into other areas of passion. Believing art and culture feed the soul, she showed her creativity, leadership and fundraising skills, with many organizations serving the arts community.

While chairing the Banff Centre Board of Governors for four years and serving on the board for seven, Jenny Belzberg was a part of the Banff Centre's move into the high-tech industry. A scholarship at the institution and the Honorary Alumni list both bear her name. She also served for 14 years on the board of the Calgary Philharmonic Society, playing a key role in preserving the orchestra. Mrs. Belzberg is a founding member, and past board chair of the Esther Honens Calgary International Piano Competition.

Another organization for which Jenny Belzberg was a founder and first chair is the Calgary Arts Partnership in Education Society, a member of a national program originating with the Royal Conservatory of Music. Also known as CAPES, this organization works with artists and teachers to apply the concept of "Learning through the Arts" to regular school curriculum and has been incorporated by more than 60 Calgary schools.

Mrs. Belzberg's support for higher learning also extends to longstanding support for post-secondary institutions. She has been a fundraiser for Mount Royal College Conservatory and sits on the Dean's Advisory Committee for the University of Calgary's Faculty of Social Work.

A dedicated volunteer, Jenny Belzberg was a member of a National Advisory Committee for the Canadian Centre for Philanthropy. On behalf of the National Society of Fundraising Executives, she chaired Calgary's National Philanthropy Day. She is also an Honorary Chair for Leadership Calgary, and has shared her expertise with the Royal Conservatory of Music and the Sheldon Chumir Foundation for Ethics in Leadership. In August 2000, she was appointed to the Board of Trustees of the National Arts Centre.

Mrs. Belzberg has been recognized for her lifelong commitments in a variety of ways. Jenny Belzberg and her husband were honoured in 1992 by the Jewish National Fund for their various contributions. In 1997, she received a medal from Her Majesty the Queen on the 25th anniversary of Her Majesty's accession to the throne and a Paul Harris Fellow medal from the Rotary Foundation of the City of Calgary Rotary International.

Jenny Belzberg was appointed a Member of the Order of Canada in 1997.

THE ALBERTA ORDER OF EXCELLENCE

Upon the recommendation of the Council of The Alberta Order of Excellence The Honourable Lois E. Hole Lieutenant Governor of Alberta and Chancellor of the Order grants Membership in The Order of Excellence to

Jenny Belzberg

in recognition of service of the greatest distinction and of singular excellence for or on behalf of the residents of Alberta.

Given at Government House at Edmonton Alberta on the 19th day of October 2000.

Under the Seal of the Order by

The Honourable Lois E. Hole,
Lieutenant Governor of Alberta,
Chancellor of The Alberta Order of Excellence.

The Honourable Samuel S. Lieberman,
Chairman, Alberta Order of Excellence Council.

Accepted by

Jenny Belzberg
Member, The Alberta Order of Excellence

CPO
calgary
philharmonic
orchestra

ESTHER HONENS
CALGARY
INTERNATIONAL
PIANO
COMPETITION

The Banff Centre
For The Arts

Artist, Cora Healy-Tosin.

Dr. Chester R. Cunningham

Inducted: 2000

DR. CHESTER CUNNINGHAM IS A HUMANITARIAN and educator whose personal convictions about justice and equality have improved the quality of life for Aboriginal Peoples in Alberta, across Canada and around the world.

Chester Raymond Cunningham was born in Slave Lake, Alberta, in 1933, the third child in a fourth generation Métis family. Chester credits his parents for instilling in him the character and strength that helped him to embrace life in a non-Aboriginal society. He attended school in Wayne and St. Albert, where he excelled in sports. In 1952, he left high school to play semi-professional baseball.

After retiring from his baseball career, Chester worked briefly in the Wayne coal mines and then spent several years working in the construction industry throughout northern Alberta. In 1964, he was hired by the Canadian Native Friendship Centre as a courtworker and program director, helping Native peoples deal with the justice system. He immediately demonstrated leadership qualities that promoted him to executive director by 1965, setting in motion a long list of achievements.

In 1970, Chester launched his own personal mission to bring about change, communication and cultural understanding among the judicial and Native communities. He was founder and executive director of Native Courtworker Services, later to be called Native Counselling Services of Alberta. From 1970 to 1997, this agency grew from four courtworkers to more than 150 employees serving all of Alberta. Within its first five years, the organization set new standards when the number of Aboriginal provincial inmates dropped from 56 per cent to 28 per cent.

To create this remarkable success, he relied on traditional ways of the Native community and involved elders whenever possible. A strong communicator, he negotiated fairly with both government bodies and Native agencies, while maintaining the best interests of each group.

Under Native Counselling Services of Alberta, the pioneering programs of Chester changed the lives of thousands. He was the first in Canada to set up such programs as the Alcohol Education Program; Liaison Programs in both provincial and federal prisons; Family and Juvenile Courtwork Program; Family Life Improvement Program; and many others in the criminal justice systems. The organization made history for a second time when it became the first non-government agency in the world to administer a correctional institution, the Stan Daniels Centre.

Chester is a founding member of the St. Albert Lion's Breakfast Club and the Native Credit Union. He has shared his knowledge and spirit with the community by sitting on numerous boards and committees. Some of these include National Parole Board; Boyle Street Co-op; John Howard Society; Alberta Native Communication Society; Canadian Native Friendship Centre; Alberta Human Rights and Citizenship Commission; Consulting Committee on Young Offender's Act; Canadian Advisory Committee, Justice and Corrections; and a committee for the Ministry of Children's Services.

He was appointed a member of the Carson Committee examining management and operation of prisons and corrections in Canada and a delegate to the 7th United Nations Conference on Prevention of Crime and Treatment of the Offender in Milan, Italy. The governments of Australia, Japan and the Soviet Union, as well as many other countries around the world, have benefited from his expertise and insight. Currently, Dr. Cunningham serves on the Provincial Court Nominating Committee; the Law Enforcement Review Board; and as Treasurer and Board Member of the Aboriginal Multimedia Society.

In recognition of his devotion and determination, Chester Cunningham has received many awards and honours. A few of these include a Queen's Medal for Achievement; Honorary Chief of the Peigan Tribe; the Aboriginal Achievement Award; the Alberta Achievement Award; a medallion from Prince Charles at Treaty 7 celebrations; and a lifetime membership for the Canadian Native Friendship Centre. The Aboriginal Students Council at the University of Alberta also recognized Dr. Cunningham for his contributions to the Native community and for his influence as a strong role model.

In 1989, he received an Honorary Doctor of Laws degree from the University of Alberta recognizing his contributions to the correctional system. He was appointed a Member of the Order of Canada in 1993.

A belief in humankind and the value placed on family and community is reflected throughout Dr. Cunningham's outstanding career. Members of his staff and the aboriginal community have gone on to become lawyers, social workers, police officers and doctoral candidates, as a result of his encouragement and faith in their abilities.

Chester and his wife Elzaida raised a family of seven, David, Calvin, Carola, Bill, Mark, Rosalie and Frank, along with countless unofficial foster children.

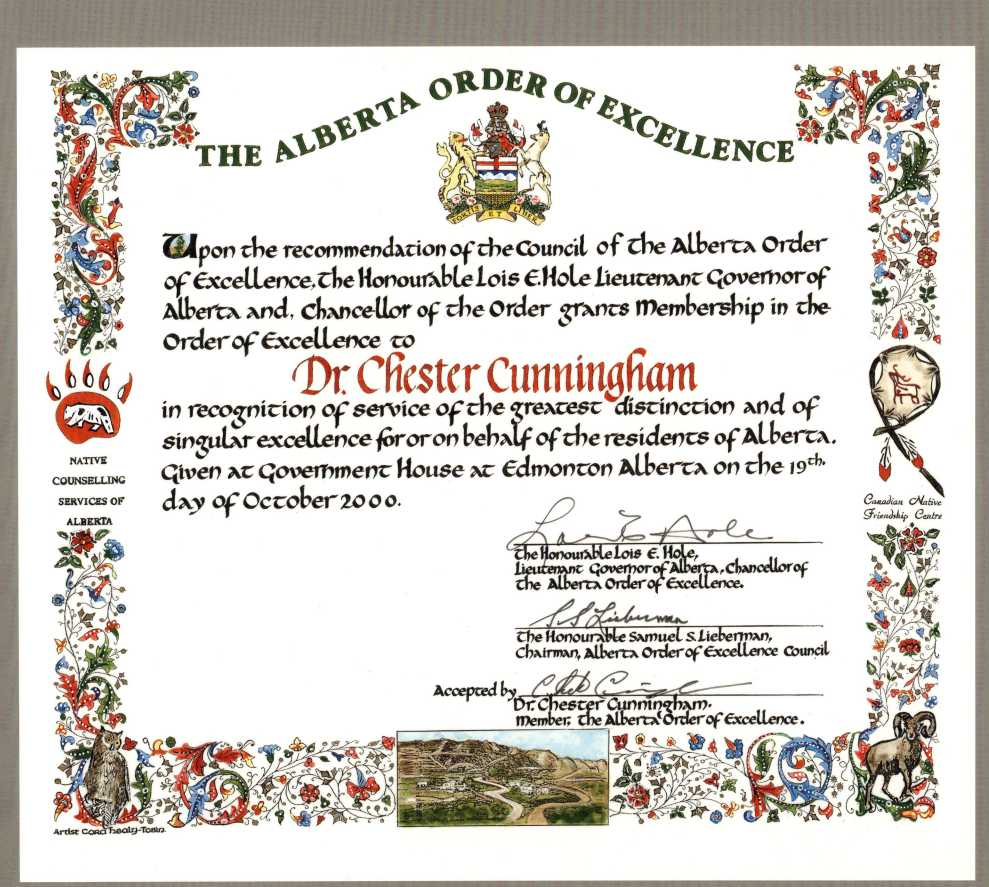

THE ALBERTA ORDER OF EXCELLENCE

FORTIS ET LIBER

Upon the recommendation of the Council of the Alberta Order of Excellence, the Honourable Lois E. Hole Lieutenant Governor of Alberta and, Chancellor of the Order grants Membership in the Order of Excellence to

Dr. Chester Cunningham

in recognition of service of the greatest distinction and of singular excellence for or on behalf of the residents of Alberta. Given at Government House at Edmonton Alberta on the 19th day of October 2000.

The Honourable Lois E. Hole,
Lieutenant Governor of Alberta, Chancellor of
the Alberta Order of Excellence.

The Honourable Samuel S. Lieberman,
Chairman, Alberta Order of Excellence Council

Accepted by
Dr. Chester Cunningham.
Member, the Alberta Order of Excellence.

NATIVE
COUNSELLING
SERVICES OF
ALBERTA

Canadian Native
Friendship Centre

Artist Cora Healy-Tobin.

Dr. D. Lorne J. Tyrrell

Inducted: 2000

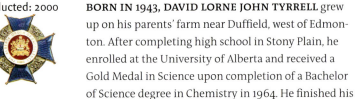

BORN IN 1943, DAVID LORNE JOHN TYRRELL grew up on his parents' farm near Duffield, west of Edmonton. After completing high school in Stony Plain, he enrolled at the University of Alberta and received a Gold Medal in Science upon completion of a Bachelor of Science degree in Chemistry in 1964. He finished his Doctor of Medicine and was awarded a Gold Medal in Pediatrics in 1968. In his second year of medicine, he received a Life Insurance of North America Studentship, providing him an opportunity to complete a combined MD and PhD program. Following an internship at the University of Alberta Hospital, Dr. Tyrrell entered Queen's University and completed his PhD in pharmacology in 1972. In 1975, he returned to Alberta to complete training in internal medicine to qualify as a Fellow of the Royal College of Physicians and Surgeons. He subspecialized in infectious diseases and in 1976 was awarded the Medical Research Council of Canada Centennial Fellowship, which has played a pivotal role in Dr. Tyrrell's medical career. The following two years of his postdoctoral training in the field of virology at the Karolinksa Institute in Stockholm, Sweden, inspired a research interest that continues to this day.

In 1986, while teaching a graduate course, Dr. Tyrrell found clues that might lead to the discovery of antiviral drugs to inhibit the hepatitis B virus. Thus began his research on the virus that was the ninth leading cause of death according to the World Health Organization. Dr. Tyrrell was joined by his colleague in chemistry, Dr. Morris Robins, in studying chronic hepatitis B, which affects approximately 300 to 350 million people. The major findings that ensued prompted one of the largest research contracts with industry ever known to a Canadian university. Glaxo Canada, now Glaxo Wellcome, supported his ongoing work and established the Glaxo Heritage Research Institute and a Research Chair in Virology at the University of Alberta. Continuing his research, Dr. Tyrrell and his team discovered antiviral therapy for chronic hepatitis B, leading to the licensing of Heptovir (Canada) and Zeffix (worldwide), which is saving many lives daily. The recognition received for this major finding include Alberta's ASTech Award for Innovation and Science in 1993; J. Gordin Kaplan Award for Excellence in Research from the University of Alberta in 1998; and the Prix Galien Canada medal for research from the Pharmaceutical Manufacturers of Canada, also in 1998. Dr. Tyrrell was awarded a Gold Medal by the Canadian Liver Foundation and the Canadian Association for the Study of Liver in 2000.

Dr. Tyrrell's dedication to research is equalled by his gift for teaching. He has been honoured by students of all levels of study, including an Outstanding Resident Award and Teacher of the Year Awards in all three phases of medical school: basic sciences, clinical and bedside teaching. He also received the University of Alberta Rutherford Undergraduate Teaching Award in 1990 and the University Cup for excellence as an educator and a researcher in 1999. In 1998, he was Alumnus of the Year, University of Alberta, Faculty of Medicine.

Dr. Tyrrell has trained many research students and postdoctoral fellows; served on more than 200 committees, task forces and research teams; and is widely published in books and medical and science journals around the world.

Dr. Tyrrell's impressive medical career includes academic appointments at the University of Alberta, one of Canada's most prestigious teaching and research institutions. These appointments include Assistant Professor in Medicine and Biochemistry in 1976, promoted to Full Professor in Medicine and Biochemistry in 1982; Director of the Division of Infectious Diseases from 1982 to 1986; and Chairman of the Department of Medical Microbiology and Infectious Diseases from 1986 to 1994. He was appointed dean of Medicine in 1994, and re-appointed in 1999 as dean, Faculty of Medicine and Dentistry.

While receiving provincial, national and international accolades for his revolutionary work, Dr. Tyrrell's close ties with his native province remain strong. A firm conviction to developing quality medical health care in Alberta and Canada has kept Dr. Tyrrell at home. Some of his numerous commitments include past president of the Association of Canadian Medical Colleges and past chair of the Provincial Advisory Committee on Health Research.

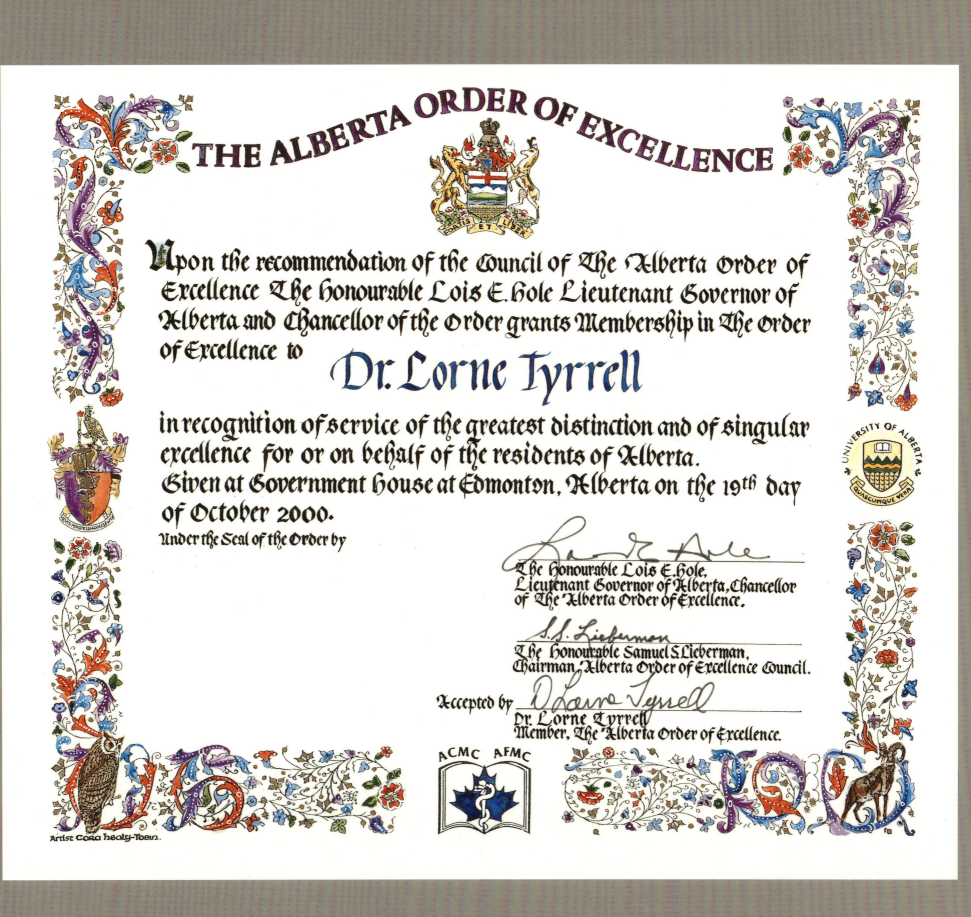

THE ALBERTA ORDER OF EXCELLENCE

Upon the recommendation of the Council of The Alberta Order of Excellence The honourable Lois E. Hole Lieutenant Governor of Alberta and Chancellor of the Order grants Membership in The Order of Excellence to

Dr. Lorne Tyrrell

in recognition of service of the greatest distinction and of singular excellence for or on behalf of the residents of Alberta.

Given at Government House at Edmonton, Alberta on the 19th day of October 2000.

Under the Seal of the Order by

The Honourable Lois E. Hole,
Lieutenant Governor of Alberta, Chancellor
of The Alberta Order of Excellence.

The Honourable Samuel S. Lieberman,
Chairman, Alberta Order of Excellence Council.

Accepted by

Dr. Lorne Tyrrell
Member, The Alberta Order of Excellence.

Artist Cora Healy-Tobin.

ACMC AFMC

Louis Armand Desrochers

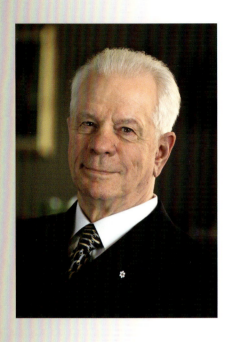

Inducted: 2001

LOUIS ARMAND DESROCHERS WAS BORN in Montréal, Québec, in 1928. For his contributions to Alberta, to Canada and to the francophone community, he is credited with connecting Canadians and building national unity.

Born into the French language culture, Louis Desrochers learned early the value of both Canadian languages. He took his primary schooling in Québec, then moved to Jasper, Alberta, with his widowed mother in 1939. With the move west, he was still able to continue his French education attending le Collège des Jésuites in Edmonton until 1942, and the Collège Saint-Jean d'Edmonton until 1947.

Beyond his commitment to the francophone community, Louis Desrochers also extended his skills to other organizations, such as the Edmonton Family Service Bureau. In a role that led to president of the organization, he helped to elevate the organization's volunteer initiative to one that provided professionally operated services to a broader community base.

As an articulate and well-respected francophone, he was appointed by then Prime Minister John Diefenbaker to the Northwest Territories Council, serving from 1960 to 1963.

During decades of community service, he served as vice-chairman of the advisory board of the Misericordia Hospital, member of the Canada Council, governor of the Glenbow-Alberta Institute and associate of the Devonian Group of Charitable Foundations. He also served as council member and second chairman of the Alberta Order of Excellence Council.

For five years, Mr. Desrochers chaired the Board of Trustees of the Edmonton General Hospital (Grey Nuns) Foundation. He was the foundation's first chair and established the fund development program for what Albertans now recognize as the Caritas Hospitals Foundation. Mr. Desrochers also serves as honorary chairman of the Edmonton Community Foundation.

Mr. Desrochers was invited to join the Trilateral Commission, an organization of world leaders and influential figures representing Europe, Japan and North America. He served on this commission from 1974 to 1981.

In 1972, he was one of the founding directors of the Institute for Research on Public Policy, an independent think tank on public policy. Mr. Desrochers subsequently served as vice-chairman of the organization, which remains active today.

He has long-standing service on many corporate boards, including the Royal Trust Edmonton Advisory Board, MacLab Enterprises, Shaw Communications Inc., Royal Trustco Limited, Northern Transportation Company Limited, Canada West Insurance Company, and l'Assurance-vie Desjardins. He also acted as director of the Bank of Montreal and was one its longest serving directors. He continues as honorary director.

For his work within Alberta and Canada, Louis Desrochers received numerous honours. He was awarded an Honorary Doctor of Laws degree from the University of Ottawa in 1971 and another from the University of Alberta in 1978. As well, he was awarded a Doctor of Science in Education from Laval University in 1972. In 1994, Louis Armand Desrochers was inducted as a Member of the Order of Canada.

Louis Desrochers married Marcelle Boutin in September 1953. The couple raised a family of four daughters and one son, all of whom are graduates of the Faculté Saint-Jean. The Desrochers live in Edmonton where they enjoy the frequent company of their family, including 13 grandchildren.

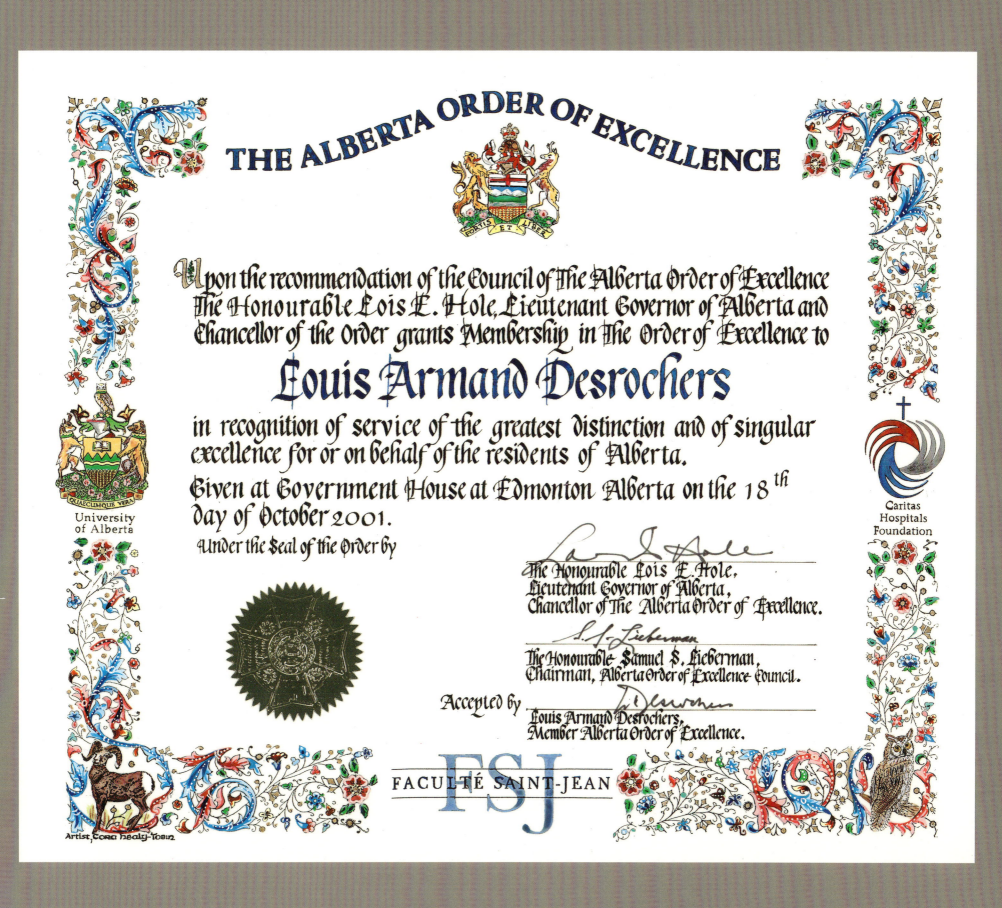

THE ALBERTA ORDER OF EXCELLENCE

Upon the recommendation of the Council of The Alberta Order of Excellence The Honourable Lois E. Hole, Lieutenant Governor of Alberta and Chancellor of the Order grants Membership in The Order of Excellence to

Louis Armand Desrochers

in recognition of service of the greatest distinction and of singular excellence for or on behalf of the residents of Alberta.

Given at Government House at Edmonton Alberta on the 18th day of October 2001.

Under the Seal of the Order by

The Honourable Lois E. Hole,
Lieutenant Governor of Alberta,
Chancellor of The Alberta Order of Excellence.

The Honourable Samuel S. Lieberman,
Chairman, Alberta Order of Excellence Council.

Accepted by

Louis Armand Desrochers,
Member Alberta Order of Excellence.

University of Alberta

Caritas Hospitals Foundation

FSJ FACULTÉ SAINT-JEAN

Artist, Cora Healy-Tobin

Colonel (Retired) Donald S. Ethell

Inducted: 2001

DONALD STEWART ETHELL WAS BORN IN 1937 in Vancouver, British Columbia. Committed to the welfare of others, Colonel Ethell's humanitarian efforts and military career have had international impact and have brought distinction to the reputation of Canadian peacekeeping.

In 1955, Donald Ethell joined the Canadian Army at the young age of 17. Private Ethell immediately received his basic training as a rifleman in the Queen's Own Rifles of Canada at Currie Barracks in Calgary. When the Queen's Own Rifles of Canada was removed from regular army service in 1970, all members of the battalion including Ethell changed their affiliation to the Princess Patricia's Canadian Light Infantry. He quickly rose through the non-commissioned officer ranks to that of warrant officer until being commissioned as an officer to Her Majesty's Forces in 1972. This move was to foreshadow a distinguished career in the military service.

Colonel Ethell consistently demonstrated his natural ability for leadership. He is a veteran of 14 international peacekeeping deployments with service in Cyprus, Lebanon, Syria, Jordan, Egypt, Israel, Central America and the Balkans.

Between two tours of duty in the Middle East, for the years 1987 to 1990, Colonel Ethell served as the director of Peacekeeping Operations at National Defence Headquarters in Ottawa. This period of time encompassed a significant increase in Canada's commitment to peacekeeping and peace-makers with Canadian Forces and individual officers being deployed to Afghanistan, Pakistan, Iran, Iraq, Namibia and Central America.

In support of Canadian-sponsored efforts to bring peace to the Central America region, Colonel Ethell frequently visited Central America to brief military and political leaders on the benefits of peacekeeping missions. This led to his secondment to United Nations headquarters in New York to conduct in-theatre reconnaissance of five Central American countries associated with the Arias Peace Plan. The Ethell plan was accepted by the UN Under-Secretary General for Peacekeeping as the initial operations plan of the UN Peacekeeping troops assigned to the area. Additionally, then Secretary of State for External Affairs, Right Honourable Joe Clark, tabled the plan in the Canadian House of Commons.

Following his tenure as the director of Peacekeeping Operations, Colonel Ethell returned to the Middle East where he served as the Chief of Staff and Deputy Force Commander of the Multinational Force and Observers during the 1990–1991 Persian Gulf War.

Colonel Ethell then returned to Canada to commence retirement leave. However, within one month, he was ordered back on duty to Yugoslavia as the head of the Canadian Delegation for Canadian Forces officers assigned to the European Community Monitoring Mission in Yugoslavia. This tour in early 1992 overlapped the commencement of yet another war in Bosnia-Herzegovina and the subsequent arrival of the large United Nations protection force. In due course, he returned to Canada and finally retired from the Canadian Forces in July 1993.

While in the service, Colonel Ethell also participated in many domestic and international peacekeeping symposia in Moscow, Madrid, New York, San Jose and Tegucigalpa. He continues to serve as a defence analyst to the Canadian Broadcasting Corporation and other media organizations.

Colonel Donald Ethell is considered to be Canada's most experienced and decorated peacekeeper. Honours and awards received include the Order of Military Merit (officer grade) in 1982 and the Most Venerable Order of the Hospital of St. John of Jerusalem (serving member grade) in June 2001. In 1986, he received the Meritorious Service Cross for his action in planning and commanding operations associated with prisoners of war and body exchanges between the Israelis and Syrians in 1984 and the passage of Palestinian prisoners from Israel to Lebanon through Syria in 1985. He also received the Canadian Peacekeeping Service Medal in 2001, as well as various campaign medals for his service on peacekeeping missions, 100th and 125th Anniversary medals, the Special Service Medal and the Canadian Forces Decoration.

Following his military retirement, Colonel Ethell found a new focus and more time for humanitarian efforts. He became involved with CARE Canada, providing consulting services to staff responsible for five refugee camps in Eastern Kenya and Somalia. Despite being witness to many atrocities throughout his military career, this exposure to "matchstick" children and many others dying of AIDS-related illness and starvation left a haunting impression. This memory remains foremost in his mind as he currently serves as Alberta's Diirector of the International Committee for the Relief of Starvation and Suffering, ICROSS. He continues his efforts in providing relief to the estimated 15,000 people in Africa who succumb to starvation or AIDS-related illnesses each week.

In addition to his concern for the tragedy in Africa, Colonel Ethell is active in pursuing issues regarding Canada's veterans. As a member of the Friends of Colonel Belcher committee in Calgary, he is committed to many activities associated with the move of the veterans from the existing Colonel Belcher Veteran Care Centre to a new care facility in 2002. Additionally, Colonel Ethell serves as one of four committee chairs for the recently formed Canadian Forces Advisory Council, which is responsible for investigating and reporting on all aspects associated with Canada's veterans. He also serves as national president of the Canadian Association of Veterans in United Nations Peacekeeping.

Colonel Ethell became president of DEthell Consulting International Inc, through which he provided experience and expertise for United Nations peacekeeping operations in Haiti, Rwanda and Angola, and with the United States Special Forces.

He has served as a member of the Queen's Own Rifles of Canada Association and Princess Patricia's Canadian Light Infantry Associations, Royal United Services Institute of Alberta, Calgary Military Museums Society and the Royal Canadian Legion.

THE ALBERTA ORDER OF EXCELLENCE

Upon the recommendation of the Council of The Alberta Order of Excellence, The Honourable Lois E. Hole, Lieutenant Governor of Alberta and Chancellor of the Order grants Membership in The Order of Excellence to

Donald Stewart Ethell

in recognition of service of the greatest distinction and of singular excellence for or on behalf of the residents of Alberta.

Given at Government House at Edmonton Alberta on the 18th day of October 2001.

Under the Seal of the Order by

The Honourable Lois E. Hole,
Lieutenant Governor of Alberta, Chancellor,
of The Alberta Order of Excellence.

The Honourable Samuel S. Lieberman, Chairman,
The Alberta Order of Excellence Council.

Accepted by

Donald Stewart Ethell,
Member, The Alberta Order of Excellence.

QUEENS
OWN RIFLES
OF CANADA

ICROSS
INTERNATIONAL
COMMUNITY FOR
THE RELIEF OF
STARVATION
AND SUFFERING

Artist Cora Healy Tobin

UN/NU
CANADA

Dr. Steven K.H. Aung

Inducted: 2002

DR. STEVEN KYAW HTUT AUNG IS A PIONEER in the integration of western, traditional Chinese and complementary medicine. His efforts have helped to make Alberta an active centre in the field of integrated and complimentary medicine. His unique approach to medicine, combined with the remarkable compassion he brings to all that he does, has made him a highly respected teacher, researcher and doctor.

Dr. Aung's professional journey began at an early age when his grandfather, a traditional Chinese medicine practitioner, asked that one of his three grandsons dedicate his life and career to integrating the best of eastern and western medicine. That early direction became a guiding force for Steven, leading him to map out an approach to medicine based on balance and harmony and rooted in the belief that medicine should be focussed on offering the best possible treatment for patients regardless of geographic divisions.

Dr. Aung pursued studies in traditional Chinese medicine as a physician and surgeon in both his native Myanmar (formerly Burma) and China, before moving to Canada. Wanting to see as much of Canada as possible and guided by his interest in studying specializations that could benefit from integration with traditional Chinese medicine, he completed residencies in Vancouver, Montréal and St. John's. His studies included internal medicine, family medicine, neurology, rheumatology, oncology and counselling. An interest in geriatric medicine eventually led him to Edmonton and the University of Alberta.

Dr. Aung took a gentle approach to introducing the notion of integrated medical care. As his own integrated medical practice grew, so did his reputation as a doctor skilled in both western and eastern approaches. His quiet persistence led to Canada's first Certificate Program in Medical Acupuncture, developed by Dr. Aung for the University of Alberta in 1991. He remains the program's chief instructor, examiner and curriculum consultant.

Dr. Aung serves as an associate clinical professor in the Departments of Medicine and Family Medicine at the University of Alberta. He also shares his expertise in acupuncture to the University of Alberta Hospitals, the Cross Cancer Institute, the Caritas Health Group, the Glen Sather University of Alberta Sports Medicine Centre and the Edmonton Oilers Hockey and Eskimo Football Teams.

In 1995, Dr. Aung brought the 3rd World Congress of Medical Acupuncture and Natural Medicine to Edmonton. It was the first time the event was held outside China. The conference returned to Edmonton in August 2000. The theme of that second Alberta-based conference reflected the lifelong goal of Dr. Steven Aung: *Integrative Medicine: Competent, Complementary and Compassionate Primary Care for the Next Millennium.*

He is active in national and international medical organizations, serving as president and founding member of the World Natural Medicine Foundation; Health Canada advisor on acupuncture standards; World Health Organization advisor on acupuncture nomenclature and Health Food Standards, cancer pain control and Herbal Medicine; Fellow, American Academy of Family Physicians; Associate Clinical Professor, Division of Surgical Sciences, New York University College of Dentistry; and Fellow, International College of Acupuncture and Electro-Therapeutics, American College of Acupuncture and Australian Medical Acupuncture College.

In addition to his medical practice and teaching work in Edmonton, Dr. Aung holds visiting professorships with a number of universities and medical colleges across Canada and around the world. Dr. Aung travels to universities in California, New York, New Zealand, Australia, Puerto Rico, Japan and China to speak to physicians, medical students and other medical practitioners interested in hearing his message and learning his techniques and approaches.

Dr. Steven Aung's life and career are strongly rooted in the tenets and practice of Buddhism and in the concept of finding balance in all things. He spends time everyday meditating and offering blessings for his patients, a practice that helps him approach his work as a doctor in the spirit of love and compassion. He practices Qi Gong, an ancient form of exercise and healing that focuses on breathing concentration and energy flow, as well as traditional Chinese calligraphy. He teaches both these disciplines, thus allowing him to share traditional Chinese concepts of wellness, balance and harmony with people from across Alberta and around the world.

Teaching also allows him to continue sharing the vision given to him as a child. "I carry the light of my grandfather's vision for balanced and integrated medicine," says Dr. Aung. "Every time I teach someone, I pass that light on to another and they pass it on to someone else. I don't just teach techniques. I also try to teach and remind others of the vital importance of compassion in medicine." His long-term goal is to further honour his grandfather's original vision and mission through the creation of a medical centre or hospital that offers fully integrated western and eastern treatments to its patients.

THE ALBERTA ORDER OF EXCELLENCE

Upon the recommendation of the Council of The Alberta Order of Excellence The honourable Lois E. Hole Lieutenant Governor of Alberta and Chancellor of the Order grants Membership in the Order of Excellence to

Steven K.H. Aung

in recognition of service of the greatest distinction and of singular excellence for or on behalf of the residents of Alberta Given at Government House at Edmonton Alberta on the 17th day of October 2002
Under the Seal of the Order by

The honourable Lois E. Hole,
Lieutenant Governor of Alberta Chancellor
of The Alberta Order of Excellence

The honourable Samuel S. Lieberman,
Chairman, Alberta Order of Excellence Council.

Accepted by~Steven K.H. Aung,
Member, The Alberta Order of Excellence.

James K. Gray

Inducted: 2002

JIM GRAY IS A RESPECTED COMMUNITY LEADER with a solid reputation for getting the job done. His energy, determination and optimism are reflected in a number of valued Calgary facilities and social programs.

Jim came to Calgary in 1956 to pursue a career in Alberta's energy sector. In 1973, he co-founded Canadian Hunter Exploration, an organization that became one of Canada's largest and most successful natural gas companies. As Canadian Hunter grew and prospered, he took care to focus on the bigger picture, creating an employee-friendly work culture and maintaining an awareness of environmental conservation and sustainability. Jim also worked to develop Alberta's stature on the international stage. He enjoyed a successful tenure as chair of the 16th World Petroleum Congress, which was staged in Calgary in June 2000.

Jim has met with equal success in his efforts as a community leader and fundraiser. As in his business career, he has earned a reputation as someone who can see beyond the immediate call to action to find an innovative, long-term solution to the issue at hand.

His work to improve the quality of life for Calgary residents began in the summer of 1962 as discussion around the city focussed on disappointing attendance at the Calgary Stampede. It occurred to Jim that participation might grow with the addition of a petroleum show. He wrote a formal proposal for the show, drummed up support for the idea among his oil industry colleagues, and succeeded in creating a successful addition to the Stampede.

The experience showed Jim that one individual's actions could make a difference, and that finding positive solutions and creating strong teams could go a long way in addressing community and social needs. It also provided him with an approach to community leadership that has served him well in the 40 years since that first endeavour. While Jim points to the strength of the teams on which he serves as the reason for his success, his contribution as a team builder and leader cannot be ignored.

He chooses to invest his energies in causes that focus on education, children and families, particularly those with a local connection. Over the years, he has volunteered with organizations such as the Science Alberta Foundation, the Achievement Centre for Youth, the Calgary Women's Emergency Shelter and the Calgary Native Friendship Centre. Jim has also supported the Calgary Academy and Renfrew Educational Services, two facilities that offer specialized educational support to children with unique learning challenges and special needs.

Jim has also worked to further his belief that productive and democratic debate are key ingredients for a healthy society.

He serves as chair of the Canada West Foundation, a Calgary-based organization that promotes discussion on political, economic and social issues of the day.

One of Jim Gray's longest community associations has been with the YMCA. This began when, as a young adult, he noticed a group of inner-city Calgary Herald paperboys with no where to channel their energies. Soon, Jim was offering the group free swimming lessons at the YMCA. He went on to help develop summer camp programs in the 1960s and 70s and, more recently, to spearhead a successful effort to build a new Calgary facility. Jim's contributions were recognized nationally in 1994 with the YMCA Fellowship of Honour. He continues to make the YMCA a part of his routine, arriving at 5:30 am for a daily swim.

After 28 years of operation, Canadian Hunter Exploration was sold in 2001. Jim remains active in the business community, serving on a number of corporate boards including Canadian National Railway, Emera, Hudson's Bay Company and Brascan Corporation. His work as a director with Temple Exploration, a new exploration company, gives him the opportunity to share his wealth of experience and balanced approach with the next generation of oil executives.

Jim's involvement with community organizations has helped him live a balanced life, something he points to as key in ensuring overall success. "I think it's a danger for people to get blinders on and focus only on business," Jim says. "Strong communities and families lead to good, strong business ethics. If we don't channel our energies to the overall quality of life we enjoy, we'll lose it."

Jim Gray has proven that fact through a lifetime of making a difference to his community, the province and the country as a whole. He received an Honorary Doctor of Laws degree from the University of Calgary in 1991, a Citation for Citizenship from the Government of Canada in 1992 and was appointed an Officer of the Order of Canada in 1995.

THE ALBERTA ORDER OF EXCELLENCE

Upon the recommendation of the Council of The Alberta Order of Excellence, The Honourable Lois E. Hole Lieutenant Governor of Alberta and Chancellor of the Order grants Membership in The Order of Excellence to

James Kenneth Gray

in recognition of service of the greatest distinction and of singular excellence for or on behalf of the residents of Alberta

Given at Government House at Edmonton Alberta on the 17th day of October 2002.

Under the Seal of the Order by

The Honourable Lois E. Hole,
Lieutenant Governor of Alberta Chancellor
The Alberta Order of Excellence.

The Honourable Samuel S. Lieberman,
Chairman, Alberta Order of Excellence Council.

Accepted by   James Kenneth Gray,
Member, Alberta Order of Excellence.

YMCA
WE BUILD
STRONG KIDS,
STRONG
FAMILIES,
STRONG
COMMUNITIES.

canadian hunter

John Murrell

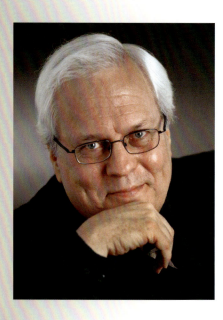

Inducted: 2002

JOHN MURRELL IS A CELEBRATED and influential Alberta playwright who has made equal contributions to the canon of Canadian literature and the Canadian arts community. His plays have been translated into 15 languages and performed in 30 countries around the world.

John's connection to the natural world lends a strong sense of place to all of his plays. From his homes and offices in Calgary and at The Banff Centre, he creates vivid stories and settings that have captured audiences around the world. His characters often reflect the Alberta personality, aiming their sights high and expecting great things from the future and the world around them.

Those stories began to take shape when John was a junior high school teacher in Hanna and, later, in Calgary. Struck by the lack of plays appropriate to his students' age and written in a Canadian voice, he set about creating works for his classes to perform. John soon left teaching to follow his passion to become a full-time playwright.

In 1975, John began work as Playwright in Residence for Alberta Theatre Projects. In 1977, he wrote *Waiting for the Parade*, a work that has become one of his best known and most often performed pieces. The story follows five women struggling to come to grips with a changing world and their own changing lives on the Calgary home front of World War II. *Waiting for the Parade* was the first of three John Murrell works to win the Chalmers Best Canadian Play Award.

His reputation as a unique voice in Canadian theatre was further enhanced with *Memoir*, a play depicting the final days of legendary French actress Sarah Bernhardt. It received national and international recognition, including an extended three-year run in Paris, and continues to be performed in Canada and around the world. John Murrell's stature as a playwright grew with terms as associate director of the Stratford Festival from 1978 to 1980 and Head of the Canada Council Theatre Section from 1988 to 1992. During that period, he added to his body of work with successful plays such as *Farther West* (1981), *New World* (1984) and *Democracy* (1990). The latter play received awards from the Canadian Authors Association and the Writers Guild of Alberta. His success continued with *The Faraway Nearby* in 1995, for which he received his third Chalmers Award. In 2002, he received the Walter Carsen Prize for Excellence in the Performing Arts.

John's ability to capture the rhythm of Canadian speech and reflect the realities of modern life has also led him to be recognized in another field— that of theatre translation. His translations of plays by authors such as Chekhov and Ibsen are highly regarded and frequently performed, bringing new life and new audiences to classic works.

In addition to writing, John Murrell has dedicated his time and expertise to arts administration and education. He teaches both by example and by lending direct support and insight to writers and actors. His generosity has helped many emerging Canadian artists hone their craft.

The Banff Centre has been an enduring fixture throughout John's career, both as an artist and arts administrator. He began as a participant and, later, Head of The Centre's Playwrights Colony. He became Theatre Arts director/executive producer in 1999, taking over leadership of the Centre's programs for theatre, opera, and dance.

Banff serves as an inspiration for John. It is a place where he feels most at home, drawing hope and vision from the awesome beauty of the setting and the energy of his fellow artists and administrators at the Centre. He maintains a busy routine, working to lead and develop artistic programs, serving as a touchstone for companies around the world that present his plays and continuing to create new works. His latest venture is Filumena, an opera he created together with Calgary composer John Estacio.

Despite his considerable reputation, many honours and varied roles, John Murrell's ultimate goal in life is a simple one: to be useful to others. He is motivated by the desire to entertain, but also to offer insight which will prove inspirational or helpful to others in their lives or relationships. "I would like life for all of us to be something extraordinary every day," says Murrell. "I like to have a sense of discovery every day—some personal or public observation that is new."

He has clearly been a success in that pursuit, offering the gifts of enjoyment and discovery to his audiences, students and fellow artists throughout his career.

THE ALBERTA ORDER OF EXCELLENCE

Upon the recommendation of the Council of The Alberta Order of Excellence, The Honourable Lois E. Hole, Lieutenant Governor of Alberta and Chancellor of the order grants Membership in The Order of Excellence to

John Murrell

in recognition of service of the greatest distinction and of singular excellence for or on behalf of the residents of Alberta.

Given at Government House at Edmonton, Alberta on the 17th day of October 2002.

Under the Seal of the Order by

The Honourable Lois E. Hole,
Lieutenant Governor of Alberta
Chancellor of The Alberta Order of Excellence.

The Honourable Samuel S. Lieberman
Chairman, Alberta Order of Excellence Council.

Accepted by
John Murrell,
Member, The Alberta Order of Excellence.

Playwrights Union of Canada

ALBERTA PLAYWRIGHTS NETWORK

THE BANFF CENTRE

The Right Honourable Donald F. Mazankowski

Inducted: 2003

DON MAZANKOWSKI IS AN ARDENT CANADIAN who has played an important role in shaping the country's modern history. While his career has taken him around the world and into the highest echelons of political and corporate governance, he remains humbly committed to his prairie roots and thankful to be a citizen of a country where anyone can get involved and make a difference.

Don was born in Viking, Alberta, to U.S. immigrant parents of Polish descent. He was raised in Viking and educated in a one-room country school. His early years on the family farm and his experiences as a young farmer and businessman fuelled Don's passion for rural life and instilled a deep understanding of the economic and political challenges facing Western Canada.

His early career was spent farming and building an automotive dealership in Innisfree, Alberta. The latter allowed Don to exercise his business acumen and talent for dealing with people. In 1960, he moved to Vegreville and opened an automotive business with his brother, Ray. His life and career took on a new direction when he met Prime Minister John Diefenbaker, who was travelling through Vegreville on a speaking tour. Inspired by Diefenbaker's insistence that the West play a meaningful role in the nation's business, Don began working behind the scenes in local politics. Five years later, in 1968, the local Member of Parliament asked Don to consider running in the upcoming election. He threw his hat in the ring and won a closely contested race to become the Member of Parliament for Vegreville.

Don successfully contested a total of seven general elections, serving his constituency for 25 years. The first nine years were spent as an opposition member, where he became an outspoken critic of transportation and economic policies that hampered trade in the West. He assumed a leadership role in 1979 when his party came to power and he was appointed Minister of Transport. He immediately set to work redrafting the National Transportation Act and instituted a series of initiatives to lessen regulatory burdens on business and create a more market-oriented economy.

He took on a wide range of responsibilities and portfolios during his political career, leading one journalist to dub him "the minister of everything." Don was appointed deputy prime minister and government House Leader in 1986 and held that position until his retirement in 1993. He left politics with a reputation as a fair and respected leader who patiently heard all sides of an issue, thus building consensus and finding workable solutions to problems. He also built a legacy of programs and policies that continue to benefit the country as a whole, including the Farm Income Protection Act, the North American Free Trade Agreement, of which Don was a strong supporter, and the Western Diversification Program, which has strengthened and broadened the West's economic base.

While his main interests have been trade and economics, Don has also applied his talents to a number of other areas in service of his fellow Canadians. In 1985, he established the Don Mazankowski Scholarship Foundation, which has since distributed more than $250,000 to some 150 youth from across Canada. His support for post-secondary education led him to serve as a member of the University of Alberta Board of Governors and to co-chair a highly successful University of Alberta fundraising campaign. He is currently a member of the University's Business Advisory Council.

Don is also involved with programs to improve the health and quality of life of Canadians. He is chairman of the Canadian Genetics Diseases Network, which brings together the nation's top scientists to share knowledge and encourage the development of treatments for a wide range of diseases. He serves as chair of the Institute of Health Economics and completed an extensive review of Alberta's health system as chair of the Premier's Special Advisory Council on Health. In addition to his service in education and health, Don shares his expertise with a number of national and international corporate boards, where he stresses the importance of making environmental protection an integral part of corporate budgets.

Don was named an Officer of the Order of Canada in 2000 and has received an Honorary Doctor of Engineering degree from the Technical University of Nova Scotia and an Honorary Doctor of Laws degree from the University of Alberta.

When asked what he most appreciates about Canada, Don points to the beauty of the land and its people. He continues to reside in Vegreville and, despite his many accomplishments, remains in awe of the opportunities his country has afforded him. He draws encouragement from working with young Canadians and urges them to follow his early example and get involved in the political process. "It's incumbent on everyone to get involved, at any level and in any capacity," he says, adding "it's amazing what can be achieved when people put their minds to it."

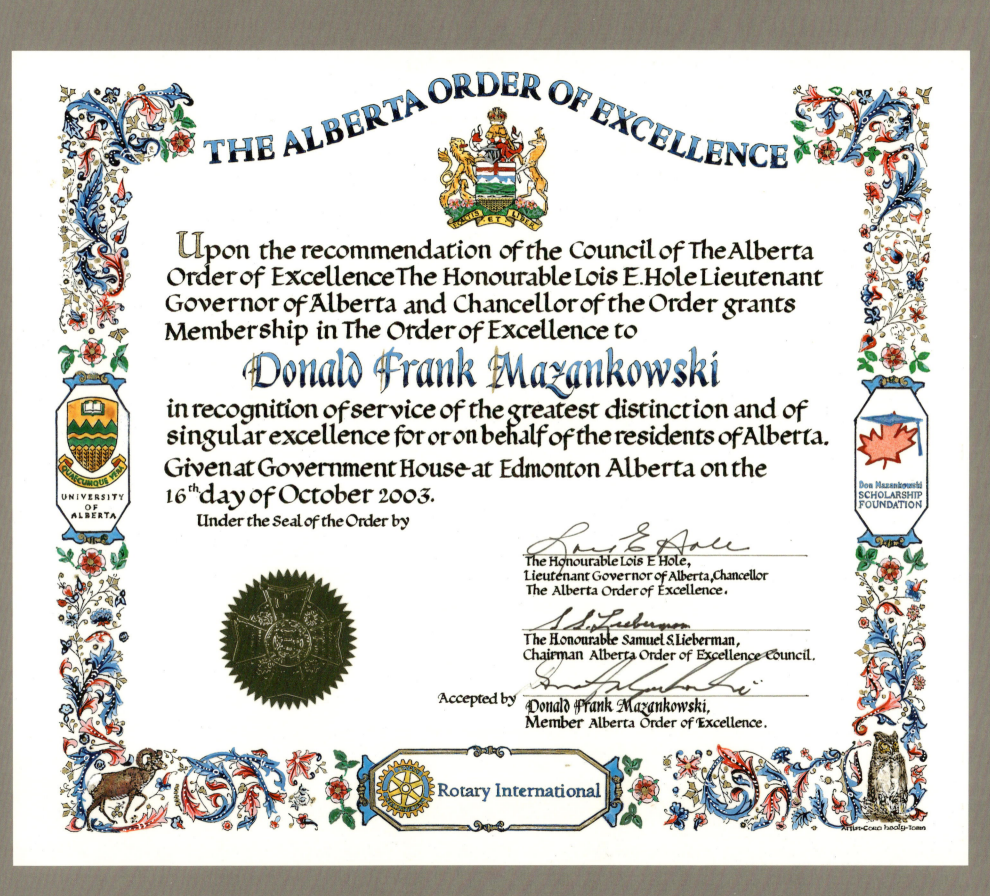

Audrey Attril Morrice

Inducted: 2003

AUDREY MORRICE HAS MANY TALENTS that have shaped her career working with brain injured Albertans, but the greatest of those talents could arguably be a powerful faith that helps her to see potential where others have given up and a remarkable instinct that allows her to transform that hope into reality.

Her natural instincts for therapy and rehabilitation first found an outlet following a move to Alberta from her home in Ontario in 1948. Audrey had travelled to Calgary to visit her sister, Lil, but made the move permanent when she met her future husband, George Morrice. They were married in Calgary in 1950.

Audrey had performed some volunteer service in nursing homes as a young adult. However, it was not until the late 1960s, when the self-taught artist volunteered to teach art to troubled youth and women with mental health problems, that her skills truly began to take shape. She saw in her clients a need for self-esteem and hope. Using a simple and practical approach, she showed them how to create works of art and helped them to build a sense of pride in their accomplishments. She might have continued with that work had she not met Mel Laine. In 1972, Audrey went to Colonel Belcher Veterans Hospital to lend support to Alice Laine, a friend and church choir-mate whose son, Mel, had sustained a profound brain injury from a hit and run accident. The young man lay badly broken and in a persistent vegetative state. Notwithstanding the doctors' opinions that the young naval radar technician's condition was most likely permanent, Audrey was convinced she could help him.

Although she had no medical training, Audrey asked for permission to work with Mel. She and Alice worked in shifts, encouraging him to make eye contact, respond and move his muscles. By 1974, Mel was well enough to leave the hospital and, with Audrey's help, began an extensive program of home care. Over the next four years, they worked together eight hours a day, seven days a week. Audrey's approach was both caring and practical. She offered unrelenting support and encouragement until Mel shared in her belief that he could recover and devised simple exercises, using everyday objects, to help Mel relearn how to move and communicate. Audrey's husband, George, used his skills as an electrical engineer to build whatever equipment was needed. Although progress was painstaking, Mel slowly regained his physical, social and communication skills.

Word spread of Mel's recovery and, by 1977, Audrey was helping others suffering from severe brain injury. In 1978, she and Alice co-founded the non-profit Association for the Rehabilitation of the Brain Injured (ARBI) and began working with three patients in the basement of Woodcliff United Church in Calgary. There was no model to help them shape ARBI, as it was Canada's first community-based brain injury rehabilitation program. Under Audrey's guidance, and with support from partners and donors, the roster of ARBI patients continued to grow, as did the variety of therapies offered. By 1989, ARBI had increased to 20 patients and moved into its own facility. While ARBI expanded to include a complement of paid professional staff, volunteers and family members continued to play an important role in each patient's team of helpers.

Audrey served as the Association's executive director and program director while continuing to work with Mel outside her ARBI duties. Seeing the need for higher-level cognitive and community integration training, she helped to found the Mel Laine Society in 1985, which later became the Brain Injury Rehabilitation Centre. In 1988, health problems forced Audrey to give up her duties as executive director. She resigned as program director in 1995 following a major heart attack but has continued to oversee Mel's care and volunteer at ARBI one day a week.

In 1998, Audrey received an Honorary Doctor of Laws degree from the University of Calgary. Other honours include the City of Calgary Citizen of the Year; Global Woman of Vision; induction in the Terry Fox Hall of Fame; the Sir Fredrick Haultain Prize for contributions to the humanities; the Government of Canada 125th Anniversary medal; the Brian Moore Volunteer Award from Canadian Brain Injury Coalition; and the Rotary International Paul Harris Award for humanitarian contributions to the peoples of the world. She is modest about her accomplishments, pointing to ARBI's many volunteers, staff and benefactors over the years as equal partners in the Association. Those who know and work with her, however, understand the unique nature of her gift and the importance of her contributions.

Audrey's pioneering work has inspired countless patients and volunteers to believe in what seems impossible and to strive for positive change. Due to her patience and determination, many Albertans now enjoy an improved quality of life and, once again are involved in meaningful activities in their communities, Mel Laine included. She has encouraged health care practitioners to consider new approaches in the treatment of brain injuries, and her work at ARBI has led to the development of similar organizations across Western Canada. Perhaps most importantly, Audrey's achievements serve as an example of what can be achieved through determination and a belief in the power of the human spirit to overcome adversity.

Mrs. Morrice is now deceased.

THE ALBERTA ORDER OF EXCELLENCE

Upon the recommendation of the Council of The Alberta Order of Excellence The Honourable Lois E. Hole Lieutenant Governor of Alberta and Chancellor of the Order grants Membership in The Order of Excellence to

Audrey Attril Morrice

in recognition of service of the greatest distinction and of singular excellence for or on behalf of the residents of Alberta.

Given at Government House at Edmonton Alberta on the 16th day of October 2003.

Under the Seal of the Order by

The Honourable Lois E. Hole,
Lieutenant Governor of Alberta, Chancellor
The Alberta Order of Excellence.

The Honourable Samuel S. Lieberman,
Chairman The Alberta Order of Excellence Council.

Accepted by

Audrey Attril Morrice,
Member The Alberta Order of Excellence.

MOUNT ROYAL COLLEGE

UNIVERSITY OF CALGARY

arbi Association for the Rehabilitation of the Brain Injured

Artist Coao Healy-Tosin

James Simpson Palmer

Inducted: 2003

JIM PALMER LEARNED A LESSON EARLY in life that profoundly shaped his life and his contributions to Alberta and Canada. Born into a prominent Prince Edward Island family with roots stretching back to Confederation, Jim was taught to take nothing for granted and to realize the advantages he enjoyed came with an obligation to better the world around him. That lesson was further engrained through the liberal arts education he received from McGill University, where he earned a Bachelor of Arts degree in 1948. He then followed a family tradition: graduating from Dalhousie University Law School in 1952 and becoming the fifth generation to pursue a legal career.

Jim moved to Alberta following an invitation from his McGill roommate, who lived in Calgary. The energy of the growing city and beauty of the Rocky Mountains captured Jim's imagination and he settled in Calgary in 1952 with his new bride, Barbara. He practiced general law with Petrie and Petrie and Texaco Exploration before joining the firm of Burnet, Duckworth in 1955. He became a partner in the firm one year later. During his career with Burnet Duckworth Palmer, Jim established himself as a leader in business, tax and international law and has played an instrumental role in the development of Alberta's oil and gas industry. His expertise and talent for seeing things from a global perspective have brought Jim international recognition in his field.

While working diligently in his legal practice, Jim has taken care to make time for community service. He has volunteered his talents in a number of sectors over the years, but perhaps in none as vigorously as post-secondary education. He firmly believes that "education is independence" and has dedicated considerable time and leadership to help young Canadians achieve that freedom. He currently sits on the Board of Governors of Dalhousie University and also served on the Board of Governors and as chancellor of the University of Calgary from 1986 to 1990. From 1990 to 1993, Jim assumed duties as chair of the University of Calgary's Building the Vision fundraising campaign and helped to surpass the campaign's $40 million goal.

Jim's contributions to the University of Calgary were recognized in 1995 with the James S. Palmer Lecture Series. In the inaugural lecture, speaker John Kenneth Galbraith covered a topic well suited to its namesake, discussing the nature of "The Good Society." Jim's own definition is simple. He believes that a good society offers its citizens access to education and affords those who can look after themselves with an opportunity to build a life and earn a living. Alongside those freedoms, he advocates the need for a caring society that provides a solid safety net for people in need. That conviction has led Jim to support a number of social organizations, including the Calgary Homeless Foundation and Habitat for Humanity. In 2002, he demonstrated the strong community leadership and personal commitment that have defined his life when he led his firm's staff in volunteering at a Calgary Habitat for Humanity construction site.

Over the years, Jim has actively supported arts and culture in his community. He was president of the Calgary Philharmonic Orchestra from 1981 to 1983 and is a committed patron of numerous Calgary arts organizations. Other former duties include Director of the Council for Business and the Arts in Canada, National Director of the Fathers of Confederation Building Trust and Director of CBC Television.

Jim is a fervent supporter of national unity and is committed to the democratic principles that built Canada. He is involved in political organizing and fundraising and, in 1979, ran as the Liberal candidate for the federal constituency of Calgary South. Jim is past provincial president of the Canadian Unity Council and former governor and chairman of the Canadian Tax Foundation.

Jim Palmer's contributions to Alberta and Canada have been recognized with a number of honours. He became a Member of the Order of Canada in 1998 and has received Honorary Doctor of Laws degrees from the University of Calgary, Dalhousie University and the University of Prince Edward Island. He received the Weldon Award from Dalhousie Law School for unselfish public service and the Distinguished Service Award from the Law Society of Alberta and the Canadian Bar Association. In 2002, he was awarded the Commemorative Medal for the Golden Jubilee of her Majesty Queen Elizabeth II.

Despite his many achievements and obligations on corporate and charitable boards, Jim continues to cherish the daily routine of his law practice. Although he allows himself some time for golf and hiking in the Rocky Mountains, he shows no interest in retiring and prefers to draw energy from the unpredictable nature of a business where "every morning the phone rings and anything can happen." In addition to his duties as Burnet Duckworth Palmer chairman, he serves as a mentor to the firm's junior lawyers. He encourages them to see that everyone is important and deserving of respect. He also charges them to pay attention to detail, work hard to find solutions and never forget their obligation to give back to the community. His students would be hard pressed to find a better teacher or role model than Jim Palmer.

Leonard Peter Ratzlaff

Inducted: 2003

LEONARD RATZLAFF IS A GIFTED AND CRITICALLY acclaimed musician who has dedicated his life to helping musicians of all ages and abilities develop their own musical skills. He has played a key role in creating the high quality of vocal music that exists in Alberta today, and his efforts have helped to establish the province as a nationally and internationally recognized center of excellence in choral study.

Leonard comes by many of his talents naturally. He was born with a fine voice and given ample opportunities to develop that gift growing up in the rich choral traditions of the Mennonite faith. He was also born into a family of teachers who provided him with a wealth of role models and helped him develop an appreciation for the finer points of what he refers to as the "family business."

Like many successful teachers, Leonard is an avid student who has maintained a lifelong commitment to learning. In the early 1970s, he earned a Bachelor of Church Music degree with a double major in Voice and Conducting from Mennonite Brethren College of Arts in Winnipeg, followed by a Bachelor of Arts degree in English and Music from the University of Winnipeg and certification in secondary education from the University of Manitoba. He taught English and Music at Mennonite Brethren Collegiate in Winnipeg and sang under the baton of his mentor, William Baerg, before moving to the University of Iowa, where he earned a Master of Arts degree in 1980 and a Doctor of Musical Arts degree in Choral Conducting in 1985.

In 1981, he took a position as assistant professor of Choral Music with the University of Alberta. Leonard's role at the University has grown over the years to include a full professorship and duties as chair of the Music Department. He has also worked to develop Canada's largest graduate program in Choral Conducting, which attracts students to Alberta from across Canada and around the world.

1981 also marked the beginning of what has grown into a long and highly productive association with two Edmonton-based choirs, the University of Alberta's Madrigal Singers and the Richard Eaton Singers. Under Leonard's direction, the Madrigal Singers have won international awards and earned critical acclaim. Those who have worked with Leonard list his greatest strength as his ability to encourage a high level of musical understanding and technical excellence while fostering an environment of kindness, integrity and respect for others. He approaches his conducting duties with a strong commitment to maintaining the highest possible technical and performance standards. He then tempers those standards with a profoundly caring and compassionate approach to teaching that allows the choir's young singers to grow as musicians and find an emotional connection with the music.

That same balance between quality of performance and quality of experience is reflected in his work with the Richard Eaton Singers. While the choir is technically considered an amateur ensemble, Leonard has been successful in creating a program where members can reach a very high performance standard and explore the most demanding works of the choral repertoire. The choir's efforts have been rewarded with high praise from critics and audiences alike. Leonard sees his work with amateur musicians as one of his life's missions. While he makes it a priority to ensure that each singer is given ample opportunity to develop his or her technical abilities, his greatest motivation comes from seeing members grow as individuals through their musical experiences.

Leonard's work has been recognized with a number of honours, including the Commemorative Medal for the Golden Jubilee of her Majesty Queen Elizabeth II in 2002; the University of Alberta Arts Undergraduate Teaching Award in 2001; induction into the City of Edmonton's Cultural Hall of Fame in 2001; and the Alberta Choral Federation Con Spirito Award in 1999. He also received the Julius Herford Dissertation Prize from the American Choral Directors Association in 1987.

Leonard contributes to the cultural health of Alberta and Canada through volunteer service in a number of capacities. He is a member and past president of the Association of Canadian Choral Conductors and in 2000 was chosen to conduct the Association's National Youth Choir of Canada. He has served on boards and committees for the Canada Council and other arts granting organizations and is a member of the International Society for Music Education. He is also a member of the Edmonton Opera Association and has served as a jury member for the Canadian Academy of Recording Arts and Sciences Juno Awards. His contributions to the arts also include his considerable work to promote and celebrate the works of Canadian composers.

Leonard continues to perform in Canada and abroad as a baritone soloist. True to his motivations as a teacher and conductor, the moments he relishes as a performer are those when he can look out at the audience and see that he has made a connection and succeeded in communicating the music's deeper meaning. When asked to offer a word of advice to young musicians, Leonard encourages them to discover that connection for themselves. He urges them to learn to appreciate just how strongly human emotion and the human experience can be expressed through music.

THE ALBERTA ORDER OF EXCELLENCE

Upon the recommendation of the Council of The Alberta Order of Excellence The Honourable Lois E. Hole Lieutenant Governor of Alberta and Chancellor of the Order grants Membership in the Order to

Leonard Peter Ratzlaff

in recognition of service of the greatest distinction and of singular excellence for or on behalf of the residents of Alberta. Given at Government House at Edmonton, Alberta on the 16th. day of October 2003.

Under the Seal of the Order by

The Honourable Lois E. Hole,
Lieutenant Governor of Alberta, Chancellor
of The Alberta Order of Excellence.

The Honourable Samuel S. Lieberman,
Chairman Alberta Order of Excellence Council.

Accepted by Leonard Peter Ratzlaff,
Member, The Alberta Order of Excellence.

QUAECUNQUE VERA
UNIVERSITY OF ALBERTA

accc
ASSOCIATION OF CANADIAN CHORAL CONDUCTORS

RES Richard Eaton Singers

Artist, Cora Healy Tobin

Alvin Gerald Libin

Inducted: 2004

ALVIN LIBIN IS A PROUD CALGARIAN and Albertan with a long record of service to the province, particularly in the area of health care research and education. His strong leadership, combined with his unwavering commitment to encouraging and promoting excellence, has made this lifelong Calgary resident a distinguished example of the Alberta spirit at its best.

Alvin was born in Calgary on 22 April 1931. He inherited a strong work ethic from his parents, who were Russian immigrants to Alberta. Alvin used that ethic and his natural talents to build a successful business portfolio with interests in real estate, oil and gas and financial services. When asked to describe his formula for success, Alvin lists the essential ingredients as "hard work, honesty and teamwork; putting the right people in the right place to do the job; and luck." Those who have had the pleasure of working with him suggest Alvin's remarkable business acumen, discipline, and strong leadership and mentoring skills as equally important contributors to his success.

In addition to building a career in the corporate sector, Alvin has developed a solid reputation as a community leader. From 1980 to 1990, he served Calgary's Foothills Hospital as chairman of the Board of Trustees. The hospital underwent considerable growth during his 10 years at the helm and developed a reputation for excellence throughout the institution, from research and education to clinical care and patient outcomes.

Alvin's ability to foster a culture of excellence can also be seen in the Alberta Heritage Foundation for Medical Research, where he served as chairman of the Board of Trustees from 1990 to 2000. Under his stewardship, the Foundation saw its original $300 million provincial government endowment grow to over $1 billion. Alvin also helped recruit strong leadership for the Foundation and cultivate the organization's high standards of excellence. Those standards define the Foundation's reputation as an internationally respected organization and serve as a powerful tool for attracting the world's best researchers to the province. Working in partnership with Alberta's three research-intensive universities, the Foundation has supported many of the exciting health research and treatment discoveries made by the province's health researchers. To date, the Foundation has granted some $750 million to health research, attracted 400 independent researchers to the province and supported over 6,000 research trainees.

In 2000, having fulfilled the legislated maximum term of office with the Alberta Heritage Foundation for Medical Research, Alvin was invited to share his skills as chair of the Alberta Ingenuity Fund, a new organization created to nurture science and engineering research and discoveries in Alberta.

Alvin is a long-term supporter of the University of Calgary, providing leadership in a number of capacities. He served as a board member of University Technologies International where he shared his business insights with entrepreneurs working in the University's spin-off companies. In addition to leading two major fundraising campaigns to support the University's health research activities, Alvin has made major investments of his own. The University's facilities now include the Libin Gene Therapy Unit, which funds research to explore new therapies for heart disease, diabetes, mellitus, arthritis and cancer, and the Libin Cardiovascular Institute, which works to integrate and strengthen cardiac research, education, treatment and patient care in Calgary and southern Alberta.

The Gene Therapy Unit and Cardiovascular Institute were made possible through the auspices of the Alvin and Mona Libin Foundation. The fact that these two important contributions bear the name of both Alvin and his wife of more than 50 years reflects the important role Mona has played in Alvin's life and their commitment to the community. In addition to funding major health care initiatives, the two are ongoing supporters of numerous community programs, including scholarships at the University of Calgary and the city's Jewish community. Alvin and Mona, who is also a native Calgarian, were high school sweethearts before marrying in 1953. Their family includes their son Robert, daughter-in-law Leeann, and grandchildren Louis, Eda and Nora.

Alvin has received numerous honours for his community service. He was named a Paul Harris Fellow by Rotary Club International and holds an Honorary Doctor of Laws Degree from the University of Calgary. In 2002, he was named an Officer of the Order of Canada. That same year, the Alberta Heritage Foundation for Medical Research created the Libin Prize in Cardiovascular Research, a fitting tribute to a man who describes his approach to the Foundation, and to fostering research in general as "excellence creates excellence." That attitude is clearly evident in the life and career of Alvin Libin, in the contributions he has made to the quality of life Albertans enjoy today and in the legacy he has created for generations of Albertans to come.

THE ALBERTA ORDER OF EXCELLENCE

Upon the recommendation of the Council of The Alberta Order of Excellence, The Honourable Lois E. Hole, Lieutenant Governor of Alberta and Chancellor of the Order grants Membership in The Order of Excellence to

Alvin Gerald Libin

in recognition of service of the greatest distinction and of singular excellence for or on behalf of the residents of Alberta.

Given at Government House at Edmonton Alberta on the 21st day of October 2004.

Under the Seal of the Order by

The Honourable Lois E Hole,
Lieutenant Governor of Alberta Chancellor
The Alberta Order of Excellence.

Dr. Robert C.P. Westbury,
Chairman, Alberta Order of Excellence Council.

Accepted by

Alvin Gerald Libin,
Member Alberta Order of Excellence.

AHFMR
ALBERTA HERITAGE FOUNDATION
FOR MEDICAL RESEARCH

Alberta INGENUITY Fund

Artist-Cora Beatty-Tobin

M. Ann McCaig

Inducted: 2004

ANN MCCAIG IS A DEDICATED VOLUNTEER who has made lasting contributions to Calgary, the province and the country. Her strongest accomplishments are seen in her work to strengthen and support post-secondary education and her eloquent advocacy of programs for children and youth.

Ann's small town prairie upbringing lies at the root of her commitment to community service. Her early years in Saskatchewan centered around family, church and community. Ann's mother and father, the local John Deere implement and Chrysler dealer, led by example. It was a world where, as Ann points out, "if you wanted something, you did it yourself. You raised the funds and had fun doing it." This environment provided Ann with a powerful combination of traits—a sense of warmth and compassion for others, tempered with a healthy dose of determination, strength and self-sufficiency.

Ann earned a Bachelor of Education degree from the University of Saskatchewan in 1961 and moved to Calgary to teach English and History. She returned to Saskatchewan, where she married her first husband in 1962 and continued to teach for a short time before turning her attention to helping with her husband's business and raising their three children: Roxanne, Jane and John. Ann also served as a youth counselor at Lakeview United Church in Regina and helped establish one of the city's first group homes. That initiative was Ann's first major fundraising project. Besides being a moving and rewarding experience, it showed her she had valuable skills to offer as a fundraiser and community advocate.

In 1970, Ann returned to Alberta with her young family and settled in Calgary. She enjoyed the energy and vitality of the city and valued its proximity to the Rocky Mountains, which have long served as a place of reflection and recreation for her. Ann's first husband, Roger, died in 1976. She worked through the challenge of the following years with characteristic strength and determination, continuing to raise her young family and serve as a volunteer. She married Bud McCaig in 1984.

The same year Ann began a new chapter in her life with Bud she also embarked on a new relationship with the University of Calgary. She was approached by her friend and mentor, Peter Lougheed, and asked to serve on the University's Board of Governors. Although daunted, she accepted the position, spurred on by Peter's insistence that it was "time to get to work," and work, she did. She served on the Board from 1984 to 1994 before becoming chancellor in 1995. With her characteristic dedication, she took on her new duties as a full-time job. At the end of her term in 1998, the University conferred upon her the title chancellor emerita in recognition of her outstanding service to the school, which has also included co-chairing the Faculty of Management's $13 million fundraising campaign and serving as vice-chair on the national Building on the Vision $40 million campaign. Ann continues to serve as one of the University's most dedicated and passionate ambassadors.

Ann's work to support post-secondary education in Alberta and across Canada includes service as a Trustee of the Killam Estate. In this role, she helps to oversee the administration and distribution of scholarships to post-graduate students at Canadian universities, as well as Killam Fellowships and Prizes for Canada's leading professors and scholars.

Ann's passion for children and youth, as well as her skill as a businesswoman, can be seen in her work as chair of the Alberta Adolescent Recovery Centre in Calgary. She is a dedicated supporter, advocate and fundraiser for the Centre, which provides residential treatment for youth aged 12 to 18 who struggle with multiple addictions. Ann's efforts are driven by the knowledge that it is a place some of its young residents have come to call "the last house on the block." Ann is currently working on a fundraising project to expand the Centre's capacity from its current limit of 30 residents.

Ann has also served as co-chair of Alberta Children's Hospital's *All for One-All for Kids* campaign, which raised $50 million for the new Calgary facility. She was chair of the Calgary Zoo's *Tusks and Tails Ball*, which raised $1 million over four years for education and conservation education at the zoo. Other community service duties include past Chairperson of the Calgary Foundation, board member of the Banff Centre Foundation, Director of the Calgary United Way, National Director of the Shaw Festival Niagara-On-The-Lake and Director of the Nature Conservancy of Canada. She has served on the Board of Suncor Energy since 1995.

She is a recipient of the Canada 125 Award, the YWCA Woman of Distinction Lifetime Achievement Award and a Paul Harris Fellowship from Rotary International. In 2001, Ann received an Honorary Doctor of Laws degree from the University of Calgary. In 2004, she was one of the inaugural recipients of the University of Calgary Education Partnership Award as part of the University's Celebration of Excellence.

Ann often draws inspiration from the words of Eleanor Roosevelt, who said, "you must do the thing you think you cannot do." Ann McCaig takes those words to heart. She does not shy away from a challenge, preferring instead to roll up her sleeves and get to work. She has done a great many things to make her community, province and country a better place to live, and, in doing so with such grace and passion, she has inspired others to do the same.

THE ALBERTA ORDER OF EXCELLENCE

Upon the recommendation of the Council of The Alberta Order of Excellence, The Honourable Lois E. Hole, Lieutenant Governor of Alberta and Chancellor of the Order grants Membership in The Order of Excellence to

Margaret Ann McCaig

in recognition of service of the greatest distinction and of singular excellence for or on behalf of the residents of Alberta. Given at Government House at Edmonton, Alberta on the 21st day of October 2004.

Under the Seal of the Order by

The Honourable Lois E. Hole,
Lieutenant Governor of Alberta, Chancellor
of The Alberta Order of Excellence.

Dr. Robert C.P. Westbury, Chairman,
The Alberta Order of Excellence Council.

Accepted by Margaret Ann McCaig,
Member, The Alberta Order of Excellence.

SUNCOR ENERGY

AARC

Les Fiducies Killam Trusts

UNIVERSITY OF CALGARY

Artist - Cara Healy - Tobin.

Eric Patrick Newell

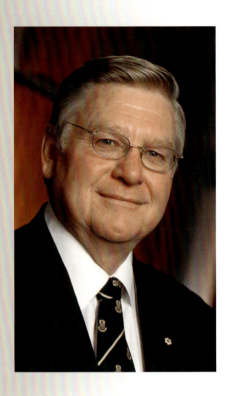

Inducted: 2004

ERIC NEWELL IS A CORPORATE LEADER and innovator who has made lasting contributions not only to the economic health of Alberta and Canada, but also to the strength and diversity of the country's workforce and the opportunities and quality of life enjoyed by his fellow Canadians. His skills as a businessman and entrepreneur coupled with his passionate support of education and commitment and compassion as a community leader have helped lay the groundwork for a stronger future for Alberta and for the country as a whole.

Eric's career began with Imperial Oil and Esso, where his skills as an engineer and manager made him a valuable asset. He was frequently sent "on loan" to sites across North America, moving through postings in 15 different cities over the first 20 years of his career before coming to Alberta in 1986. His temporary assignment with the Syncrude oil sands development in northern Alberta became permanent, and Eric and his wife, Kathy, settled their family in Fort McMurray. Eric's responsibilities with Syncrude quickly grew to include service as president, CEO and chairman of the Board of Directors.

Through his strong leadership of Syncrude and his groundbreaking work with the National Oil Sands Task Force, Eric was instrumental in communicating the vast potential of the oil sands, thereby bringing this potential to market and developing a new blueprint for Canada's energy industry. He retired from Syncrude in 2003, leaving the corporation, the province, and the Canadian industry as a whole with a solid plan for continued growth and prosperity.

While working to fully develop the economic potential of Alberta's oil sands, Eric also committed himself and his organization to mining the enormous potential of Alberta communities and Albertans themselves. His influence can be seen in Syncrude's strong sense of corporate social responsibility, which includes education and community development initiatives, strong health and safety programs and a commitment to environmental stewardship. Eric's commitment to consensus building and finding cooperative solutions has earned him the respect and trust of the Aboriginal community, the energy industry, and government and community leaders.

Eric's community and volunteer efforts in the areas of education and workforce development are equally well regarded. Under his leadership, Syncrude became Canada's largest industrial employer of Aboriginal people, and his ongoing work with the Aboriginal community has helped develop educational opportunities and open up new career paths for future generations.

Eric has worked extensively to encourage Alberta businesses to work in partnership with post-secondary institutions to develop scholarships and strengthen the quality of programs and experiences available to all Alberta students. His long-standing association with the University of Alberta includes service as chair of the Board of Governors. He was named chancellor in June 2004.

In addition to his duties with the University of Alberta, Eric continues to serve as chair of Careers: the Next Generation, an organization Eric created in 1989 in response to projected trade workforce deficits in Alberta. Since its inception, the program has helped some 100,000 young Albertans from across the province develop career plans and has given thousands more the opportunity to take on internship positions.

Eric's extensive volunteer and community service has also included duties as Chair of the Conference Board of Canada, Director of the Canadian Millennium Scholarship Foundation, Co-chair of the Alliance for Responsible Environmental Alternatives, member of the Aboriginal Human Resources Development Council; Co-chair of the 2000 Governor General's Canadian Study Conference, Honorary Chairman of the Edmonton Business Council for the Visual Arts, Board of Directors member of the Keyano College Foundation and Chairman of the Alberta Winter Games.

He has been honoured with numerous recognitions and awards for his contributions, including Honorary Doctor of Laws degrees from the University of British Columbia, the University of Alberta and Athabasca University; the 125th Commemorative Medal of Canada; the Canadian Business Leader award from the University of Alberta; and numerous awards from public education organizations. Eric's commitment and integrity earned him distinction as Alberta's most respected CEO in a 2001 poll of 1,300 senior executives from across the province. In 2000, he was named an Officer of the Order of Canada.

Despite his many prestigious awards and recognitions, Eric is humble about his accomplishments, pointing to the strong teams he has been fortunate to assemble and work with. When asked to describe his formula for success, he shares a philosophy that, like the man himself, is intelligent, forward-looking and compassionate. He suggests that the role of a leader is to articulate a shared vision, help people realize they are part of a larger community and the need to work as a team to achieve success. Anyone wishing to see that theory put into practice need only study the career and contributions of Eric Newell and the economic and social legacies he has helped to create for Albertans and all Canadians.

THE ALBERTA ORDER OF EXCELLENCE

Upon the recommendation of the Council of The Alberta Order of Excellence, The Honourable Lois E. Hole Lieutenant Governor of Alberta and Chancellor of the Order grants Membership in The Order of Excellence to

Eric Patrick Newell

in recognition of service of the greatest distinction and of singular excellence for or on behalf of the residents of Alberta.

Given at Government House at Edmonton, Alberta on the 21st day of October 2004.

Under the Seal of the Order by

The Honourable Lois E. Hole,
Lieutenant Governor of Alberta
Chancellor of The Alberta Order of Excellence.

Dr. Robert E P Westbury,
Chairman Alberta Order of Excellence Council.

Accepted by Eric Patrick Newell,
Member The Alberta Order of Excellence.

University of Alberta

CAREERS the Next Generation

Syncrude

Artist-Cora Healy-Tobin

Bryan Perkins

Inducted: 2004

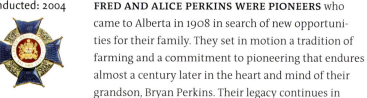

FRED AND ALICE PERKINS WERE PIONEERS who came to Alberta in 1908 in search of new opportunities for their family. They set in motion a tradition of farming and a commitment to pioneering that endures almost a century later in the heart and mind of their grandson, Bryan Perkins. Their legacy continues in the remarkable energy, intelligence and innovation with which Bryan approaches his life's work. From a farm rooted in history, he has helped foster a promising future for agriculture in the province.

Bryan was born on 22 June 1946 in Edmonton and raised on the family farm outside Wainwright. He enjoyed a typical rural upbringing, working the farm with parents Jack and Vern and siblings Susan and Mark, and taking part in scouting and local sports. He attended the University of Alberta where he earned a BSc in Agriculture in 1969. He began farming that year and married his wife, Sharon. Sharon taught school before turning her attention to raising their young family and helping out with their farming operation and fertilizer and chemical business.

In addition to running the farm, Bryan kept busy as a volunteer. He served with the Wainwright Credit Union; the Wainedge Gas Co-op; on the board of Grace United Church, as a trainer, coach and manager of local hockey and swimming teams; and as an active volunteer for minor and amateur hockey organizations. Bryan's keen business sense, natural diplomacy and strong public speaking skills also made him a valuable asset to a number of industry organizations. He served as Chairman of the Agricultural Diversification Alliance; Vice-President of the United Grain Growers; an early member and then President of the Western Hog Growers Association; Director of United Oilseeds Products; board member of the Alberta Agricultural Research Institute; and Chairman of the Board of Fletcher's Fine Foods.

As Bryan's participation in the industry grew, so too did Perkins Farm. The family sold its fertilizer and chemical business in the mid-1980s and focussed on the pig and grain operation. In the mid-1990s, Bryan began developing an innovative and successful approach to farming that would have a positive effect on hundreds of family farms across Alberta.

Today, Perkins Farms Inc. includes land farmed by Bryan and Sharon, their children, Bryan's brother Mark and family, Sharon's brother-in-law Matt and family, and their close friend Ken Wasmuth. They are all part of a unique organization called Sunhaven Farms, which is made up of approximately 150 farm families. Each family operation maintains its independence while also belonging to one of four local groupings of farms that work together. These four groups, in turn, make up the larger Sunhaven Farms. Grain grown by group members goes to Venture Feedmill at Irma, which is run on a non-profit basis by Sunhaven. The group also includes individuals and local businesses. Bryan serves as president of Sunhaven, as well as each of the smaller farm groups.

The benefits of this approach are many. It allows independent operators to pool resources and take advantage of economies of scale. It also helps to mitigate the risks of diversifying an operation as members can pool knowledge and take advantage of expertise within the group in areas such as nutrition, marketing, risk management and agribusiness. They can also access outside expertise as a group, thereby expanding their collective pool of knowledge. A further benefit comes from the collective scale of Sunhaven, which allows for a value-added approach to production and gives each farm the ability to access bigger markets and opportunities.

Bryan acknowledges that this approach demands a willingness to work together and delegate some decision making to the group. He finds the benefits far outweigh any negatives. He points to the collective energy and talent of the group as one of its greatest strengths and enjoys being around members who are enthusiastic and positive about farming. He is also rewarded by seeing young farmers become excited about agriculture and committed to staying in the community.

Bryan's own energy and enthusiasm for his profession show no signs of flagging. He is chairman of the Board of Directors for the Prairie Swine Centre in Saskatoon, which furthers research in a range of areas from animal welfare and nutrition to agricultural engineering. He also fundraises for agricultural scholarships and for the Swine Research Centre at his alma mater.

Bryan's focus on the future and his caring nature are evident when asked what he hopes for his grandchildren: "I hope they'll farm if that's what they want," he says "but, more than anything, I want them to be people who know how to appreciate and share love with their family and their community, who understand some things about nature and respect the land and the people around them."

When asked what he values most about Alberta, Bryan points to the "great entrepreneurial spirit of Albertans and the diverse opportunities that exist for all different kinds of people, ventures and trades." Those qualities are what drew settlers to the province at the beginning of the last century, and they will continue to define Alberta in the 21st century, thanks to the vision, commitment and innovation of leaders like Bryan Perkins.

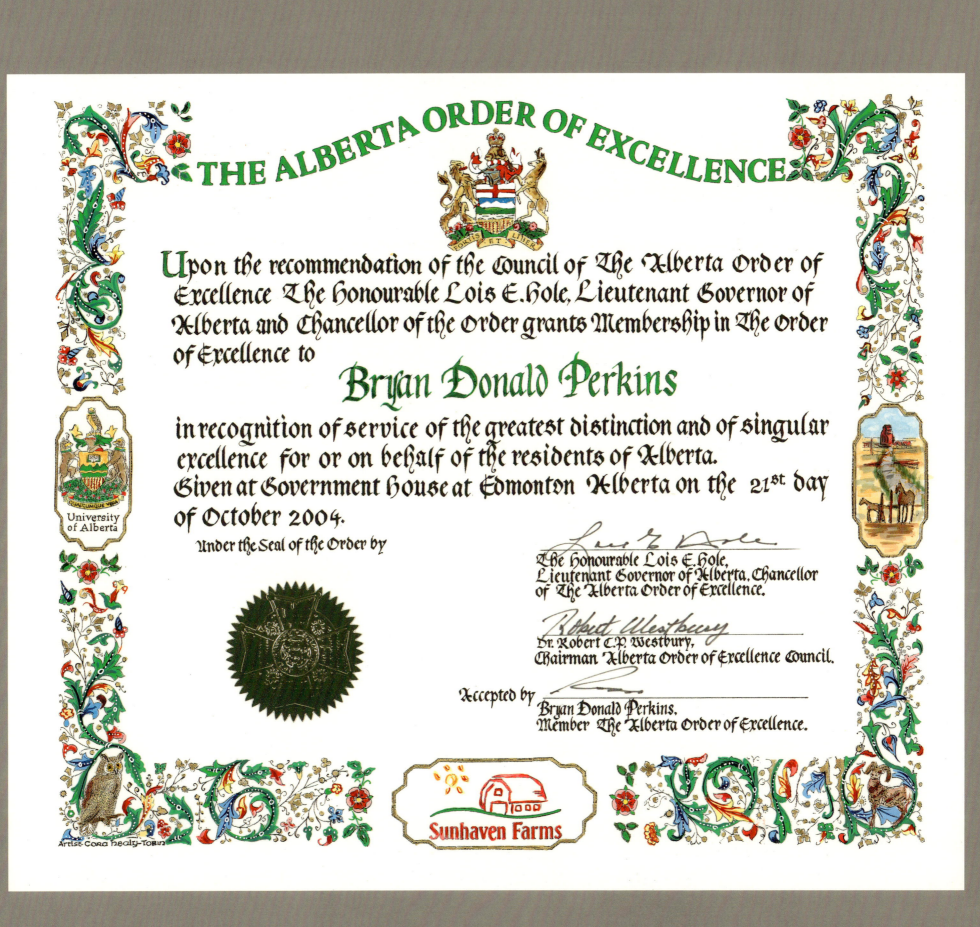

THE ALBERTA ORDER OF EXCELLENCE

Upon the recommendation of the Council of The Alberta Order of Excellence The Honourable Lois E. Hole, Lieutenant Governor of Alberta and Chancellor of the Order grants Membership in The Order of Excellence to

Bryan Donald Perkins

in recognition of service of the greatest distinction and of singular excellence for or on behalf of the residents of Alberta.

Given at Government House at Edmonton Alberta on the 21st day of October 2004.

Under the Seal of the Order by

University of Alberta

The Honourable Lois E. Hole,
Lieutenant Governor of Alberta, Chancellor
of The Alberta Order of Excellence.

Dr. Robert C.P. Westbury,
Chairman Alberta Order of Excellence Council.

Accepted by

Bryan Donald Perkins,
Member The Alberta Order of Excellence.

Artist Cora Healy-Tobin

Sunhaven Farms

Barbara Caroline Poole
John Edward Poole

Inducted: 2004

JOHN AND BARBARA POOLE REPRESENT valued members of the corps of dedicated volunteers and supporters that have fuelled Alberta's diverse social, cultural and community endeavours. As individuals, they are bright, engaging and passionate advocates for the many causes and organizations they embrace. Together, they formed an energetic, compassionate and insightful team that created important and lasting benefits for their fellow Albertans. Their induction marks the first time that a couple or team has been jointly named to the Alberta Order of Excellence.

John and Barbara come from similar backgrounds. Raised during the Depression, they grew up appreciating the value of hard work and of extending a helping hand to others. John's family moved from Regina to Edmonton in 1932, hoping to improve the fortunes of its struggling construction business. In 1939, Barbara's father moved the family to Calgary from her hometown of Coronation, Alberta, in search of better opportunities for his medical practice. Both attended university where they received Bachelor degrees—John's in Civil Engineering from the University of Alberta in 1937 and Barbara's in Interior Design from the Faculty of Architecture at the University of Manitoba in 1952.

They met in the winter of 1952 during a ski trip to Banff and were married that same year. The Pooles settled and began raising a family in Edmonton where John had already begun making his mark as an engineer. His first job, as a structural engineer with the City of Edmonton Power Plant working on Edmonton Pumping Station #1, was the first in a long series of projects that would help shape the city and province. John soon joined the business his father had started in 1906 and, with the exception of a period during World War II when he was recruited to Defense Industries Limited in Montréal to assist in the war effort, he spent his career helping to build Poole Construction into an industry leader. In 1948, John and his brother, George, purchased the company from their father. Over the next 30 years, they worked with their talented team members to create numerous landmark projects in Alberta, across Canada and in the United States. With Don Love, they founded Oxford Properties, which became a major developer, and they were also founding partners in Shaw Communications. John served as a director of the TD Bank and other boards.

In 1977, the two co-chairmen sold Poole Construction to their employees in a move that offered financial independence for the brothers and their families. John refuses to take credit for the progressive approach to the sale, which provided a unique and profitable future for staff of the newly renamed PCL Construction. Barbara offers an alternative view: that the positive staff relationships the company enjoyed and the unique nature of the sale reflect the thoughtful and generous approach John has always taken to business and to life.

During John's years with Poole Construction, both he and Barbara were active members of the community. Selling the company allowed them to take on their community interests and endeavours in a new way.

In 1989, they decided to give back to Edmonton by rejuvenating the Edmonton Community Foundation, which was inactive and without funds. John and Barbara's family, George Poole and Robert Stollery each contributed to the project while their friend, E. John Slatter, served as Secretary and supervised the reorganization. The Edmonton Community Foundation today is a great success story with assets over $150 million and $45 million distributed to education and various charities.

It is difficult to compile a complete list of their volunteer efforts and community investments, as they have been frequently offered quietly and without fanfare. Their energy, dedication and generosity can be seen in a wide-range of areas, including arts organizations, such as the Edmonton Symphony, the Alberta Ballet, the Citadel Theatre, the Glenbow-Alberta Institute and the Lieutenant Governor of Alberta Arts Award Foundation; educational institutions, such as the University of Alberta, Grant MacEwan College, the Lester B. Pearson College of the Pacific and the Banff Centre; health organizations, such as the University of Alberta Hospital Foundation and the Alberta Foundation for Health Research; and environmental organizations, such as the Nature Conservancy of Canada, to which they contributed critical assistance to protect natural ranch lands adjacent to Waterton National Park.

Having been deeply involved in a high school Teen Club in Calgary, Barbara started one in Edmonton's Crestwood Community and, with John, devoted many Friday evenings to their activities. On the national stage, Barbara has shared her passion for the arts as a governor for the National Theatre School of Canada and the Canadiana Fund, and as a national council member for the Canadian Society of Decorative Arts.

Their extensive record of community involvement has been recognized with numerous awards and honours. John was awarded an Honorary Doctor of Laws degree from the University of Alberta and was named an Officer of the Order of Canada in 1996. He received many business and engineering honours in recognition of his contributions to the industry. Both John and Barbara received Queen Elizabeth II Golden Jubilee Medals and share joint honours, such as the Northern Lights Award of Distinction from the Edmonton Chamber of Commerce, the Distinguished Citizens Award from Grant MacEwan College and induction into the Edmonton Cultural Hall of Fame.

Together, John and Barbara shared a love of nature and outdoor pursuits. They were avid skiers and hikers and travelled extensively, including numerous cycling tours of Europe. As a husband and wife team, they shared a unique combination of personality traits: a kind and generous nature, an infectious sense of optimism and of humour, and a dedication to community service that has made a difference in the quality of life enjoyed by Edmontonians, Albertans and all Canadians.

John Edward Poole is now deceased.

THE ALBERTA ORDER OF EXCELLENCE

Upon the recommendation of the Council of The Alberta Order of Excellence
The Honourable Lois E. Hole, Lieutenant Governor of Alberta and
Chancellor of the Order grants Membership in The Order of Excellence to

Barbara C. Poole and John E. Poole

in recognition of service of the greatest distinction and of singular
excellence for or on behalf of the residents of Alberta.

Given at Government House at Edmonton Alberta on the 21st day
of October 2004.

Under the Seal of the Order by

The Honourable Lois E. Hole,
Lieutenant Governor of Alberta Chancellor
The Alberta Order of Excellence.

Dr Robert E.P Westbury,
Chairman, The Alberta Order of Excellence Council.

Accepted by
Barbara C. Poole and John E. Poole,
Members, The Alberta Order of Excellence.

University of Alberta

UNIVERSITY of MANITOBA

Artist-Cora Healey-Tobin

Robert W. Chapman, Sr.

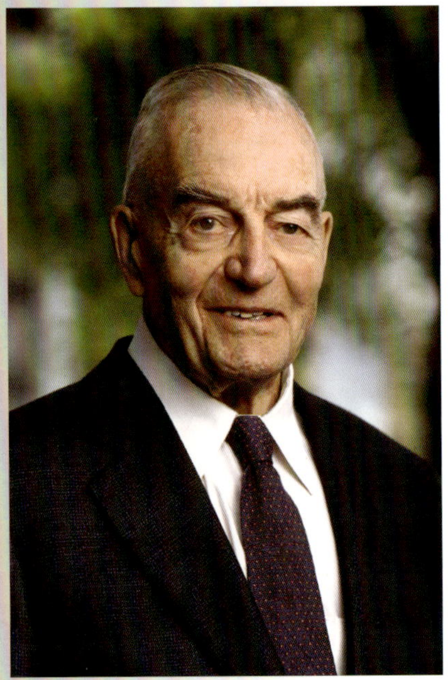

Inducted: 2005

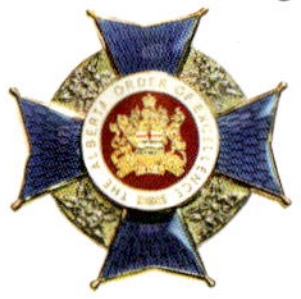

ROBERT CHAPMAN IS A LONG-STANDING member of the Edmonton business community who has played a leading role in developing many of the city's seminal business and social service organizations. His extensive resume of service to Edmonton and Alberta spans almost 70 years and touches on a wide range of sectors. While Robert's activities and interests have been diverse, they all speak to his singular commitment to making his city and province a better place to live.

Robert came to Edmonton in 1918, when his father moved the family from Medicine Hat to pursue opportunities for his insurance business. He joined Chapman Weber Ltd. in 1936 and quickly developed an interest in the aviation industry. Here, he worked to expand the company's role as a major aviation insurance broker in Alberta.

Robert put his budding business career on hold in the early 1940s to join the Loyal Edmonton Regiment. He received an honourable discharge for medical reasons, but his knowledge of aviation allowed him to continue serving the war effort by working as a civilian advisor with military airports across Western Canada. After the war, Robert continued serving as a Loyal Edmonton reservist. In 1945, he married Dorothy White, and they began raising a family.

Over the years, Robert expanded his business interests to include Capilano Motors, Chapman Weber Motors, Mayfair Developments, Chapman Developments and Edmonton Travel. He also worked to build on the health of businesses in Edmonton and across the province through his 60 years of involvement with the Chamber of Commerce. In his service as president of the Edmonton and Alberta Jaycees and Chamber of Commerce, and as a member of the National Chamber of Commerce Executive, Robert helped open doors for many businesses around Alberta and across the country. He took that work a step further in 1971 when he became the first chair of the Alberta Opportunity Company. For the next 14 years, he took great pleasure in helping countless Alberta businesses take flight.

Robert has given equal attention to fostering the opportunities available to Edmontonians in need of social supports. In the late 1930s, he helped create the Edmonton Council of Social Agencies and, later, the Edmonton Community Chest and the Edmonton Family Welfare Bureau. These agencies were among the first viable social service agencies to take root in Edmonton. They not only provided much needed help for a city recovering from the effects of the Great Depression, but also served as the basis for a number of the city's current social service agencies. Robert has also volunteered with the Salvation Army for more than 40 years at both the local and national levels.

His extensive list of community work also includes duties as founding chair of the Medical Services Research Foundation, and as a founder and board member of the Citizen's Committee. Over the years, Robert has also shared his energy and expertise as a member of more than 40 charitable and community organizations, including the University of Alberta, the Boys and Girls Club of Edmonton, the Charitable Foundation of Alberta, the Edmonton Regional Airport Taskforce, the Conference Society of Alberta, and the Canadian Arthritis and Rheumatism Society.

Mr. Chapman has received numerous honours, including the Order of Distinguished Auxiliary Service from the Salvation Army, and a Community Achievement Award from the Alberta government. In 1991, he was appointed Honorary Colonel of the Loyal Edmonton Regiment.

Robert Chapman approaches every challenge with the same trademark qualities that have defined his career and his life: with great energy and optimism for the future, and with a desire to create new opportunities for the city and the province he is proud to call home.

Robert W. Chapman is now deceased.

THE ALBERTA ORDER OF EXCELLENCE

Upon the recommendation of the Council of The Alberta Order of Excellence The Honourable Norman L. Kwong Lieutenant Governor of Alberta and Chancellor of the Order grants Membership in The Order of Excellence to

Robert William Chapman, Sr.

in recognition of service of the greatest distinction and of singular excellence for or on behalf of the residents of Alberta.

Given at Government House at Edmonton Alberta on the 20th day of October 2005.

Under the Seal of the Order by

The Honourable Norman L. Kwong,
Lieutenant Governor of Alberta, Chancellor
The Alberta Order of Excellence.

Dr. Robert E.P. Westbury,
Chairman, The Alberta Order of Excellence Council.

Accepted by *R W Chapman*

Robert William Chapman Sr.,
Member, The Alberta Order of Excellence.

Dr. Gerald Warren Hankins

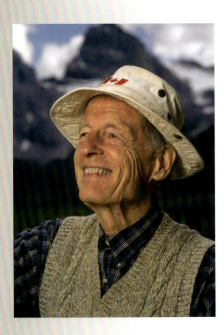

Inducted: 2005

DR. GERALD HANKINS IS A DEDICATED and compassionate man who shares the best of his talent and spirit with those around him. He has brought distinction to his community, province and country through his work as a missionary doctor and writer and through his commitment to serving others.

Gerald Warren Hankins was born in Calgary, Alberta, on 16 October 1923 to Ralph and Gladys Hankins. His parents divorced when he was four, leaving Gladys to raise Gerald and his brother Murray. Without marketable skills, Gladys had great difficulty supporting her two boys, and they struggled through the Depression and the poverty it brought to many. As a teenager, Gerald developed a love of the Rocky Mountains and would often ride his bike from Calgary to Canmore to hike and help out in work parties at the Youth Hostel. It marked the beginning of a lifelong association with, and love for, the town of Canmore.

After graduating from Western Canada High School in Calgary, Gerald attempted to join the war effort, despite being under age. Later, he joined the Royal Canadian Air Force and after training for aircrew, served as a radio navigator with the Royal Air Force Squadrons 96 and 176 in Britain, India and Burma. In 1943, his airplane suffered engine failure and crashed, leaving Gerald with a severe back injury. It was an event that would serve to transform his life on two important fronts. During his 10-month recuperation in Scotland, Gerald developed an interest in the medical profession. He also experienced a growing sense of faith that would greatly influence his life.

After the war ended, Gerald returned to Canada and began studies at the University of Alberta. On 22 June 1948 he married Alison Matthews. He earned a BSc in 1949 and then a medical degree in 1951. After post-graduate training in Surgery in England, Gerald and Alison settled in Calgary and Gerald established a general surgery practice at the Calgary General and, later, at the Foothills Hospital. Over the years, their family grew to include five children.

The Hankins family was a regular fixture at Calgary's First Baptist Church. Gerald's growing faith also began leading him toward overseas service as a medical missionary. In 1966, he took part in a two-week mission to Mexico with the Christian Medical Society but felt it important to wait until the children were grown before undertaking a more extensive assignment.

In 1970, he accepted the invitation to provide vacation cover for his former classmate, Dr. Helen Huston, at the United Mission to Nepal hospital she had established a year earlier. That two-month assignment turned into a commitment to complete a four-year term. Those four years eventually turned into twelve.

Gerald, Alison and their youngest daughter, Jennifer, lived in Nepal from 1974 to 1986 where Gerald performed surgery and taught junior Nepali doctors. After a couple of years experience, he realized there were few, if any, textbooks of practical surgery that would help doctors working in Third World countries. Working under an editor living in Kenya, he and 10 other surgeons contributed to a textbook called Primary Surgery. It became a massive project that took five years to complete. The end result was *Primary Surgery Vol 1 & 2*, an invaluable and eminently practical resource that continues to see frequent use in Third World hospitals. While Dr. Hankins is humble about his contributions to the work, he served as one of its key contributors.

Dr. Hankins returned to Canada in 1986. In 1987, and again in 1989, Gerald completed short medical relief assignments in Inuvik, NT. He retired from active medical practice in 1990, having set his sights on a new career. His years working on the surgery textbook had sparked a love of writing.

In 1992, he published the biography of Dr. Helen Huston and then followed up with biographies of three other distinguished Albertans: Dr. Arthur Jenkyns, Dr. Otto Schaefer and Dr. Gary McPherson. All four had received the Order of Canada. A fifth work on Calgary's Mustard Seed Street Ministry followed in 2004. He has also written numerous articles, poems and stories. Gerald Hankins' contributions to the province extend beyond his medical service and his work to share the stories of remarkable Albertans. Over the years, Gerald has offered his energy and support to a number of organizations, including Physicians for Global Survival, the Mustard Seed Street Ministry, CAUSE Canada, King's Fold and the Inter-Varsity Christian Fellowship. He and Alison also support the Dr. Fred G. McNally scholarship at Western Canada High School and the E. Catherine Barclay scholarship at the University of Calgary.

THE ALBERTA ORDER OF EXCELLENCE

Upon the recommendation of the Council of The Alberta Order of Excellence The Honourable Norman L. Kwong, Lieutenant Governor of Alberta and Chancellor of the Order grants Membership in The Order of Excellence to

Gerald W. Hankins

in recognition of service of the greatest distinction and of singular excellence for or on behalf of the residents of Alberta.

Given at Government House at Edmonton Alberta on the 20th day of October 2003.

Under the Seal of the Order by

The Honourable Norman L. Kwong,
Lieutenant Governor of Alberta
Chancellor of The Alberta Order of Excellence.

Dr. Robert C.P. Westbury,
Chairman Alberta Order of Excellence Council.

Accepted by Dr. Gerald W. Hankins,
Member, The Alberta Order of Excellence.

Dr. Margaret (Marmie) Perkins Hess

Inducted: 2005

MARMIE HESS HAS BEEN DESCRIBED as a quintessential Western Canadian and her remarkably diverse range of skills, passions and life experiences illustrate this description. She has led a life as challenging and dynamic as the land she loves. Her contributions to Alberta and Canada range from her work in the fields of education, business and the environment through her tireless promotion of Albertan and Canadian culture, art and history.

Marmie Hess was born in Calgary, Alberta, on 3 May 1916. Early in life, she acquired the nickname "Marmie" and continues to be known by that name in the diverse circles of friends, teams and colleagues that make up her extended family. Marmie's youth was equally shaped by the strong sense of community responsibility she received from her family and by her great love of the land.

After attending St. Hilda's School and Western Canada High School in Calgary, Marmie attended the University of Alberta and then transferred to the University of Toronto where she completed a Bachelor of Arts degree in 1938. During WWII, she taught art at the Alberta Provincial Institute of Technology and the Banff School of Fine Arts before completing postgraduate studies at the University of Iowa in 1947. In the years that followed, Marmie put her education to use through her desire to find and preserve the art and history that surround us and her interest in how the land shapes us as Canadians.

Marmie's academic career focussed on studying and preserving the art and environment of Canada's Aboriginal people, including Western Plains, Dene, Pacific West Coast, Inuit and Circumpolar cultures. She became a respected lecturer, travelling around the world sharing her expertise. In 1970, Marmie opened Calgary Galleries Ltd. to share her love and encourage awareness of Aboriginal art. Over the years, she has donated considerable time and expertise to Albertan, Canadian and other national museums. In 1988, the Government of Canada recognized her contributions to the Inuit by naming the archeological site on Ekkalluk River the Hess Site.

While building her academic career, Marmie also found time to further her love of the Western way of life. In 1952, she acquired the historic Spencer Creek Ranch in the foothills of Alberta and built its reputation as a successful horse breeding and cattle operation. She has played an active role as a founding member of the Kananaskis Citizen's Advisory Board. In 1999, she served on the committee for the Re-enactment of the RCMP March West, where she proved both her love of the West and her mettle by taking part in the march at age 83.

Marmie's contributions also extend to the area of education. The University of Calgary houses the Margaret P. Hess Collection, a nationally significant resource of historical books, journals and pamphlets. She helped to establish the Arctic Institute of North America at the University of Calgary, as well as a revolving fund in support of select University of Alberta Press publishing endeavours. Marmie has helped recruit international students for the University of Lethbridge and has also served as a senator for the Universities of Calgary and Lethbridge.

Marmie's record of community service covers a wide range of organizations, including the Calgary Exhibition and Stampede, the Calgary Red Cross, the United Way, the Calgary Zoological Society, the Rotary Club of Calgary, the RCMP Committee for Drug Abuse Resistance Education (DARE) program, the Calgary Regional Arts Foundation and the Calgary Chamber of Commerce. She also continues to support St. Hilda's School and served as chair for the St. Hilda's/ Strathcona-Tweedsmuir Centennial Celebration in 2005.

Marmie was named a Member of the Order of Canada in 1982 and an Officer in 1993. She holds an Honorary Doctorate of Fine Arts from the University of Lethbridge and Honorary Doctor of Laws degrees from the University of Calgary and the University of Alberta. She received the Rotary International's Paul Harris Fellowship in 1989 and is an Honorary Fellow of the Royal Canadian Geographical Society. In 2000, she received the YWCA Women of Distinction Lifetime Volunteer Achievement Award and in 2004 received the Grant MacEwan Lifetime Achievement Award from the City of Calgary.

THE ALBERTA ORDER OF EXCELLENCE

Upon the recommendation of the Council of The Alberta Order of Excellence The Honourable Norman L. Kwong, Lieutenant Governor of Alberta and Chancellor of The Order grants Membership in The Order to

Margaret 'Marmie' Hess

in recognition of service of the greatest distinction and of singular excellence for or on behalf of the residents of Alberta.

Given at Government House at Edmonton Alberta on the 20th day of October 2005.

Under the Seal of the Order by

The Honourable Norman L. Kwong,
Lieutenant Governor of Alberta, Chancellor
of Excellence of The Alberta Order.

Dr. Robert C.P. Westbury,
Chairman, Alberta Order of Excellence Council.

Accepted by Margaret Hess
Dr. Margaret 'Marmie' Hess,
Member, The Alberta Order of Excellence.

OFFICER OF THE ORDER OF CANADA

Rotary International

© Artist, Com Healy Tobia

Elsie Kawulych

Inducted: 2005

ELSIE KAWULYCH IS A LEADER in Alberta's Ukrainian community who has made a lasting contribution to the multicultural fabric of the province. Her resume of accomplishments ranges from her pioneering work to preserve and promote Ukrainian culture to her many contributions to the educational and recreational opportunities enjoyed by youth across the province and to her commitment to building strong community supports in her home town of Vegreville.

Elsie was born on 21 September 1932 to John and Helen Kubrak. Her parents had immigrated to Canada from their homeland of Ukraine in search of a better life for themselves and their children. Many times in her youth, Elsie had to overcome barriers that young Ukrainian women faced growing up in that era. She demonstrated her great perseverance and determination by becoming one of the first women from Vegreville's Ukrainian community to be accepted into university. With this, she went on to earn a Bachelor of Science degree in Home Economics from the University of Manitoba.

Elsie chose a profession that allowed her to combine her passion for sewing and handicrafts with her natural love for teaching. She returned to Alberta in 1955 and became a Home Economist for the Alberta government. She spent much of the late 1950s travelling extensively throughout east central Alberta teaching and advising families on everything from nutrition and food safety to sewing and homemaking. In 1958, Elsie married Mike Kawulych and began teaching home economics in Mundare and Vegreville.

As her family grew to include five children, so did Elsie's involvement in the community. She served as a 4-H leader and judge, specializing in sewing and public speaking. She volunteered with the Boy Scouts, Air Cadets and countless other youth recreation programs, and also served as a Girl Guide leader and district commissioner, as well a Tester for the Duke of Edinburgh awards. In the late 1980s, Elsie was called upon to use her energy and public speaking skills as a member of a group selected to represent Western Canada during a national unity mission to Québec.

Elsie has been a long-standing volunteer for the Canadian Cancer Society, serving as a provincial board member and logging countless hours on local and regional initiatives. She currently serves as chair of the Vegreville Senior Housing Board. In recognition of her many volunteering efforts, Elsie has received numerous awards including the Alberta Volunteer Achievement Award, the Alberta Hetman Award, the Volunteer of the Year Award for Vegreville and the Queen's Golden Jubilee Medal.

While Elsie has offered valuable support to a wide range of endeavours over the years, her greatest contribution to the province can be found in the great energy and hard work she has poured into the preservation and promotion of Ukrainian culture. She is a long-standing member of the Ukrainian Catholic Women's League and also enjoys a solid reputation as a respected Ukrainian dance teacher and authority on traditional patterns for Ukrainian dance costumes. She has also served as director of the Alberta Ukrainian Dance Association and as a member of the Alberta Folk Arts Council.

In 1973, Elsie began work to help develop what has become an iconic expression of Alberta's Ukrainian culture as a charter member of Vegreville's Pysanka festival. In 1984, Elsie took on new duties as a charter member of the Friends of the Ukrainian Village Society. Her many efforts have helped the Ukrainian Cultural Heritage Village become a world-class living museum. She currently serves as chair of the Village's Advisory Board.

More than a way to preserve her own cultural heritage, Elsie sees the Village and the other work she does to promote Ukrainian culture as ways to build acceptance of, and appreciation for, the great cultural diversity that exists in the province.

When asked to describe what she most values about being an Albertan, Elsie points out that the province is a place where you can achieve anything you want to if you are hardworking and determined. Elsie Kawulych is proof of that. Her hard work and determination have done more than fulfill her parents' early hopes for their daughter. Her efforts have also helped create lasting tributes to the contributions made by all of Alberta's early Ukrainian settlers.

THE ALBERTA ORDER OF EXCELLENCE

Upon the recommendation of the Council of The Alberta Order of Excellence The honourable Norman Kwong, Lieutenant Governor of Alberta and Chancellor of the Order grants Membership in the Order of Excellence to

Elsie Kawulych

in recognition of service of the greatest distinction and of singular excellence for or on behalf of the residents of Alberta. Given at Government house at Edmonton Alberta on the 20th day of October 2005.

Under the Seal of the Order by

Vegreville Senior Housing

UKRAINE

The honourable Norman L. Kwong,
Lieutenant Governor of Alberta, Chancellor
of The Alberta Order of Excellence.

Dr. Robert C.P. Westbury,
Chairman Alberta Order of Excellence Council.

Accepted by

Elsie Kawulych,
Member, The Alberta Order of Excellence.

Ronald Neil Mannix

Inducted: 2005

RONALD MANNIX HAS DEVOTED considerable efforts to preserving the wealth of advantages he feels privileged to have enjoyed as a native Albertan and Calgarian. His work with his family's business has literally helped to build Alberta, while his record of community leadership has helped many of his fellow Albertans find the same balance he strives for in his own life.

Ron was born in Calgary on 25 February 1948 to Frederick C. and Margaret R. Mannix. He grew up learning about the family business his grandfather Frederick S. Mannix began in 1898 as one of Western Canada's first construction firms. When Ron joined the business in 1973, the newly-minted Bachelor of Commerce graduate from the University of Alberta took his place in a business that had diversified to include ventures such as oil and gas exploration and production, venture capital, coal mining, pipelining and railroad maintenance services. Ron and his brother Frederick P. Mannix began efforts to take the third generation of the family business to the global stage.

While he worked to grow the family businesses, Ron also took care to give back to the community, largely in a very quiet and private way, and always with a greater purpose in mind. His thoughtful approach to his community work is evident in the initiatives he has supported over the years.

Ron has encouraged a wide range of community initiatives through his work as a former chairman, director and shareholder of the family's Carthy Foundation, as a past director and chairman of the Scripps Foundation International Board, as a former chairman, director and current member of the Max Bell Foundation, and also as a founder, former member and director of Strathcona Tweedsmuir School Foundation. Whenever possible, he has worked to focus his energies on initiatives that contribute to a balanced community where healthy bodies, strong minds and resilient spirits are encouraged in equal measure.

This balanced approach can be seen, in particular, in the work of the Norlien Foundation, which he created in 1998. The Foundation works to support four major initiatives that contribute specifically to the body, mind and spirit of his fellow Albertans, including health-related programs like the One World Child Development Centre and programs that encourage healthy pre-natal development and prevent Fetal Alcohol Spectrum Disorder, as well as a variety of educational, musical and environmental protection initiatives.

Ron believes that music has the most universal ability of all the arts to strengthen the human spirit. That belief, along with the love of keyboard music he inherited from his mother, led to efforts that have made Calgary an internationally-recognized centre for keyboard music. Ron served as founder of the Calgary International Organ Competition and Festival and creator of Calgary's Cantos Music Foundation, which offers a museum-style exhibit and experience of the history of keyboard instruments. Over the years, he has also provided his energy and skill to the Jack Singer Concert Hall and the Esther Honens International Piano Competition. He has been a driving force behind the rebuilding of numerous organs in the city and the building of a Bach concert organ for the University of Calgary's Rozsa Centre.

Ron also supports keyboard programs in over one quarter of Calgary's elementary schools and plans to expand the program further so that more children have the opportunity to develop a love of music. Other music programs have been developed and used to help the seniors' community.

Ron's contributions to education in Alberta also include his support of numerous programs at the University of Calgary, Strathcona Tweedsmuir School and the Centre for Entrepreneurship and Family Enterprise at the University of Alberta School of Business. His guidance, along with that of his fellow program supporters in the Alberta Business Family Institute (which he helped found), has turned the University of Alberta into a centre of excellence that boasts more resources invested into this field of study than any other university in the world. Ron's many contributions to his alma mater over the years were recognized in 2005 when he received an Honorary Doctor of Laws degree from the University of Alberta.

His further support and efforts to help build Canada in many ways, through his family enterprise and previous work with industry associations, such as the Canadian Council of Chief Executives and Coal Association of Canada, and through his philanthropic efforts. In 2005, he became an Officer of the Order of Canada.

Ron is currently helping to introduce a fourth generation of the Mannix clan to the business, using some of the family's philanthropic activities as a training ground in corporate governance and business principles. If that generation can master the same level of energy, dedication and leadership that Ron brings to his work, the Mannix family businesses and philanthropy will continue contributing to the health and well-being of Albertans for many years to come.

In addition to his brother Fred and sister Maureen, Ron's family includes his wife, Nancy, and his five children and one granddaughter.

THE ALBERTA ORDER OF EXCELLENCE

Upon the recommendation of the Council of The Alberta Order of Excellence The Honourable Norman L Kwong, Lieutenant Governor of Alberta and Chancellor of the Order grants Membership in The Order of Excellence to

Ronald Neil Mannix

in recognition of service of the greatest distinction and of singular excellence for or on behalf of the residents of Alberta.

Given at Government House at Edmonton Alberta on the 20th day of October 2005.

Under the Seal of the Order by

The Honourable Norman L Kwong,
Lieutenant Governor of Alberta, Chancellor
The Alberta Order of Excellence.

Dr. Robert C.P. Westbury,
Chairman, Alberta Order of Excellence Council.

Accepted by Ronald Neil Mannix,
Member, Alberta Order of Excellence.

Collection Programs Community
CANTOS MUSIC FOUNDATION

Coril Holdings Ltd.

Father Charles Michael McCaffery

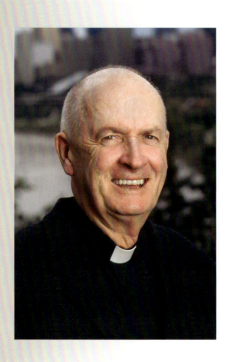

Inducted: 2005

FATHER MICHAEL MCCAFFERY IS A MODEL both of what it means to serve others and what it means to be an Albertan. Throughout his life and his career as a Roman Catholic priest, he has demonstrated a remarkable ability to reach and comfort those around him. He has also shown the great sense of energy, individuality and pioneering spirit that defines the Alberta character.

He was born Charles Michael McCaffery in Bassano, Alberta, on 17 September 1935. Mike, as he is known, spent his early years in Brooks. His parents, Dr. Hugh and Isobel McCaffery, created a home that offered a solid social conscience and sense of compassion for others, tempered with a healthy dose of light-hearted humour. Mike's family life also helped to plant the seeds of the strong ecumenical approach that would define his work as a priest. His mother was Anglican, his father was a devout Catholic, one of his great-grandfathers was a Presbyterian minister, and a favourite uncle was Mormon. To Mike, the common elements of the various beliefs were more apparent that any differences.

Throughout his career, Mike's path has been as unique as the man himself. His questioning nature led him to leave his early studies at St. Joseph's Seminary in Edmonton to work for the Social Action department of the Canadian Conference of Catholic Bishops, where he searched for a fuller expression of the church's social teachings. He later returned to Edmonton and was ordained at St. Joseph's Seminary in 1961. Father Mike began creating a ministry characterized by his sharp-witted, seven-minute homilies; his ability to deliver compassionate pastoral care to those in pain and crisis; and his strong desire to help those marginalized by society.

It was the time of the Second Vatican Ecumenical Council and Father Mike was eager for the changes being discussed by the Council. In 1969, he took a break from parish duties to pursue a Master of Sociology degree at Fordham University in New York. He worked for an ad agency in New York and as an information officer for the Canadian Consulate before moving to Vancouver to work with recovering heroin addicts. He took on duties in Edmonton studying alcoholism in isolated northern communities and furthered his studies at Notre Dame University in Indiana. In 1976, he was drawn back to Edmonton and his pastoral work. He taught Pastoral Theology at Newman Theological College before returning to full-time parish work in 1983. He became chancellor of the Archdiocese of Edmonton in 1993.

Father Mike serves as a fifth-step listener for recovering alcoholics, listening to their stories and helping them come to terms with their actions. In the late 1970s, he co-founded a workshop called "New Beginnings" which has helped countless participants deal with feelings of loss and grief stemming from divorce, separation and death. He has also served a wide range of community initiatives, including the United Way's Success by Six, the Junior Chamber of Commerce and the Progress Club of South Edmonton. In 1989, he was awarded a Paul Harris Fellowship for his many years of service to the Rotary Club.

A retirement tribute and roast was held in Father Mike's honour in Edmonton in 2003. Some 1,250 people bought tickets to raise $325,000 to fund a Chair in his honour at Newman Theological College. In keeping with its namesake's strengths, the Chair will deal with pastoral theology and the contemporary issues faced in ministries today.

Father Mike jokes that he is still trying to figure out why he became a priest, showing both his sense of humour and his humility. The thousands of people whose lives have been enriched by his care and support over the years certainly know why. He has a unique ability to reach the hearts and souls of those around him, and he has put that gift to great use throughout his career.

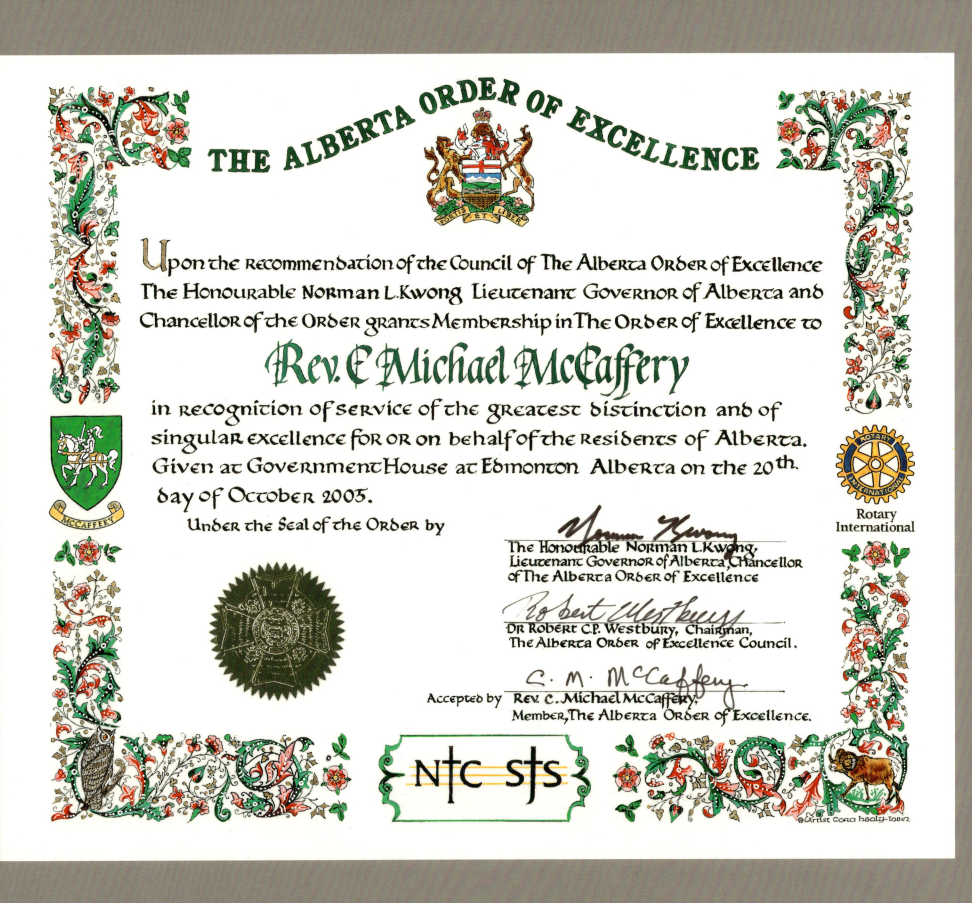

Dr. William A. Cochrane

Inducted: 2006

DR. WILLIAM COCHRANE'S CAREER has spanned the fields of medicine, biomedical research, education and business. His considerable facility in, and dedication to, each of these fields has produced lasting contributions to the health and well being of people across Canada.

William Arthur Cochrane was born in 1926 to Arthur and Olive Cochrane and grew up in Toronto's working-class east end. He inherited a solid work ethic from both parents and a strong drive from his mother, who always emphasized the importance of education to both Bill and his brother, Ted.

Bill was a keen student who was inspired by his family's doctor to pursue medical studies. He graduated from the University of Toronto in 1949 and completed post-graduate work at leading medical schools in the United States and England before returning to Toronto to establish a private paediatrics practice. He specialized in treating difficult cases and also began research into carbohydrate disorders at Toronto's Sick Kids Hospital. He soon decided to dedicate his full energies to research and teaching.

Dr. Cochrane and his wife, Phyllis, moved their young family to Halifax in 1958 where Bill established the first full-time medical research program in paediatrics at the Children's Hospital and became professor of Paediatrics at Dalhousie University. He divided his time between teaching medicine and conducting pioneering research into paediatric metabolic disorders. Dr. Cochrane also put his natural talents as a leader and businessman to work in the building and development of the I.W. Killam Hospital for Children in Halifax and began forming his own vision of how doctors should be trained.

He was given the opportunity to make that vision a reality in 1967 as founding dean of Medicine for the University of Calgary. Dr. Cochrane happily took on the challenge of building a medical school from the ground up, instituting a new integrated and interdisciplinary approach to medical education that has since become the norm across Canada.

For the next 11 years, Dr. Cochrane served in a number of leadership roles at the University of Calgary, including dean of Medicine, professor of Paediatrics, president and vice chancellor. His time at the University was interrupted in 1973 for a brief secondment to the Alberta government where he served as deputy minister of Health.

In 1978, Dr. Cochrane took his career in a new direction when he returned to Ontario as chairman and chief executive officer of Connaught Laboratories. During his tenure with the company, Connaught became a major international developer of flu vaccines for the World Health Organization and other international health agencies. The company's developments, which included insulin, plasma products and vaccines, served to improve the quality of life of people across Canada and around the world.

After 10 years at the helm of Connaught, Dr. Cochrane returned to Calgary where he took on new challenges as president of W.A. Cochrane and Associates. The move only strengthened his reputation as a leading force in the Canadian biotechnology and research communities. His unique blend of medical and entrepreneurial skills has helped many scientists move their biomedical research from the lab to commercial applications.

During his career, Dr. Cochrane has shared his leadership with a range of organizations, from the National Biotechnology Advisory Committee, the Alberta Research Council, the Alberta Economic Development Authority and the Alberta Science and Research Authority, to private sector ventures such as Vencap Equities Alberta, Oncolytics Biotech, Q.S.V. Biologics and Resverlogix Biotech Inc. His extensive contributions to the non-profit sector include service to the Ronald McDonald Children's Charities Foundation, the Canada/China Child Health Foundation, the Calgary Rotary Club and the Banff Centre.

Dr. Cochrane was named an Officer of the Order of Canada in 1989. He holds many other honours, including a National Merit Award for his contribution to biotechnology in Canada, ASTech Foundation and Bio-Alberta awards for his contributions to Alberta's science and technology sector and three honorary degrees from universities in Canada. In 1971, he was made an honorary Medicine Chief of the Stoney Nation of Morley, Alberta in recognition of his contributions to the health of Aboriginal people. In 2005, the Alberta Medical Association named Dr. Cochrane one of Alberta's "Physicians of the Century."

While some might see his careers as a doctor and entrepreneur as being disparate, Dr. Cochrane describes them as being dependant on one's ability to "deal with people and keep the team balanced." He adds that his greatest satisfaction comes from being connected to the success of others.

Dr. William Cochrane's role in the successes of Canada's medical, educational and biomedical communities is evident in the many schools, labs and businesses across the country that have benefited from his vision and leadership. He has a unique ability to envisage change and make it a reality and that skill has changed his province and his country for the better.

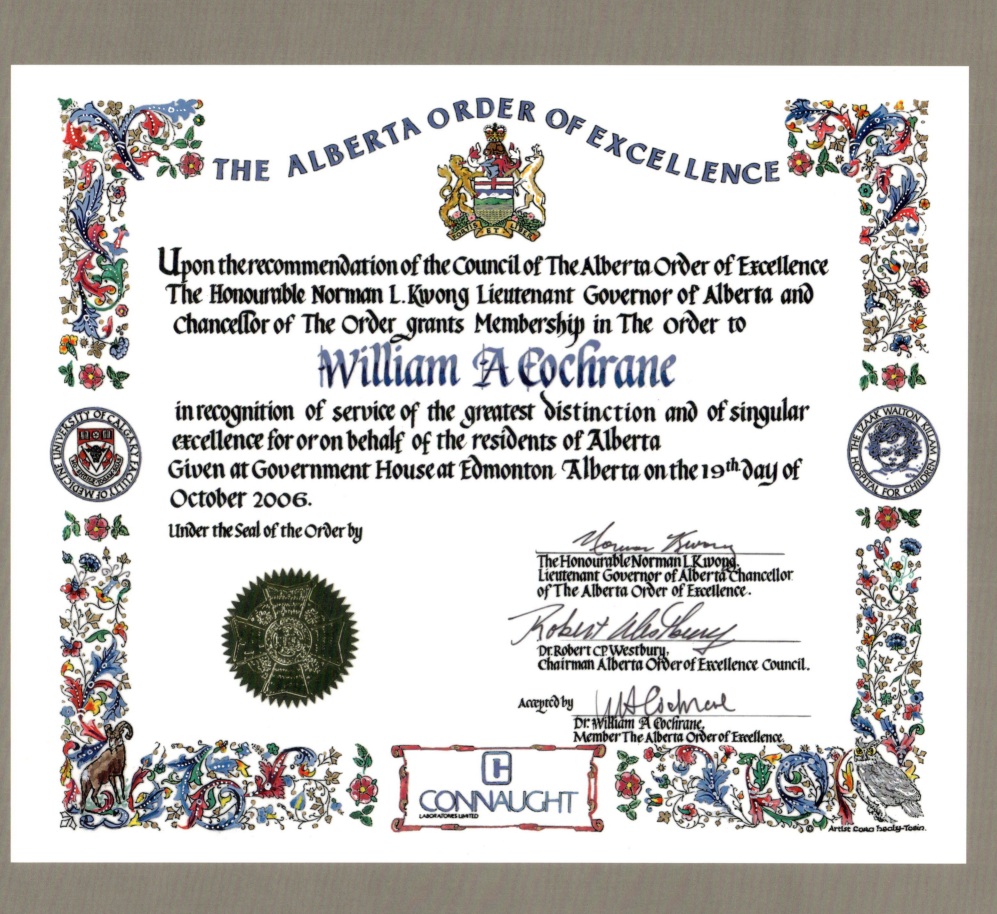

THE ALBERTA ORDER OF EXCELLENCE

Upon the recommendation of the Council of The Alberta Order of Excellence The Honourable Norman L. Kwong Lieutenant Governor of Alberta and Chancellor of The Order grants Membership in The Order to

William A Cochrane

in recognition of service of the greatest distinction and of singular excellence for or on behalf of the residents of Alberta

Given at Government House at Edmonton Alberta on the 19th day of October 2006.

Under the Seal of the Order by

The Honourable Norman L. Kwong,
Lieutenant Governor of Alberta Chancellor
of The Alberta Order of Excellence.

Dr. Robert C.P. Westbury,
Chairman Alberta Order of Excellence Council.

Accepted by

Dr. William A Cochrane,
Member The Alberta Order of Excellence.

CONNAUGHT
LABORATORIES LIMITED

Artist Coro Healy-Tobin.

Bertha (Berdie) Fowler

Inducted: 2006

BERTHA (BERDIE) FOWLER IS A DEDICATED Alberta community leader and volunteer who has helped to forge new openings territory for Alberta businesswomen and spurred the development of many programs and services in her home of Camrose. Her contributions range from her work as co-founder and editor of the award-winning *Camrose Booster* weekly publication, to her service on provincial, business and industry boards, to her commitment to serving women and families in her community.

Berdie was born in Bittern Lake, Alberta, on 1 July 1920 to Lester and Lilian Anderson. She and her two sisters grew up on the family farm where their responsibilities included feeding the chickens and gathering eggs. The emphasis at home, however, was always that school should remain the first priority. After graduating from Camrose High School, Berdie chose to pursue post-secondary education. Since she was too young to be accepted into nursing school, Berdie enrolled in business college to improve her chances of finding employment in the difficult labour market of the 1930s.

In 1939, Berdie graduated from the Camrose Lutheran College (now the Augustana Campus of the University of Alberta). In 1940, she married William F. (Bill) Fowler, whom she first met in high school and with whom she also attended college. In 1945, following Bill's service to various postings with the Royal Canadian Air Force, Berdie and Bill were eager to return to Camrose to raise their four children, Bonnie, Blain, Beth and Bruce.

After spending 12 years as a full-time wife and mother, Berdie joined Bill to start the *Camrose Booster* in 1952. The free weekly paper has enjoyed great success and has remained family-operated since its creation. Today, their son Blain is owner and publisher. Berdie remains involved with the paper, writing her award-winning column, Pen Points, as she has done for many years.

Over the years, Berdie has taken time from her duties with family and the paper to contribute to numerous community and volunteer organizations. In the late 1960s, she was chair of the founding board of the Camrose Children's Day Care Centre—the first public day care centre established in Alberta outside of Edmonton and Calgary. At that time, there was public opposition to such a facility on the basis that it would encourage mothers to work outside the home—then generally believed to be a bad thing. The concept was eventually accepted and the Centre opened in 1968. Berdie served as the president of the Board of Directors for the first two years and remains a proud booster of the Day Care Centre.

Berdie's long record of community service includes duties as alderman for the City of Camrose from 1974 to 1977. She has also worked to enhance the quality of life in her community as a dedicated volunteer with organizations such as the Camrose and District Crime Stoppers, the Camrose Association for Community Living, the Augustana Faculty of the University of Alberta, the Battle River Community Foundation, the Camrose Public Library and various community literacy programs.

Though much of Berdie Fowler's volunteer work has focused on ensuring women are given fair opportunities in business and in the community, she refers to herself as a humanist rather than a feminist, believing that people should be appointed to positions based on their ability and suitability for that job.

Her own abilities led her to become the first woman on the board of the Alberta Opportunity Company. She was also the first woman to serve on the Apprenticeship and Trade Certification Board and has been president of the Business and Professional Women's Club of Camrose.

In 1972, Berdie was the first woman ever to be elected as president of a chamber of commerce in Alberta and only the second in all of Canada. She has been an active member of the Alberta Chamber of Commerce, where she served as chair of the education committee. As a past president and life member of the Camrose Chamber of Commerce, Berdie has remained active in promoting Camrose as a vibrant community. She lives by her late husband's motto: "Be of service; think beyond yourself."

Berdie's commitment to service has been recognized with numerous awards and honours, including the Alberta Centennial Medallion and the Canada 125 medal. In 1992, she received the Distinguished Alumna Award from her alma mater, Augustana University College. Her efforts with the *Camrose Booster* were honoured with the Independent Free Papers of America Outstanding Contributions Award, the Joseph M. Sklenar Editorial Award.

Through her tireless work, Berdie Fowler has become a pioneer for Alberta women and the gold standard in Camrose and East-Central Alberta in defining and promoting community excellence.

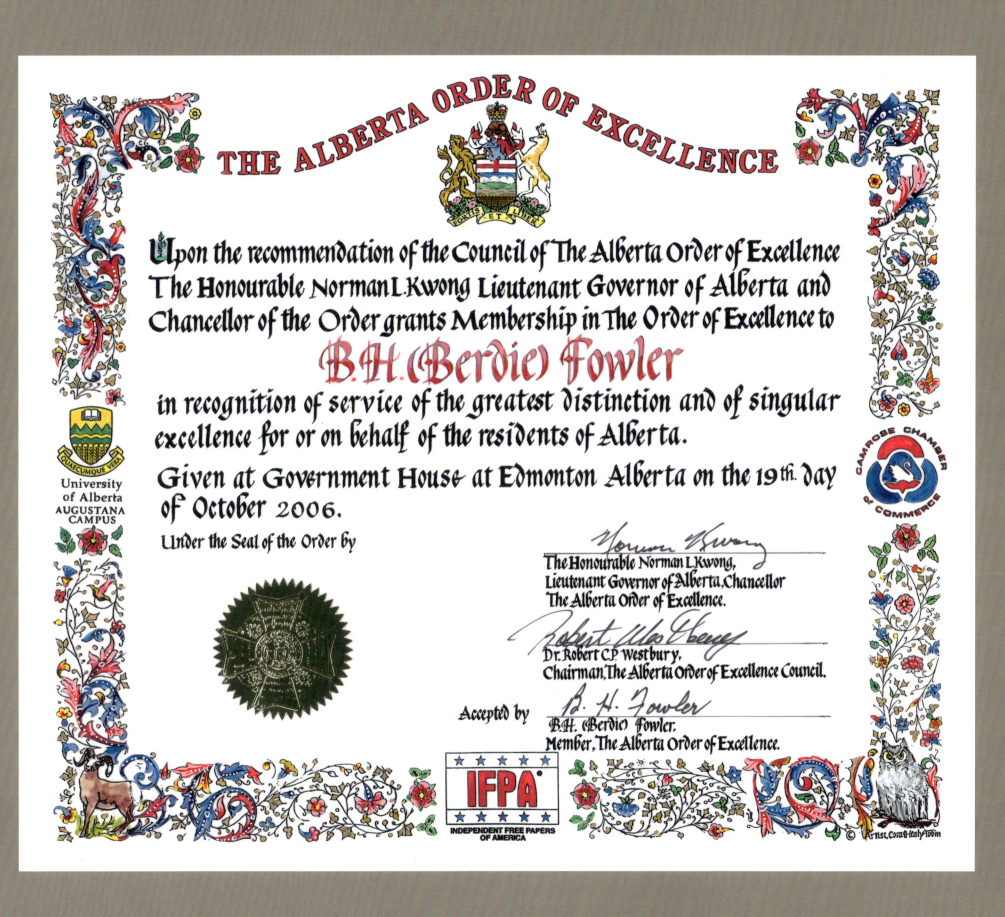

THE ALBERTA ORDER OF EXCELLENCE

Upon the recommendation of the Council of The Alberta Order of Excellence The Honourable Norman L. Kwong Lieutenant Governor of Alberta and Chancellor of the Order grants Membership in The Order of Excellence to

B.H. (Berdie) Fowler

in recognition of service of the greatest distinction and of singular excellence for or on behalf of the residents of Alberta.

Given at Government House at Edmonton Alberta on the 19th. day of October 2006.

Under the Seal of the Order by

The Honourable Norman L. Kwong,
Lieutenant Governor of Alberta, Chancellor
The Alberta Order of Excellence.

Dr. Robert C.P. Westbury,
Chairman, The Alberta Order of Excellence Council.

Accepted by

B.H. (Berdie) Fowler,
Member, The Alberta Order of Excellence.

University of Alberta
AUGUSTANA CAMPUS

CAMROSE CHAMBER of COMMERCE

IFPA
INDEPENDENT FREE PAPERS OF AMERICA

© Artist, Consi-Healy-Tobin

Richard F. Haskayne

Inducted: 2006

RICHARD (DICK) HASKAYNE'S MANY CONTRIBU- tions to Alberta reflect his considerable work ethic, his reputation for upholding the highest standard of personal and business ethics and his considerable pride in his province. He has been an important contributor to Alberta's business community and the quality of life and opportunities enjoyed by all Albertans, particularly those in rural Alberta.

Dick's strong ethical compass and sense of community comes from his childhood in Gleichen, Alberta. He was born on 18 December 1934 as the province was struggling through the final years of the Great Depression. His parents, Robert and Bertha Haskayne, were English immigrants who operated butcher shops in Gleichen and Bassano and who followed their hearts when it came to helping families unable to afford meat. Working alongside his parents and his older brother, Stan, Dick learned valuable lessons about having compassion for others, maintaining scrupulously honest practices while working hard to create a successful business.

After graduating from high school, Dick debated staying on to run the family butcher shops or accepting an offer to play junior hockey in Medicine Hat. Eventually, he decided to study at the University of Alberta. He graduated with a Bachelor of Commerce degree in 1956, moved to Calgary and began articling to qualify as a chartered accountant. Dick married Lee Murray in 1958 and became a chartered accountant one year later.

Dick's early days as a chartered accountant helped to lay the groundwork for his later career. He performed audits for a wide range of companies, describing the work as "an excellent opportunity to get inside an operation and see the big picture...the principles of what the numbers mean." His ability to see the big picture allowed him to expand his résumé to include duties as president of major companies, such as Hudson's Bay Oil and Gas, Interhome Energy and later chairman of the Board of MacMillan Bloedel, Nova, TransAlta Corporation and Fording. Dick's peers in the business community have described his work at these organizations as "classic business case studies." Dick modestly describes his approach as "doing the right thing and respecting the responsibility the business sector has to society."

In 2001, the University of Calgary recognized Dick's leadership by creating the Richard F. Haskayne Chair in Accounting. The following year, the school's Faculty of Management was renamed the Haskayne School of Business.

Throughout his career, Dick has taken care to ensure a healthy balance between work, family and giving back to the community. He has applied his enthusiasm and determination to various duties, including chair of the Board of Governors for the University of Calgary, as trustee of the Alberta Heritage Foundation for Medical Research, as a board member of the Hotchkiss Brain Institute and the Alberta Bone and Joint Institute, and as an Advisory Committee member for the Order of Canada. He has also supported community, health and arts organizations, including the United Way, the Calgary Foothills Hospital, the Alberta Children's Hospital Foundation, the Canadian Cystic Fibrosis Society, the Canadian Cancer Society, the ALS Society, the Olympic Trust of Canada, the Calgary Philharmonic Orchestra, Theatre Calgary, the Esther Honens International Piano Festival and the Banff Centre. As well, throughout his life, Dick has continued to support numerous organizations with a focus on community, health, arts and education.

Dick lost his wife, Lee, to ALS in 1993. He married Lois Heard in 1995, joining a family that includes five children and 11 grandchildren.

In 2005, Dick and Lois created the Haskayne Gleichen Cluny Bassano Community Fund and Scholarship Awards in honour of his beloved home town. They also maintain several other scholarships for rural students attending the University of Calgary, Mount Royal College and SAIT. These programs all make significant contributions to the opportunities and quality of life enjoyed by rural Canadians.

Dick Haskayne has received numerous awards and recognitions, including honorary Doctor of Laws degrees from the Universities of Alberta and Calgary, the Award of Excellence in International Business from the University of Calgary, a lifetime achievement award from the Institute of Chartered Accountants and membership in both the Canadian Business Hall of Fame and Canadian Petroleum Hall of Fame. He was appointed an Officer of the Order of Canada in 1997. In 2004, he joined the very small number of Canadians who have received the Woodrow Wilson Award for Corporate Citizenship from the Woodrow Wilson International Centre for Scholars of the Smithsonian Institution.

Dick has always taken care to follow the advice of his father, who always told him "good ethics make good business. You never know who is watching." Dick's fellow Albertans have been doing more than simply watching his actions. They have been learning and benefiting from his considerable integrity, dedication and generosity of spirit. His contributions will continue to have a positive impact on Alberta and Canada for generations to come.

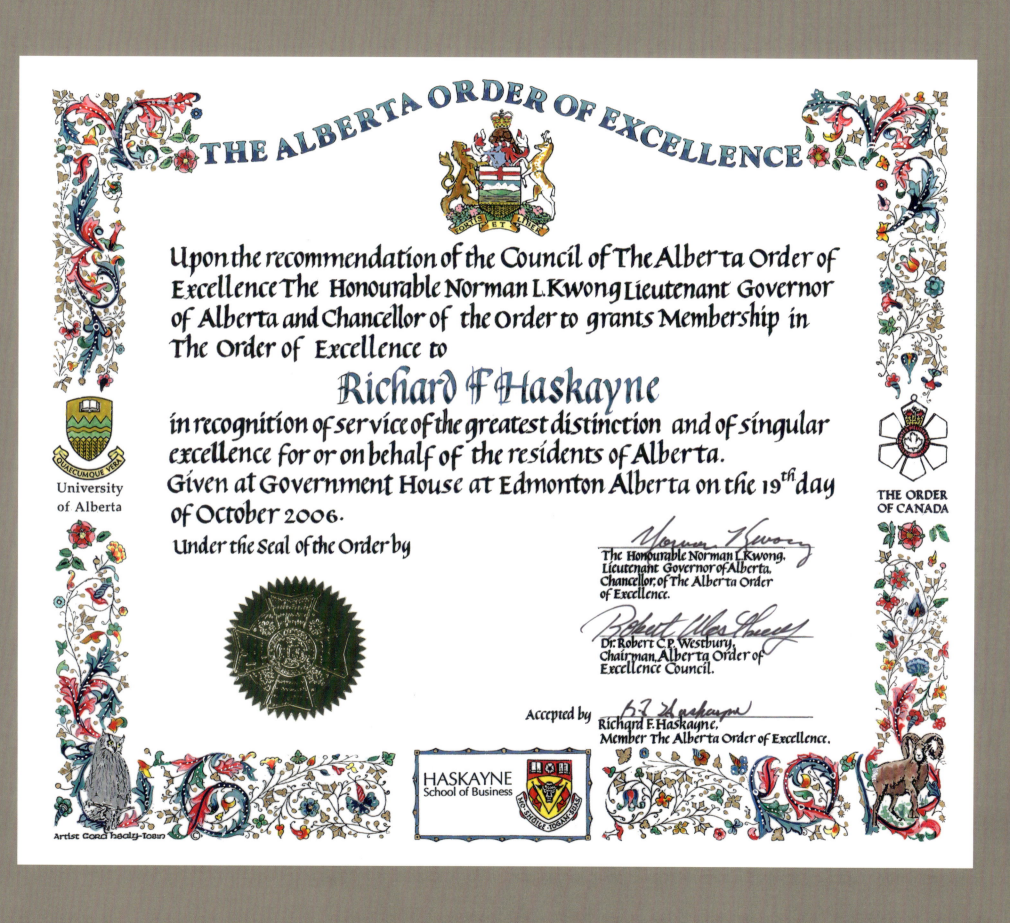

THE ALBERTA ORDER OF EXCELLENCE

Upon the recommendation of the Council of The Alberta Order of Excellence The Honourable Norman L. Kwong Lieutenant Governor of Alberta and Chancellor of the Order to grants Membership in The Order of Excellence to

Richard F Haskayne

in recognition of service of the greatest distinction and of singular excellence for or on behalf of the residents of Alberta.

Given at Government House at Edmonton Alberta on the 19th day of October 2006.

Under the Seal of the Order by

The Honourable Norman L. Kwong,
Lieutenant Governor of Alberta,
Chancellor, of The Alberta Order
of Excellence.

Dr. Robert C.P. Westbury,
Chairman, Alberta Order of
Excellence Council.

Accepted by

Richard F. Haskayne,
Member The Alberta Order of Excellence.

University of Alberta

THE ORDER OF CANADA

HASKAYNE
School of Business

Artist Gord Healy-Tobin

Harry Hole

Inducted: 2006

HARRY HOLE'S LEADERSHIP, INTEGRITY and dedication to his fellow Albertans are well-recognized in Edmonton and beyond. Throughout his years as an astute businessman, Harry devoted much of his time and effort to various professional boards and community organizations. A stalwart supporter of Alberta's hospitals, universities, theatres and other organizations, Harry Hole has made evident his commitment to making the province a better place to live.

Harry was born in Edmonton, Alberta on 14 September 1921. His parents, Annie and Harry Hole Sr, had both immigrated to Canada from England hoping to find greater opportunities. They met and married in Edmonton and soon began raising a family. Hoping to provide their children with the very opportunities they had sought for themselves, they impressed the value of education upon Harry and his eight siblings. Viewing their opportunity to attend post-secondary school as a privilege, and not an option, all nine Hole children attended the University of Alberta.

Harry developed his strong work ethic at an early age. He and his six brothers maintained the same paper route for the *Edmonton Journal* for nearly two decades, saving their earnings to help pay for university. He graduated from the University of Alberta in 1944 with a BSc in Civil Engineering and then served with the Royal Canadian Engineers as a Lieutenant until discharge in 1946.

Upon his return from the army, Harry worked in his father's plumbing and heating business, Lockerbie & Hole. In 1949, he married Muriel Sweetnam, whom he had met at the University of Alberta, where Muriel studied nursing. Harry and Muriel's family grew to include four daughters, Elaine, Mary, Janice and Karen.

During the 1950s, while Muriel served her community as a public health nurse, Harry continued to apprentice under his father, developing his expertise as an engineer and businessman. He eventually became the head of the family business when Harry Hole Sr. passed away. Harry worked to position the firm of Lockerbie & Hole as the leading mechanical engineering company in Alberta and as a national leader in the industry.

As business expanded and opportunities arose, Harry decided to remain in Alberta. He lived by Francis Winspear's advice: "This is where the action is." Lockerbie & Hole has remained an Edmonton-based company, employing a host of talented Albertans and building projects nationally and internationally.

Well-respected for his business skills, Harry also expanded his activities into other areas of the community. He has had a positive influence in areas related to business and trade, public health and safety, the arts and advanced education. As president of Edmonton Northlands, he played an important role in the development of the Northlands Coliseum, an Edmonton landmark and leading exhibition facility. He has lent his leadership and support to many organizations, including his alma mater, the University of Alberta, Concordia University College, the Grant MacEwan College, the Citadel Theatre and various Edmonton hospitals.

Between 1993 and 2003, Harry served as Honorary Colonel of 15 (Edmonton) Battalion, where he worked hard at improving facilities for local military units. He has contributed to, and worked with, the Edmonton Community Foundation and recently retired as president of the Edmonton Police Service Foundation, which he established and chaired. His efforts have helped to make Edmonton a better and safer place to live and work.

Harry Hole has also shared his energy and experience with numerous other organizations. His long roster of public service includes work with the Grant MacEwan Foundation, the Edmonton Space and Science Centre Foundation, the Edmonton Chamber of Commerce, the Salvation Army Red Shield Campaign, United Way and the Stollery Children's Hospital.

Harry has served as director of numerous businesses and associations, including the Canadian Imperial Bank of Commerce, Melco Developments Ltd as well as various petroleum, natural gas and development related corporations. Harry was proud to honour his father's heritage as a Londoner when he became a member of Lloyds of London, the world's leading insurance exchange. He received an Honorary Doctor of Laws from the University of Alberta in 2005.

Harry's activities and contributions in both time and financial support are almost endless. While his activities and interests have been diverse, they all speak to his commitment to the province. His many contributions have created a legacy that will inspire future generations of Albertans.

James Deverell Horsman

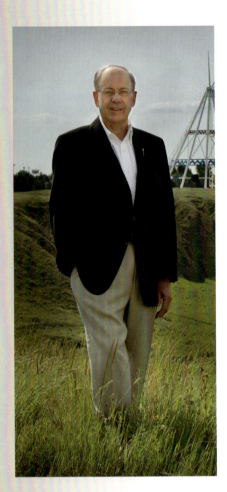

Inducted: 2006

JIM HORSMAN'S SERVICE TO ALBERTA includes his many contributions during five consecutive terms as a Member of the Legislative Assembly and 14 years as a Minister of the Crown, his efforts to strengthen post-secondary education in the province, and his distinguished service representing Alberta and Canada on the international stage. He has been a driving force behind many programs and institutions that shape the quality of life enjoyed by Albertans.

Jim was born in Camrose, Alberta, in 1935. During the Second World War, he lived in nearby Meeting Creek with his grandparents while his father, George, served overseas and his mother, Kathleen, served as the first postmistress at the Suffield Defence Research Establishment. After the war, Jim's family moved to Moose Jaw, Saskatchewan, where his father worked as a CPR fireman and engineer. The family grew with the arrival of Jim's sister, Lynn.

Jim was an active and avid student who, although naturally introverted, excelled at debating and public speaking. He left Moose Jaw to study at the University of British Columbia where he earned a Bachelor of Commerce degree in 1959, followed by a Law degree in 1960. He began his career articling in Calgary and may well have stayed there were it not for a visit to a cousin, who was a veterinarian practicing in Medicine Hat. While there, Jim met a local lawyer who needed a partner. He jumped at the prospect and joined the practice. Shortly after settling in Medicine Hat, Jim met a young high school teacher named Betty Whitney, the daughter of a pioneer Alberta ranch family. They were married in 1964 and began raising a family. Those early years marked the beginning of a remarkable association between Jim and a community he has long been proud to serve.

He began with a small legal practice that covered everything from drafting wills to defending criminal cases. Jim enjoyed the work, particularly opportunities to argue cases in court. He also began to foster a growing interest in public life. Jim became an activist with the Alberta Progressive Conservative Party and served as the vice president for Southern Alberta before throwing his own hat in the ring as a candidate. He made two unsuccessful attempts before becoming the MLA for Medicine Hat in 1975.

Jim's years at the Alberta Legislature included terms as Minister of Advanced Education and Manpower, Minister of Federal and Intergovernmental Affairs, Attorney General and Provincial Secretary, Government House Leader and Deputy Premier. His considerable legacies from this period include his leadership of Alberta's negotiations during both the Canada/USA Free Trade Agreement and NAFTA and his work as Alberta's key representative during the 10 years of discussions following the repatriation of the Constitution of Canada. He also established the Alberta Heritage Scholarship Fund, which has endowed over 10,000 Alberta students annually since it was first introduced in 1981 and successfully promoted private sector support for Alberta universities and colleges and technical institutions.

Jim continued to serve Albertans after leaving politics in 1993, including work as Alberta's chief negotiator on the issues of free trade within Canada. Jim also served as chancellor of the University of Lethbridge and continues to support the University's leading work in water and environmental research. He was a founding member of the Alberta Ingenuity Board and has served Albertans as a member of the Lieutenant-Governor of Alberta Arts Awards Foundation. Over the years, Jim has represented the province as a national and international speaker on constitutional law, senate reform and free trade and as a member of the Advisory Board of the Association for Canadian Studies in the United States.

Jim's contributions to Medicine Hat over the years include a term as chair of the Medicine Hat College Board of Governors and many other activities in support of the school. He chaired the 1995 Medicine Hat Flood Relief Committee and has served with the local Kinsmen Club, the Chamber of Commerce, St. John's Presbyterian Church and countless teams devoted to projects from renovating the local court house, library and YMCA to developing sports facilities. Jim and Betty provide scholarships and student leadership awards to three Medicine Hat high schools, as well as scholarships for University of Lethbridge political science students.

His many honours include membership in the Order of Canada, an Honorary Doctor of Laws degree from the University of Lethbridge, the Queen Elizabeth II Silver and Golden Jubilee Medals, the Governor-General's 125th Anniversary Medal and the Alberta Centennial Medal.

Jim has always remained unassuming in the face of his many accomplishments. He is known and respected as much for his humility, great sensitivity and ability to listen to others as he is for the remarkable things he has done on behalf of his fellow Albertans.

THE ALBERTA ORDER OF EXCELLENCE

Upon the recommendation of the Council of The Alberta Order of Excellence The Honourable Norman L.Kwong Lieutenant Governor of Alberta and Chancellor of the Order grants Membership in The Order of Excellence to

James D Horsman

in recognition of service of the greatest distinction and of singular excellence for or on behalf of the residents of Alberta.

Given at Government House at Edmonton Alberta on the 19th day of October 2006.

Under the Seal of the Order by

The Honourable Norman L.Kwong,
Lieutenant Governor of Alberta
Chancellor, The Alberta Order of Excellence.

Dr.Robert C.P. Westbury Chairman,
The Alberta Order of Excellence Council.

Accepted by

James D. Horsman,
Member, The Alberta Order of Excellence.

University of
Lethbridge

© Artist Gord Healey-Tobir.

The Honourable Samuel Sereth Lieberman

Inducted: 2006

JUDGE SAMUEL LIEBERMAN IS KNOWN for his impressive military and judicial careers, as well as his considerable contributions to his community. A coastal command pilot during World War II, he began his legal career upon his return to Alberta from active service.

After spending several years as a successful lawyer, he eventually became the first judge of the Jewish faith in the province. Judge Lieberman can be credited with creating ground-breaking changes to certain aspects of the legal process in Alberta which were adopted across Canada. Outside of his contributions to the legal system, Judge Lieberman has volunteered his energy and talents to numerous organizations in order to better his community, province and country.

Samuel (Sam) Lieberman was born in Edmonton on 14 April 1922. In 1940, at the age of 18, he left university and joined the Royal Canadian Air Force. He served as a pilot in R.A.F. coastal command for two overseas operational tours between 1941 and 1945 and attained the rank of Squadron Leader. With no leave available between tours, Judge Lieberman had not seen his family during his four years of service abroad. His desire to return home, and the encouragement of British friends to leave the military, return to Canada and attend university, led Judge Lieberman to return to his native Alberta in 1945. Subsequently, he received his BA in 1947 and his LLB in 1948 from the University of Alberta.

It was while attending a service club convention in Winnipeg in 1949 that Judge Lieberman met his future wife, a student at UCLA and native of Chicago. After a long-distance telephone courtship and several short visits, Judge Lieberman married Nancy Berman on 15 July 1950. The couple settled in Edmonton where their family grew to include three children: David Jonathan, Jo Ann and Audrey Gail.

Judge Lieberman has made significant contributions to the Canadian legal system, both as a lawyer and a jurist. Following his graduation from law school in 1948, he articled with his father's law firm and was admitted to the Bar of Alberta one year later. In 1962, he was appointed Queen's Counsel.

Judge Lieberman continued to practice with his father's firm, specializing in insurance law until 1966 when he was appointed Judge of the District Court of the District of Northern Alberta. Four years later, he was appointed Justice of the Trial Division of the Supreme Court of Alberta (now the Court of Queen's Bench of Alberta). He thus had the dual distinction of becoming both Alberta's first judge of the Jewish faith and the first Jewish judge to be named to the Supreme Court of the province. In 1967, he was appointed to the Court of Appeal of Alberta where he remained until his mandatory retirement in 1997.

Judge Lieberman has certainly left his mark on his chosen profession. In 1967, under the aegis of the Attorney General of Alberta, he established the Alberta Board of Review to deal with those persons who were found not fit to stand trial, or who were found not guilty of a crime by reason of insanity. It was the first such board in Canada to be set up under the provisions of the Criminal Code and became the prototype for other similar boards across the country. In addition, Judge Lieberman chaired the committee presenting the first proposal for Legal Aid to the Alberta Legislature. He became the first chair of the Legal Aid Society of Alberta, which facilitates equality of access to the legal system for all Albertans. In 1970, he chaired the Alberta Boundaries Commission and in 1998 he was appointed chair of the Alberta Bingo Review Commission.

After his retirement, Judge Lieberman continued to assist the community by chairing the Alberta Criminal Injuries Review Board. He also joined a major law firm, Miller Thomson, where he has been a respected counsel, providing advice to the firm's young lawyers.

Judge Lieberman has given freely of his time, energy and commitment to a variety of organizations, among them B'nai Brith, the Edmonton Eskimos Football Club, the Canadian Council of Christians and Jews and the Kiwanis Club.

In addition, Judge Lieberman has also served as president or director of numerous boards and organizations, including the Sir Winston Churchill Society of Edmonton and the Canadian National Institute for the Blind. He has been named an honorary life member of the Israeli Institute of Technology and honorary director of Canada's Aviation Hall of Fame.

From 1952 to 1956, Judge Lieberman served as aide-de-camp to the late Lieutenant-Governor J.J. Bowlen. He also served as chair of the Council of the Alberta Order of Excellence between 1997 and 2003.

Judge Lieberman has received numerous awards and recognition for his commitment and dedication to his province and country. For his military efforts, he was awarded Canadian Forces Decoration. He has also been awarded the Centennial Medal, the Jubilee Medal, the 125th Anniversary Medal, the Queen's Jubilee Medal and the Alberta Centennial Medal. In 1990, he was awarded an Honorary Doctor of Laws degree from the University of Alberta.

THE ALBERTA ORDER OF EXCELLENCE

Upon the recommendation of the Council of The Alberta Order of Excellence The Honourable Norman L. Kwong Lieutenant Governor of Alberta and Chancellor of the Order grants Membership in The Order of Excellence to

Samuel S Lieberman

in recognition of service of the greatest distinction and of singular excellence for or on behalf of the residents of Alberta Given at Government House at Edmonton Alberta on the 19th day of October 2006.

Under the Seal of the Order by

The Honourable Norman L. Kwong,
Lieutenant Governor of Alberta, Chancellor
The Alberta Order of Excellence.

Dr. Robert C.P. Westbury,
Chairman, Alberta Order of Excellence Council.

Accepted by

Samuel S. Lieberman,
Member, Alberta Order of Excellence.

Dr. Raymond V. Rajotte

Inducted: 2006

DR. RAYMOND RAJOTTE IS A DEDICATED member of Alberta's medical community, who is equally respected for his pioneering work in diabetes research in islet transplantation and his exceptional service as a mentor to generations of Alberta scientists and surgeons.

There were indications of the scientist he would become during Ray's early years on the family farm outside Wainwright, Alberta. He inherited determination and a pioneering spirit from his father and grandparents who arrived from Québec to homestead in 1908. He was also an inquisitive and innovative young man who reveled in the self-sufficiency that came with rural life. While attending Notre Dame College in Saskatchewan, he was deeply influenced by the words of Father Athol Murray, who urged each student to "set high goals for yourself."

Ray moved to Edmonton in 1965 to attend the X-ray Technologist program at the Northern Alberta Institute of Technology and was part of its first graduating class. During his early years working at the Edmonton General Hospital, Ray met a young nurse named Gloria. They were married in 1966 following a whirlwind romance.

At the Edmonton General, Ray also met Dr. George Bondar who involved him in research projects at the hospital. Ray's work developed into an interest in biomedical engineering and he decided to further his education at the University of Alberta. He tailored his studies to both medicine and engineering, earning a BSc and MSc in Electrical Engineering.

Dr. Rajotte's research in cryobiology took a significant turn early in his career when he attended a presentation on islets, the small structures in the pancreas responsible for insulin production. Driven by curiosity, he began experimenting with ways to freeze islets for future use in research or transplantation. He would often use his engineering training and innovation to build whatever equipment was needed, including an early version of a microwave oven. In 1975, he completed a PhD in Biomedical Engineering, with a thesis that showed islets could be successfully cryopreserved. Dr. Rajotte credits the success to his mentor, Dr. John Dosseter, who "taught him how to do research that would withstand the test of time." Following his PhD, Dr. Rajotte completed post doctoral training at several top research laboratories in the United States. He was recruited back to the University of Alberta to join the Departments of Surgery and Medicine.

He began assembling a team of clinical scientists with the skills needed to successfully transplant islets into patients suffering from type 1 diabetes. In 1989, his team carried out Canada's first islet transplant, using technology Dr. Rajotte developed during his PhD work. Their third transplant patient enjoyed long term insulin independence. By 1999, the Islet Transplantation Group demonstrated a 100-percent success rate in freeing severe diabetics from insulin injections. The process, which became known as the Edmonton Protocol, has been adopted by transplantation centres worldwide.

Dr. Rajotte's current appointments at the U of A include: Director of the Surgical-Medical Research Institute, Director of the Islet Transplantation Group, Graduate Student Co-ordinator for the Department of Surgery, Professor of Surgery and Medicine and Adjunct Professor in the Department of Biomedical Engineering.

Throughout his career at the U of A, Dr. Rajotte's research has progressed alongside his teaching duties. His leadership in the graduate program helped establish the school as one of the top graduate surgery programs in North America. Perhaps the greatest testament to Dr. Rajotte's strengths as a mentor is the fact that many of his students were members of the original Edmonton Protocol team and now serve as U of A leaders.

His former students are also among the world-class group of researchers Dr. Rajotte is leading as Scientific Director of the newly created Alberta Diabetes Institute. The team's goal is to strengthen Alberta's reputation as a world leader in diabetes research and to move from developing treatments to finding a cure. Nothing would be more fulfilling for a self-described "Alberta boy" who is thankful for the remarkable teammates and the many opportunities afforded to him by his alma mater and his home province.

Dr. Rajotte was listed among Alberta Venture Magazine's "50 Greatest Albertans of the Last 100 Years" and has received numerous honours, including the Queen's Golden Jubilee Medal, the Canadian Medical Association Medal of Honour, induction into the Royal Society of Canada, election as an Honorary Fellow of the Royal College of Physicians and Surgeons of Canada, and a Meritorious Service Medal from the governor-general of Canada. He is humble about the accolades, pointing to the teams that have stood beside him throughout his career.

When asked to describe the motivation behind his work, Dr. Rajotte lists "the challenge of it and the fact that everything is always moving forward." He adds that "you need to be curious and persevere as it may take some time before you realize your goal." The breakthroughs he has produced to date are proof that those two qualities can indeed produce great results. The many Alberta scientists he has mentored over the years will ensure the province continues as a research leader well into the future.

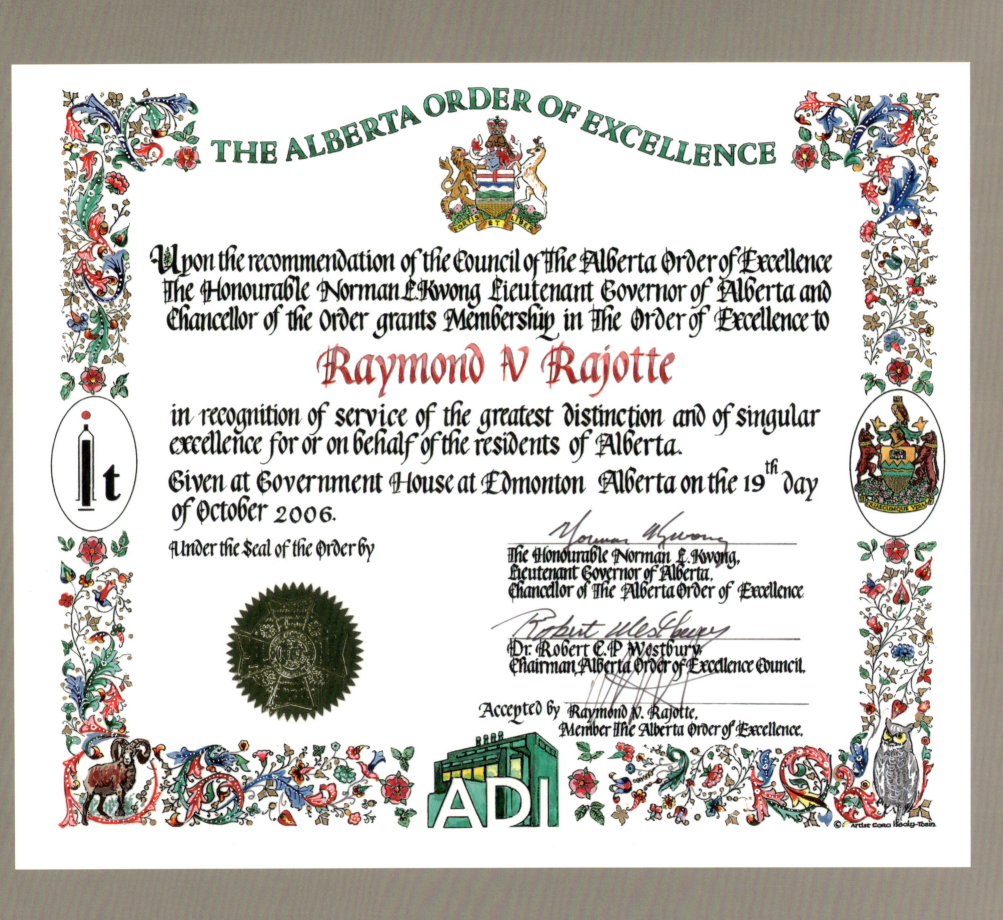

THE ALBERTA ORDER OF EXCELLENCE

Upon the recommendation of the Council of The Alberta Order of Excellence The Honourable Norman L. Kwong Lieutenant Governor of Alberta and Chancellor of the order grants Membership in The Order of Excellence to

Raymond V Rajotte

in recognition of service of the greatest distinction and of singular excellence for or on behalf of the residents of Alberta.

Given at Government House at Edmonton Alberta on the 19th day of October 2006.

Under the Seal of the Order by

The Honourable Norman L. Kwong,
Lieutenant Governor of Alberta.
Chancellor of The Alberta Order of Excellence

Dr. Robert C.P Westbury
Chairman Alberta Order of Excellence Council.

Accepted by Raymond V. Rajotte,
Member The Alberta Order of Excellence.

ADI

Dr. Matthew Warren Spence

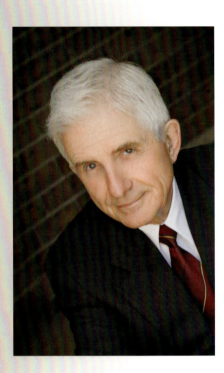

Inducted: 2006

DR. MATTHEW SPENCE IS A RESPECTED medical clinician, researcher and administrator who has been instrumental in developing Alberta's international reputation as a health research leader. As president and CEO of the Alberta Heritage Foundation for Medical Research, he created innovative and widely emulated strategies for health research funding that have fostered emerging areas of research and attracted top researchers to the province. His work has served to enhance the health and well being of his fellow Albertans and all Canadians.

Matt Spence was born in Chatham, Ontario, on 18 November 1934 while his parents, Clarence and Olive Spence, were returning to Western Canada from Ithaca, New York. The family stopped in Chatham to welcome their second child into the world and soon resumed their journey west, settling first in Saskatoon, then Edmonton, with regular sojourns at the family farm in Rimbey, Alberta.

Like his father, Matt greatly enjoyed farm life, describing it as an ideal place for a young boy to grow up. He refers to his mother as the quintessential "Western Mom," which he defines as a woman with clear visions of her children receiving a post-secondary education. As a result, all three Spence children earned multiple university degrees. As a boy, Matt had dreams of becoming a fireman or a milkman, but by the time he approached university, it was medicine that interested him most.

He earned a degree in medicine from the University of Alberta, followed by a PhD in neurochemistry from McGill University. Dr. Spence spent the early part of his career as a physician-researcher and educator in Montréal. It was there that he met and married his wife Cynthia, a nurse at a Sherbrooke hospital where Dr. Spence was completing his intern rotations.

In the early 1970s, Dr. Spence was given an opportunity to build on his growing strengths as a physician and researcher when he was recruited to work at the I.W. Killam Hospital for Children and Dalhousie University in Halifax. He focused on both paediatrics and brain chemistry and began to build a noteworthy research career. During his time in Halifax, Dr. Spence lent his growing knowledge and expertise to many national organizations including, the Canadian Association for the Mentally Retarded, the Canadian Society for Clinical Investigation and numerous committees within the Medical Research Council. His research efforts were recognized when he received a prestigious Medical Research Council Associateship Award.

In 1990, Dr. Spence was offered the position as president and CEO of the Alberta Heritage Foundation for Medical Research (AHFMR). Dr. Spence jumped at the opportunity to return to his native Alberta and to head an organization that he considered to be pioneering medical research in Canada. As leader of the Foundation, he played a key role in its work to develop and invest in Alberta's growing research strengths, including efforts to expand the ranks of the province's health researchers and to encourage young Albertans to consider a career in medical research.

During his 13-year tenure with the Foundation, Dr. Spence championed improvements in health services research and population health research. As a result of his work, many outstanding researchers have been attracted to the province to conduct world-class research. This has resulted in funding from outside the province and has helped to make Alberta a leader in health research. Largely due to Dr. Spence's efforts, AHFMR has been highly-rated by three international boards of review, making Alberta the envy of other provinces and countries around the world. Thanks to his leadership, current and future generations of Albertans will enjoy significant benefits from AHFMR research.

Even during the busiest years of his research career, Dr. Spence continued to provide his services to Canadians as a physician. He has also generously given his time and expertise to numerous professional organizations, including the Medical Research Council, the Canadian Health Services Research Foundation, the Canadian Institutes for Health Research and the Canadian Foundation for Innovation. In 2005, Dr. Spence's considerable contributions to his province were recognized when he was named one of Alberta's "Physicians of the Century." Among other awards and recognition, Dr. Spence received an Honorary Doctor of Laws degree from the University of Alberta and was appointed to the Order of Canada in 2004.

As a passionate ambassador for health research, Dr. Spence has brought tremendous respect, honour and recognition to the province of Alberta. He came to the Alberta Heritage Foundation for Medical Research with a vision to make Alberta a major powerhouse in the health research field. That vision is being realized. Thanks to his energy, hard work and dedication, Alberta can now claim a significant international presence in many areas of health research. That claim would not be possible without the considerable contributions of leaders like Dr. Matthew Spence.

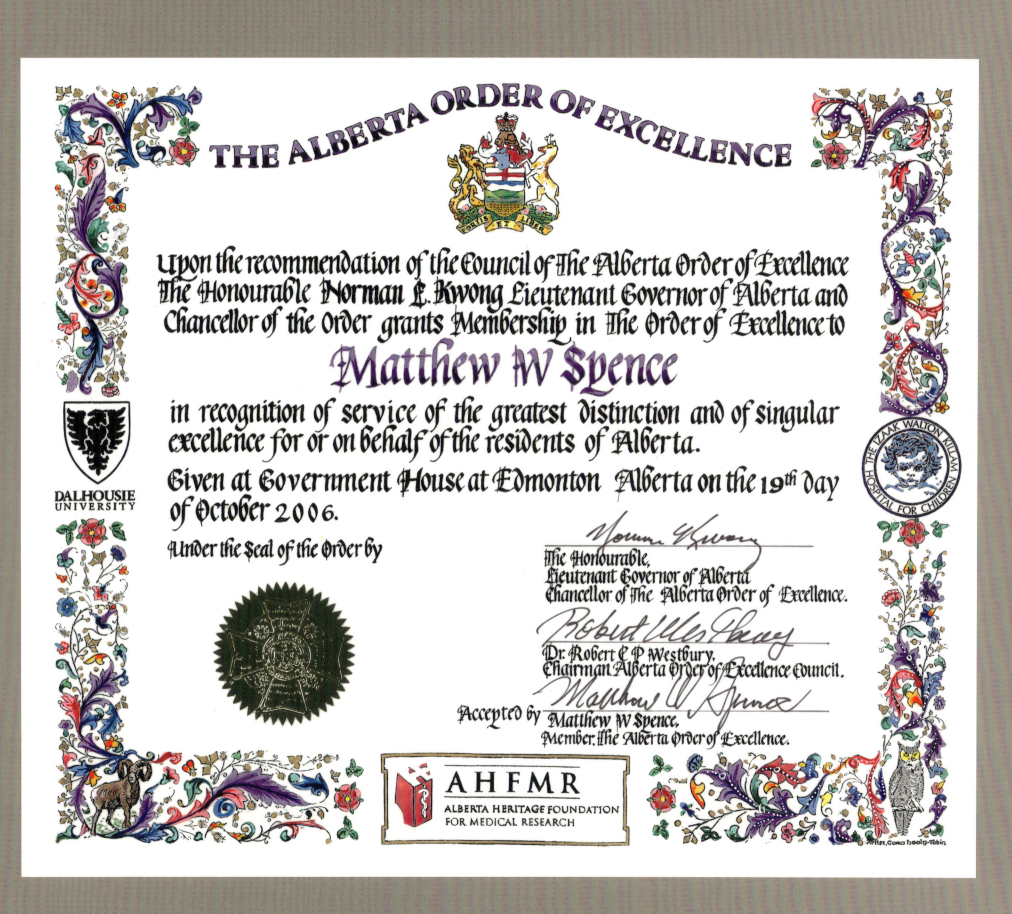

THE ALBERTA ORDER OF EXCELLENCE

Upon the recommendation of the Council of The Alberta Order of Excellence The Honourable Norman L. Kwong Lieutenant Governor of Alberta and Chancellor of the Order grants Membership in The Order of Excellence to

Matthew W Spence

in recognition of service of the greatest distinction and of singular excellence for or on behalf of the residents of Alberta.

Given at Government House at Edmonton Alberta on the 19th day of October 2006.

Under the Seal of the Order by

The Honourable,
Lieutenant Governor of Alberta
Chancellor of The Alberta Order of Excellence.

Dr. Robert C P Westbury,
Chairman, Alberta Order of Excellence Council.

Accepted by Matthew W Spence,
Member, The Alberta Order of Excellence.

DALHOUSIE UNIVERSITY

THE IZAAK WALTON KILLAM HOSPITAL FOR CHILDREN

AHFMR
ALBERTA HERITAGE FOUNDATION FOR MEDICAL RESEARCH

Ian Tyson

Inducted: 2006

IAN TYSON IS AN INTERNATIONALLY ACCLAIMED western music singer and songwriter who has created some of Alberta's and Canada's most enduring standards. His career has spanned five decades, and his music has inspired renowned artists such as Bob Dylan, Neil Young and Gordon Lightfoot. Over the years, Tyson has continued to create music that encapsulates life in the west. Through vivid descriptions of Alberta and cowboy culture, Ian Tyson has become a leading spokesman for western pride and helped establish a unique soundtrack to capture the Alberta experience.

Born in Victoria, British Columbia, in 1933, the second child of George and Margaret Tyson, Ian learned to ride horses on a small farm owned by his father, an insurance salesman who had emigrated from England in 1906. As a teenager, he left home for southern Alberta and competed in the rodeo circuit until a foot injury put him in the hospital. It was during his recovery in a Calgary hospital that Tyson first learned to play the guitar.

Soon after, at the age of 24, Tyson continued east to Toronto to pursue a music career. It was during the folk music revival of the 1960s that he met singer/songwriter Sylvia Fricker. Together, they formed the eponymous duo "Ian and Sylvia" and enjoyed great success, receiving rave reviews and playing to sold-out crowds in prestigious venues, such as New York's Carnegie Hall.

It was during this time that *Four Strong Winds* was released. The title track became an instant hit; over 50 versions were recorded in the first five years after its release, and it has remained a folk standard. Neil Young recorded *Four Strong Winds* in 1979 and called the song "the most beautiful record I ever heard in my life." Johnny Cash recorded the song shortly before his death, and it was included on his posthumous album released in 2006. The song has also become an Alberta standard. A 2005 radio listener's poll named *Four Strong Winds* the greatest Canadian song of the 20th century.

After forming the iconic country rock band "Great Speckled Bird" with Sylvia, Tyson hosted the national Canadian television music show, "Nashville North," (which was later renamed "The Ian Tyson Show") from 1970 to 1975. Soon after, he once again made Alberta his home, settling in Pincher Creek where he began ranching and living the life about which he was so proud to write and sing.

After three years of working his ranch, he recorded the album *Old Corrals & Sagebrush*, a mixture of traditional cowboy songs and new western music. His breakthrough album, 1986's *Cowboyography*, earned platinum status in Canada. As the popularity of Tyson's music resurged, he began travelling and performing at concerts across North America. Even during this busy time, Tyson stayed true to his roots, maintaining Alberta as his home and working on a ranch in Pincher Creek. In fact, it is the gravel road that runs from his present ranch in the foothills of the Rockies that inspired Tyson's 2005 album, *Songs from the Gravel Road*. Releasing this album at the age of 71, Tyson has shown that an active cowboy life keeps his creative pulse beating as strongly as ever. His discography remains an enduring collection of Canadian classics.

Tyson has said he made it a point to try to reach as many people as possible through his music, including people not directly from the ranch culture. His goal has been to write songs to which different people could all relate. The popularity and longevity of his many albums, along with the awards and recognition that followed, are proof that Tyson has been able to achieve that goal.

Through his music, Ian Tyson tells the story of rural Alberta and today's West. He depicts the challenges of a rancher's life, the beauty of the Rockies and the cowboy's strong work ethic.

Tyson's authentic career path serves as a model for Canadian musicians starting out in the industry today. His dedication to music and the genre is firmly recognized. By always focusing on his home and his passions, Tyson has served as a mentor for new artists, such as Albertan Corb Lund.

Tyson has used his skill and passion for music to benefit the community. He has performed at fundraising concerts across Alberta, Canada and internationally to raise awareness of and support for many causes, including child safety and education. As a compassionate rancher and environmentalist, Tyson has also joined his fellow Southern Albertans in work to preserve the natural landscape of rural Alberta.

He was inducted into the Canadian Country Music Association Hall of Honor and Hall of Fame in 1989, to the Juno Hall of Fame in 1992, the Canadian Broadcast Hall of Fame in 2000 and the Prairie Music Hall of Fame the following year. He holds honorary doctorate degrees from the University of Calgary and Athabasca University, and he became a Member of the Order of Canada in 1994.

Tyson's long list of honours speaks to his impact in Alberta, in Canada and abroad. Yet, despite his international acclaim, Tyson's heart lies in Alberta; he states simply, "I'll always be a Westerner and I'll always be a cowboy."

THE ALBERTA ORDER OF EXCELLENCE

Upon the recommendation of the Council of The Alberta Order of Excellence The honourable Norman L. Kwong Lieutenant Governor of Alberta and Chancellor of the Order grants Membership in The Order of Excellence to

Ian Tyson

in recognition of service of the greatest distinction and of singular excellence for or on behalf of the residents of Alberta.

Given at Government house at Edmonton Alberta on the 19th day of October 2006.

Under the Seal of the Order by

The Honourable Norman L. Kwong
Lieutenant Governor of Alberta, Chancellor
of The Alberta Order of Excellence.

Dr Robert C.P. Westbury.
Chairman, Alberta Order of Excellence Council.

Accepted by

Ian Tyson,
Member, The Alberta Order of Excellence.

Artist Cora Healy-Tobin ©

Evelyn L. Buckley

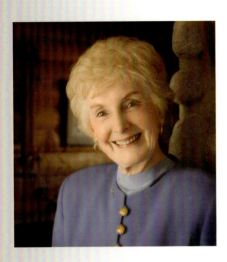

Inducted: 2007

SOME OF ALBERTA'S GREAT BUILDERS focus on the bricks and mortar that give shape to a community. Others turn their attention to the sense of compassion and inclusion that give a community heart. In her career as a community builder, Evelyn Buckley has found a way to do both.

Evelyn was born on 13 May 1934 and raised on a farm east of Calgary. Her search for community began early in life. Although her family was not religious, Evelyn felt drawn to the sense of belonging and purpose that church represents. At the age of five, she began polling neighbours about their religious affiliations and asking to be invited to take part in their services. This was more than an indication of Evelyn's natural inquisitiveness. It marked the beginning of a search for meaning and connection with others that would shape her life's work.

Evelyn chose nursing as a career and graduated with a diploma from the Calgary General Hospital in 1955. The choice was a natural fit for her nurturing and compassionate nature. Less of a fit was the administrative nature of her surgical ward duties, which did not allow her the time she craved to talk with and comfort patients.

In 1957, Evelyn married Clarence Buckley and soon found her days full with the challenges that came with running the family ranch. They began their life together in a small log cabin with no running water and little insulation. Evelyn's drive to learn helped her through the early years. She soon became a jack of all trades who could capably juggle the skills needed to work the ranch and raise a family that grew to include four children: Richard, Michael, Ken and Colleen. She also found the time to serve as an English as a Second Language instructor for the YWCA.

By the 1970s, Evelyn's busy ranch life included hosting international students who came to Alberta through Rotary International and other programs. This period also marked the beginning of her work to strengthen community health care supports and services. She returned to school and graduated with a Social Work Diploma from Mount Royal College and worked with autistic children at the Calgary Children's Hospital. She also served as executive director of the Multiple Sclerosis Society of Canada.

Evelyn began to focus on building compassionate and inclusive communities for long-term care and palliative care patients. She also worked on behalf of Albertans dealing with mental health issues and handicapped people needing accessible and affordable housing. As a member of the Carewest Board, she started to develop a model of a long-term care community that would offer residents both a feeling of home and a sense of purpose and belonging. Her vision was to create a place that "replaced nursing stations with kitchen tables." Her passion became to turn institutions into caring and inclusive homes and communities.

Evelyn was able to make that vision a reality through her work with the Bethany Care Society. As a board member, she led the creation of innovative long-term care projects, including the Harvest Hills Centre, which has been recognized as one of the best architecturally designed Alzheimer's homes in North America. She also served as a tireless advocate of long-term care issues and a promoter of good health care governance. Evelyn's work with Bethany Care eventually led to a unique partnership with the Chinese Christian Nursing Home Association. Thanks, in no small part, to Evelyn's energy and dedication, Calgary is home to the Wing Kei Nursing Home, which offers culturally appropriate, home-style care to Chinese long-term care patients.

Over the years, Evelyn has played a hands-on role with many other organizations dedicated to fostering healthy communities and raising the standard of health care in Alberta. She has completed tenures as a member of the provincial government Mental Health Review Panel and the Alberta Government Health Disciplines Board. She has volunteered with a range of organizations, including the Catholic Health Association of Alberta, the Alberta Long-Term Care Advisory Committee and the MD of Rockyview Planning Committee. She has also worked to preserve the history of the Alberta ranch country she and Clarence have been proud to call home.

Other projects have taken Evelyn's focus to the international stage. She served on the board of Kenya Connection, a pioneering micro-credit program that helps women start businesses and move toward economic independence. As a volunteer with Hearts and Hands, she travels to Guatemala to combat lung disease caused by the open stoves that are used in the homes of some of the country's poorest people.

Evelyn's diverse interests and remarkable energy are also reflected in her long-standing volunteer work for the United Church of Canada. In 1995, these efforts were recognized with an Honorary Doctorate of Divinity from St. Andrews College, University of Saskatchewan. Her other awards and honours include an Integrity Award and Paul Harris Fellowship from the Rotary Club of Calgary.

In her work as a United Church lay preacher, she often tells congregations that "sometimes you have to trust and move forward without knowing the path ahead or what will happen." Evelyn Buckley has traveled a unique path, answering a powerful call to serve others and her community. Along the way, remarkable things have happened because of her caring spirit, her great determination and her desire to build a better world.

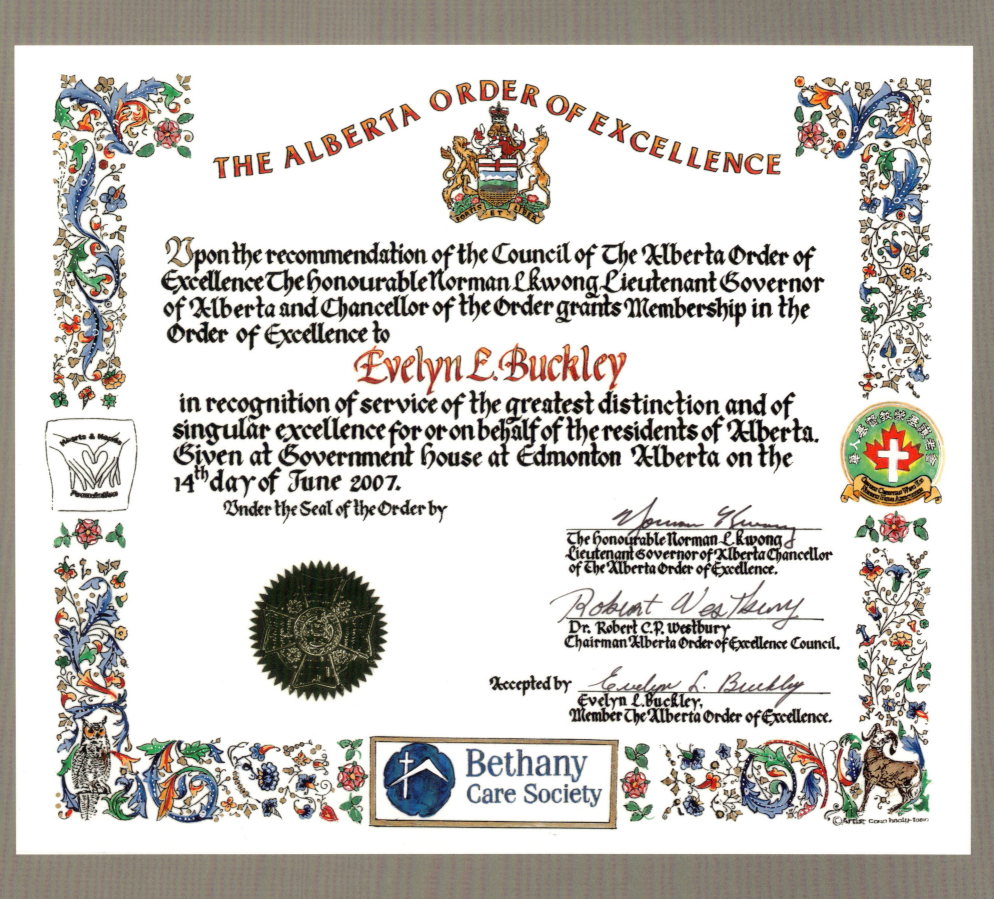

THE ALBERTA ORDER OF EXCELLENCE

Upon the recommendation of the Council of The Alberta Order of Excellence The honourable Norman L Kwong Lieutenant Governor of Alberta and Chancellor of the Order grants Membership in the Order of Excellence to

Evelyn L. Buckley

in recognition of service of the greatest distinction and of singular excellence for or on behalf of the residents of Alberta. Given at Government house at Edmonton Alberta on the 14th day of June 2007.

Under the Seal of the Order by

The honourable Norman L Kwong
Lieutenant Governor of Alberta Chancellor
of The Alberta Order of Excellence.

Dr. Robert C.P. Westbury
Chairman Alberta Order of Excellence Council.

Accepted by

Evelyn L. Buckley,
Member The Alberta Order of Excellence.

Bethany Care Society

©Artist Cora Knolly-Toan

Chief Victor Stanley Buffalo

Inducted: 2007

VICTOR BUFFALO IS A RESPECTED ALBERTA leader and entrepreneur. His pioneering work has helped First Nation businesses across Canada to thrive. His passion for education has opened new doors for Samson Cree First Nation members.

Victor Buffalo was born in Hobbema, Alberta, on 7 December 1941. He had little time to enjoy family life with parents, Edgar and Helen, and his siblings. At the age of seven, Victor was sent to residential school and, although he was only miles from his home, he was worlds away from a loving family. Victor lived an isolated life, lonely and disconnected from his Aboriginal heritage. He found solace in reading and developed considerable discipline and independence due to the strict routine of the school. At 20, Victor left residential school profoundly affected by the experience and carrying a fierce determination that would shape his life.

In 1964, Victor earned a Diploma in Chemical Technology from SAIT and began working in the field, first for Canada Tungsten Mining and then Canadian Celanese. Two years later, Victor met and married his wife, Rema. In her, Victor found a life partner who would provide him with the love and support he had sorely missed in his early years. They had a traditional ceremony, which elders said would produce a lasting marriage. The elders were right. Over the years, Victor and Rema's family grew to include four children: Heather, Steven, Brenda and Kevin.

After working in mining for a number of years, Victor began to serve as a community development officer for the Indian Association of Alberta. Victor and Rema moved their family from Edmonton back home to Hobbema, where Victor served as a land administrator for the reserve. With George Manuel of the National Indian Brotherhood as his mentor, Victor became increasingly involved in band politics. He served twice as a band councilor before being elected Chief of the Samson Cree Nation in 1980.

In the early 1980s, Victor took on a landmark project for Canadian Aboriginal communities. As one of the guiding forces behind Peace Hills Trust, he led the creation of Canada's first Aboriginal-owned financial institution. Victor faced obstacles as the Trust developed, including disbelief on many fronts that a First Nation could or should run a bank. The lack of trained Aboriginal managers and staff was another obstacle. Victor met both challenges with characteristic determination.

Peace Hills Trust opened its doors in 1981. The institution began offering personal and business loans and investing in Aboriginal projects. Meanwhile, Victor set about training Aboriginal staff and building the management capacity of the Trust's board of directors. By the time Peace Hills Trust celebrated its 25th anniversary in 2006, the institution had grown to include eight branches and some $400 million in assets, as well as a seventy percent Aboriginal workforce. Countless Aboriginal businesses startups and expansions across the country, from farming and ranching operations to business and tourism operations, can trace their success to support from Peace Hills Trust.

Chief Buffalo's determination has led to the development of other economic development opportunities for the Samson Cree, from Samson Oil and Gas to the Samson Lake Louise Mall. His business acumen has also been put to good use as a member of numerous boards of directors, including Western Lakota Energy Services, the Aboriginal Program Advisory Committee at the Banff Centre for Management, the National Aboriginal Industries Committee and the National Aboriginal Diabetes Association.

While his economic development contributions have been considerable, Victor's greatest passion has arguably been to expand educational opportunities for all Samson Cree First Nation members. In the 1980s, he established the Samson Education Trust Fund. The Fund took Hobbema from having no schools on reserve to four state-of-the art schools covering kindergarten to Grade 12. The Fund also encourages Samson Nation members to complete university degrees and trades training. As more people pursue these opportunities, Chief Buffalo has enjoyed the pleasure of seeing his people graduate in a range of disciplines from technical diplomas to master's degrees and doctorates.

Chief Buffalo opened another important door for the Samson, and all Canadian Aboriginal people, with a 2005 landmark lawsuit that allowed the Samson Cree to gain control of the $340 million in oil and gas revenues that had been managed by the federal government. The dollars were placed in a trust fund that will contribute to the First Nations' continued journey toward economic independence. In 2006, Victor Buffalo was inducted into the Aboriginal Business Hall of Fame by the Canadian Council for Aboriginal Business. In 2005, he received an Alberta Centennial Medal in recognition of his many contributions to the province.

Victor lost his life partner when Rema passed away in 2007. He describes her as the guiding force in his life and takes great pride in the accomplishments of their children, who have all pursued post-secondary education and taken on leadership roles within the Aboriginal community. Chief Buffalo continues to honour his own lifelong commitment to learning by pursuing a Bachelor or General Studies degree from Athabasca University, with a focus on Psychology. He is also working to build up social structures on the reserve and develop a strategic plan that will ensure increased stability and opportunities for the Nation well into the future.

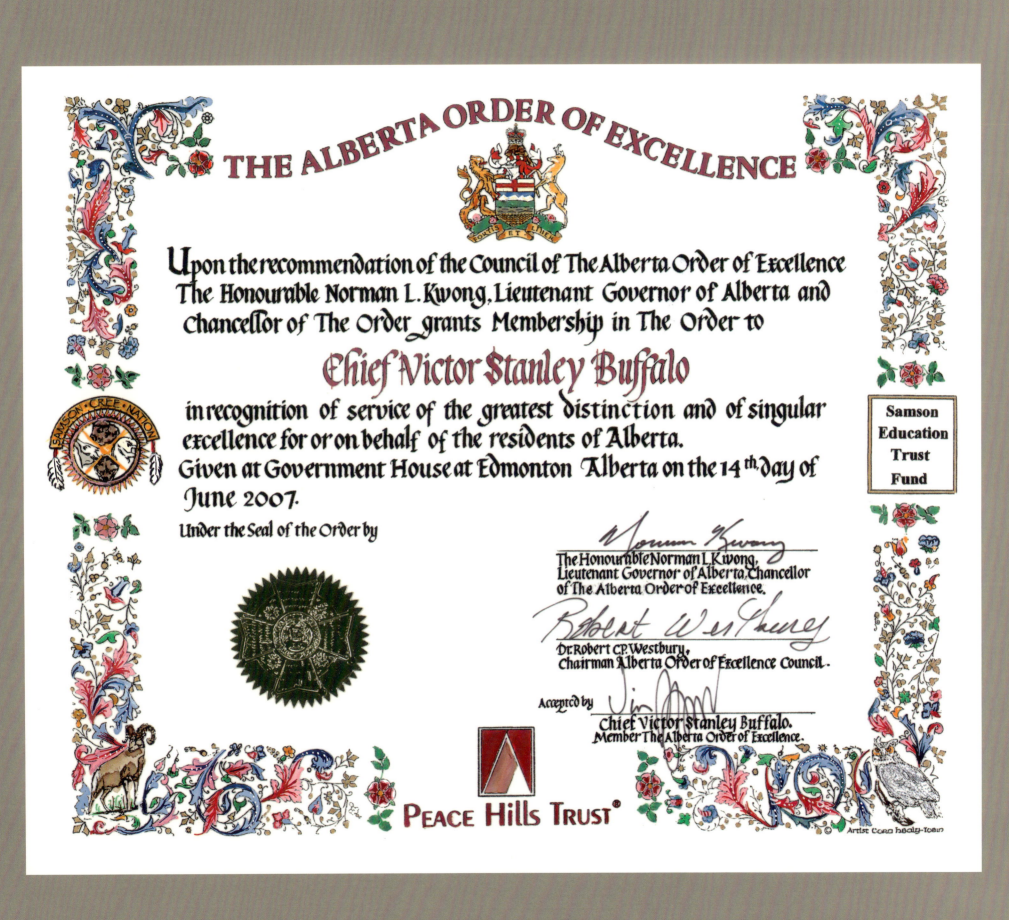

THE ALBERTA ORDER OF EXCELLENCE

Upon the recommendation of the Council of The Alberta Order of Excellence The Honourable Norman L. Kwong, Lieutenant Governor of Alberta and Chancellor of The Order grants Membership in The Order to

Chief Victor Stanley Buffalo

in recognition of service of the greatest distinction and of singular excellence for or on behalf of the residents of Alberta.

Given at Government House at Edmonton Alberta on the 14th day of June 2007.

Under the Seal of the Order by

The Honourable Norman L Kwong,
Lieutenant Governor of Alberta, Chancellor
of The Alberta Order of Excellence.

Dr. Robert C.P. Westbury,
Chairman Alberta Order of Excellence Council.

Accepted by

Chief Victor Stanley Buffalo.
Member The Alberta Order of Excellence.

Samson
Education
Trust
Fund

Peace Hills Trust

© Artist Cora Healy-Toan

Lt. General Donald C. Laubman

Inducted: 2007

LT. GENERAL DONALD C. LAUBMAN is a decorated Canadian Air Force veteran and one of the most celebrated Canadian pilots of Second World War. He has played a leadership role in building the reputation of the Canadian military, particularly in Europe, and has also been an effective leader in the creation of community programs enjoyed by his fellow Albertans.

Don Laubman was born in Provost, Alberta, on 16 October 1921. His family lived in Camrose and Westlock before settling in Edmonton. The eldest of seven children, Don enjoyed a typical childhood that included time-honoured pursuits, such as building model airplanes. It also involved a brush with legendary Alberta bush pilot, Wop May, which peaked Don's interest in flying and led to many hours standing at the fence of the Edmonton Municipal Airport watching planes take off and land.

After high school, Don found a job at a downtown Edmonton grocery store located across the street from the Royal Canadian Air Force recruiting office. Shortly after Canada entered the Second World War, Don visited the office. Thinking that a university education was a requirement for pilots, he offered his services as a photographer. He was surprised to find that a pilot's wings were within his grasp and signed up on 9 December 1939.

Donald Laubman was called up for active duty on Friday, 13 September 1940. His humility elicits a quiet response when he is asked if he was a natural pilot. However, his service record speaks volumes. By 1941, he was working as an instructor as part of the British Commonwealth Air Training Plan, and in 1943 he was sent to the United Kingdom and assigned to 412 Squadron, 126 Wing. Squadron Leader Don Laubman and his team offered distinguished service, flying key operational missions from D Day onward. On 14 April 1945, shortly before VE Day, Don was forced to abandon his aircraft and spent the next three weeks as a prisoner of war.

Donald Laubman was twice awarded the Distinguished Flying Cross in recognition of his leadership abilities, courage and devotion to duty. His aerial combat record during the war earned him the title of Canada's fourth ranking RCAF ace.

A significant new chapter of Don's life opened on his return to Canada in 1945. He met a group of friends who decided to celebrate the war's end with a trip to Banff. He was walking down Banff Avenue when he met a friend's sister who introduced him to Margaret Gibson. Don and Margie were married in 1946 and began raising a family that grew to include son Robert and daughter Leslie.

Don's career with the Canadian Forces continued in peace time. He re-enrolled in 1946 and continued building a respected career as a pilot, serving as a founding member and Flight Commander of the famed Blue Devils Air Defence Group Aerobatics Team then as a Squadron Leader and Wing Commander. Increasingly, senior postings led to an exchange with the United States Air Force in the Pentagon and service as a member of the Directing Staff of the Air Force Staff College. He was later promoted to Air Commodore at National Defence Headquarters, Brigadier General and First Commander of Canadian Forces Europe. Don retired in 1972 as Lieutenant General and Chief of Personnel of the Canadian Forces. His approachable style and easy manner lead one associate to dub him the "most popular general in the Canadian Forces."

Upon leaving the Forces, Don began a new career with Canadian Tire and managed stores in Thompson, Manitoba and Saskatoon, Saskatchewan before opening the first Canadian Tire store in Red Deer in 1979.

While running the store, Don found opportunities to put his leadership abilities to work for the community and played a founding role in the development of many Red Deer area service organizations. He was instrumental in founding the Red Deer and Central Alberta Crime Stoppers organization. He served as chairman of the Red Deer Crime Stoppers Board of Directors and as a board member for Crime Stoppers International. He also served as president of the Red Deer Rotary Club, board member of the Red Deer Chamber of Commerce, and founding board member of both the Red Deer Community Foundation and the Red Deer Regional Hospital Foundation.

As a board member and chairman of the David Thompson Health Region Foundation, Don was instrumental in helping to raise significant funds for health care programs and hospital upgrades in central Alberta. Don later served as vice chair of the inaugural board of the Lending Cupboard Society, which provides Red Deer area residents with medical equipment for home care use. Don Laubman was named Red Deer Citizen of the Year in 2005.

Don is remarkably quiet about his accomplishments. He prefers to credit his leadership and community successes to the quality of people he has been honoured to work with over the years. When asked what he values most about being an Albertan, his answer is one that befits a pilot and community visionary of his stature. His favourite thing about the province he is proud to call home is the big, blue Alberta sky.

THE ALBERTA ORDER OF EXCELLENCE

Upon the recommendation of the Council of The Alberta Order of Excellence The Honourable Norman L.Kwong Lieutenant Governor of Alberta and Chancellor of the Order grants Membership in The Order of Excellence to

Donald E.Laubman

in recognition of service of the greatest distinction and of singular excellence for or on behalf of the residents of Alberta Given at Government House at Edmonton Alberta on the 14th day of June 2007.

Under the Seal of the Order by

The Honourable Norman L.Kwong,
Lieutenant Governor of Alberta Chancellor
The Alberta Order of Excellence.

Dr. Robert C.P. Westbury,
Chairman Alberta Order of Excellence Council.

Accepted by

Donald C.Laubman,
Member, Alberta Order of Excellence.

Rotary International

DHR
DAVID THOMPSON
HEALTH REGION

Artist Conn health Team

David W. Leonard

Inducted: 2007

DAVID LEONARD IS AN INSIGHTFUL historian and dedicated archivist who has played a key role in the preservation and understanding of Alberta's history. He has been particularly effective in preserving the history of Alberta's northwest Peace River Country.

David was born in Fairview, Alberta, on 17 February 1945 and raised in Sexsmith. His father and mother, Bill and Grace, came to the Peace Country from Iowa in the early 1930s and resided in Hines Creek, Webster and Whitelaw. After serving in the Second World War, Bill took land under the Veterans Lands Act and chose two quarter sections at Teepee Creek, east of Sexsmith. The couple made their home in Sexsmith and raised three children, Donna (Menzies), Ann (Leighton) and David.

The love of Alberta's north that would come to shape David's career did not manifest itself in his early years. He was a strong student, who was active in the community, joined Air Cadets and played baseball for the local team. He also served as a community reporter for the Grande Prairie Herald-Tribune. However, after high school, David was anxious to venture beyond the Peace Country and explore other places.

He moved to Edmonton in 1964 to attend the University of Alberta where he discovered a passion for history and a particular interest in Britain and Ireland. David obtained a Bachelor of Arts Honours degree in 1968 and then a Master of Arts degree in Modern Irish History in 1969. After two years as an archivist at the Provincial Archives of Alberta, David moved to England to begin PhD studies in Modern Irish History at the University of Sheffield. He received his doctorate in 1975.

Shortly after returning to Canada, David became the Assistant City of Edmonton Archivist, a position he held until December 1978, when he became the first Territorial Archivist of the Northwest Territories, stationed in Yellowknife. In February 1981, he returned to Edmonton to assume the position of Head of the Government Records program at the Provincial Archives.

During the 1980s, David became an active member of the Society for the Protection of Architectural Resources in Edmonton and spent many years as a volunteer, offering walking tours of historic districts of the city and working to educate building owners and others about the value of preservation. He also began volunteering with the Historical Society of Alberta, the Alberta Records Publication Board and the Archives Society of Alberta.

The 1980s marked the beginning of David's interest in the history of northwest Alberta. While working at the Provincial Archives, he came across a general land distribution map of Canada and was struck by an anomaly in the Peace Country. It was common to see population growth along railways, but northwest Alberta broke with that trend, showing wide-scale settlement in the absence of a railway. David was fascinated and wondered what would compel people to pick up and move so far north. He began researching the region and joined with heritage groups in working to set up archives and protect historic sites.

In 1992, David published the first of several histories of the Peace River Country, *The Lure of the Peace River Country*, co-authored with Victoria Lemieux. In 1995, he followed with *Delayed Frontier: The Peace River Country to 1909*. As his volunteer work on the history of Alberta's North continued, David took on increasingly senior positions with the Provincial Archives. He served as the Provincial Archivist from 1993 to 1996. He also began teaching archives and records management courses at the University of Alberta's School of Library and Information Studies.

In 1996, David transferred from the Provincial Archives to the Alberta Historic Sites Service, where he assumed the role of Project Historian for Northern Alberta. His careful research of northwest Alberta history continued with the publication of numerous works. In 2006, David completed an important piece of the puzzle he first discovered looking at the land distribution map twenty years earlier. *The Last Great West: The Agricultural Settlement of the Peace River Country to 1914* provides a window into the conditions and personal stories that brought settlers to the northwest. David's work included the painstaking examination of 6,789 land files created by the Department of the Interior on each settler in the region. While some might find the task daunting, David found endless fascination in the personal histories the files revealed. The statistical data he compiled captures many stories that might otherwise be lost. The data has been digitized and made available to all through Grande Prairie Regional College.

When asked to list the skills necessary for a successful archivist and historian, David includes thorough, accurate work habits and an affection for the community being studied. By that, or any other definition, David Leonard is a consummate archivist. His knowledge of Alberta history is as solid as his passion for sharing it with others. His work has helped uncover and preserve the stories that make up Alberta history, from singular moments in the province's development to pieces that capture elements of everyday life. He has helped us understand who we are as Albertans and helped us share our stories with the world.

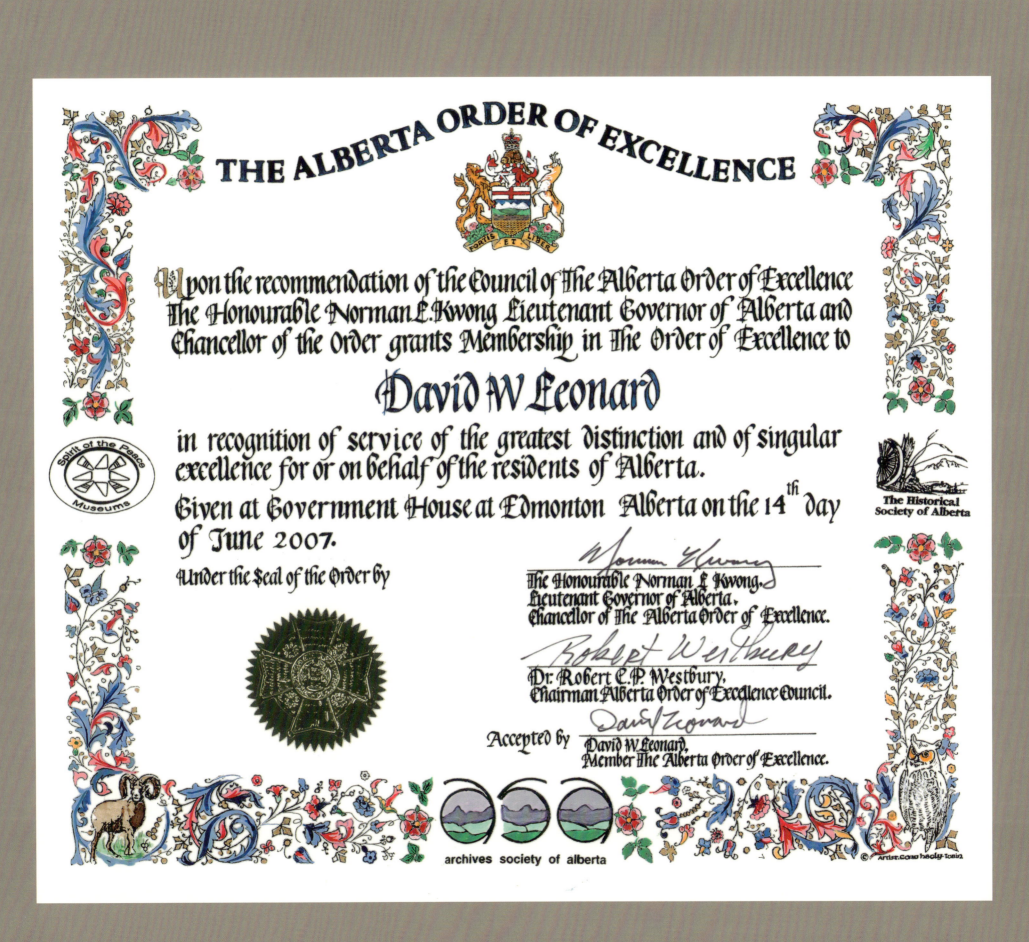

THE ALBERTA ORDER OF EXCELLENCE

Upon the recommendation of the Council of The Alberta Order of Excellence The Honourable Norman L. Kwong Lieutenant Governor of Alberta and Chancellor of the Order grants Membership in The Order of Excellence to

David W Leonard

in recognition of service of the greatest distinction and of singular excellence for or on behalf of the residents of Alberta.

Given at Government House at Edmonton Alberta on the 14th day of June 2007.

Under the Seal of the Order by

The Honourable Norman L Kwong,
Lieutenant Governor of Alberta,
Chancellor of The Alberta Order of Excellence.

Dr. Robert C.P. Westbury,
Chairman Alberta Order of Excellence Council.

Accepted by David W Leonard,
Member The Alberta Order of Excellence.

Spirit of the Peace Museums

The Historical Society of Alberta

archives society of alberta

Gary William (Wilcox) McPherson

Inducted: 2007

GARY MCPHERSON IS AN ADVOCATE and role model for Albertans and Canadians living with disabilities. He is a pioneer whose life and actions have inspired positive change in the areas of sport, business, politics, and building strong communities.

Gary was born in Edson, Alberta, on 28 June 1946, the first child of Dorothy and David Wilcox. His parents had met and married overseas while David was serving with the Canadian Forces and then returned to his native Alberta after the war. In 1948, the family moved to Edmonton and welcomed a second child, Joanne. Two years later, the Wilcox family was shattered when David died of a massive heart attack at the age of 32. Dorothy went on to marry Roderick McPherson, who adopted Gary and Joanne. A son, Scott, joined the family and the McPherson's moved to the Yukon where Gary enjoyed an active life.

That life changed dramatically during a holiday to Edmonton in October 1955. Gary became ill and was rushed to hospital where the family was told Gary had polio. Paralysis overtook his arms, legs and diaphragm, leaving him unable to move or breathe on his own. Two weeks later, Gary was transferred from the isolation ward at the Royal Alexandra Hospital to the polio ward at the University of Alberta Hospital. Although the family moved within six months to Edmonton, Gary's condition was too fragile to allow him to live with them. The hospital would serve as Gary's home for the next 34 years.

Gary worked his way from dependency on an iron lung to increasingly longer periods using a respirator. He also regained minimal movement in his left hand and leg. He eventually mastered the frog breathing (glossopharyngeal breathing) technique, which allowed him to function without a respirator during the day, although he remained dependant on the respirator to breathe at night. Gary's active schedule included studying, spending time with family and friends and taking in events, particularly anything that indulged his great passion for sports.

Gary's interest in sports led to his involvement as coach of the hospital's competitive mixed slow-pitch team. He discovered wheelchair sports through a rather unique chain of events. Gary and some of his fellow polio patients had become licensed amateur radio operators and arranged for an antenna on the hospital roof. When a mail strike threatened to derail planning for the 1968 Canadian Wheelchair Games in Edmonton, their amateur radio station hosted weekly cross-Canada amateur radio hook ups so that games' organizers could communicate. Gary got to know leaders in the field and eventually became one in his own right. With his mother providing administrative support, he took on duties as president of the Edmonton Paralympic Sports Association. Later, he became the executive director and eventually president of the Canadian Wheelchair Sports Association. He also served for eight years as the general manager of the famed Alberta Northern Lights Wheelchair Basketball team.

When Rick Hansen's Man in Motion World Tour came to Alberta in 1986, Gary's determination, combined with his ability to build relationships and motivate others, led to significant fundraising and public awareness for the cause. Gary's interest in sport also led to his appointment as an adjunct professor with the Department of Physical Education and Sport Studies at the U of A.

Another prominent element of Gary's extensive resume includes his work as a leader and advocate for the disabled community. During his decade as chair of the Premier's Council on the Status of Persons with Disabilities, Gary was successful in developing a strong network to connect government with community organizations and strengthen policies and programs for disabled Albertans. More recent activities include service as chair of the Steadward Centre for Personal and Physical Achievement and vice-chairman of the Alberta Paraplegic Foundation.

Although Gary has devoted much energy and commitment to sports and advocacy work, he has also been involved in an eclectic mix of other endeavours. He helped develop a data services company that grew from a small enterprise in the hospital to a business that included 27 staff members. At 21, he joined the Junior Chamber of Commerce where he honed his leadership and public speaking abilities and served on the Board of Directors. In recent years, he has combined his parallel interests in business and community development as executive director of the Canadian Centre for Social Entrepreneurship in the School of Business at the U of A. He has long been involved in provincial politics as a volunteer and campaign organizer. In 2006, he threw his own hat in the ring as a candidate in the Alberta Progressive Conservative Party leadership race.

If you ask Gary to choose the most significant of the many roles he has played, he quickly points to that of husband and father. He got together with his wife, Valerie Kamitomo, at a 1981 New Year's Eve party at the hospital where Gary lived and Val worked. They were married in 1988 and Gary moved out of the hospital and into their new home nine months later. A daughter, Keiko, and son, Jamie, soon followed.

Gary's diverse accomplishments have garnered him many honours, including the Order of Canada and an Honorary Doctor of Laws degree from the University of Alberta. In 2004, he was named one of the top 100 Edmontonians of the Century, and in 2005 he was named one of the Top 100 Contributors to Sport in Alberta over the past century.

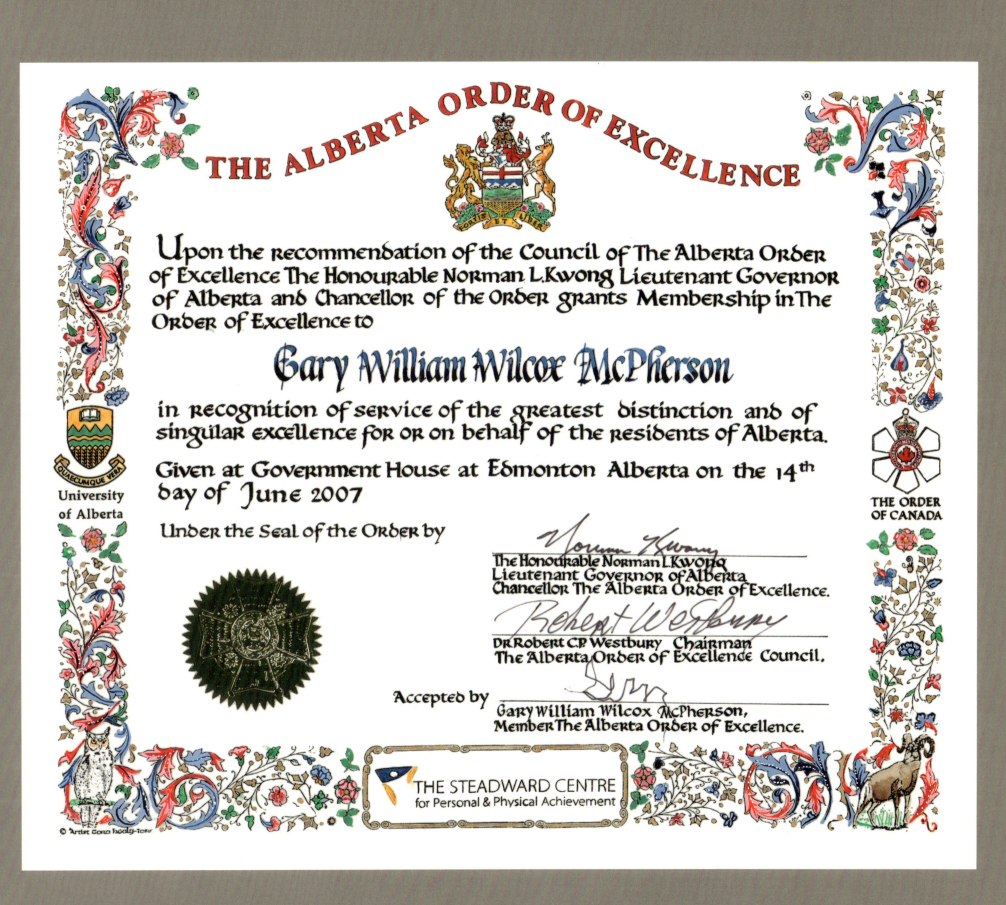

THE ALBERTA ORDER OF EXCELLENCE

Upon the recommendation of the Council of The Alberta Order of Excellence The Honourable Norman L. Kwong Lieutenant Governor of Alberta and Chancellor of the Order grants Membership in The Order of Excellence to

Gary William Wilcox McPherson

in recognition of service of the greatest distinction and of singular excellence for or on behalf of the residents of Alberta.

Given at Government House at Edmonton Alberta on the 14th day of June 2007

Under the Seal of the Order by

The Honourable Norman L. Kwong
Lieutenant Governor of Alberta
Chancellor The Alberta Order of Excellence.

Dr Robert C.P. Westbury Chairman
The Alberta Order of Excellence Council.

Accepted by

Gary William Wilcox McPherson,
Member The Alberta Order of Excellence.

University of Alberta

THE ORDER OF CANADA

THE STEADWARD CENTRE
for Personal & Physical Achievement

© Artist Gono hooly-Tone

Douglas H. Mitchell

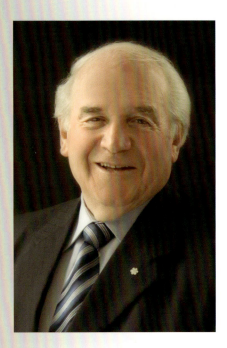

Inducted: 2007

DOUGLAS MITCHELL IS A RESPECTED business and community leader who has brought great energy and commitment to a wide range of organizations. He has made invaluable contributions to the strength and viability of amateur and professional sports in Canada.

Doug was born in Calgary, Alberta, and raised in the city's Crescent Heights neighbourhood. Like many young Canadian boys, he grew up playing school and recreation league sports and dreaming of becoming a great hockey or football player. Unlike most, he was able to fulfill both those dreams.

After high school, he attended Colorado College on a hockey scholarship and completed a Bachelor of Arts degree in Business Administration. Doug then decided to study law at the University of British Columbia. Here, he proved his great focus and versatility by completing his legal studies while playing football for the UBC Thunderbirds and then the BC Lions. During his years at UBC, Doug exhibited two qualities that would come to define his later career. Playing the traditional supporting role of a middle linebacker meant focusing his energies on doing what is best for the team rather than seeking out personal glory. Keeping on top of demanding scholastic and sports schedules meant using his time wisely and focusing his energy on where it would have the greatest impact.

While at UBC, Doug also made an important decision that would change his life. He found his best friend and life partner when he married Lois Boulding. Doug played briefly for the Hamilton Tiger Cats; however, the desire to settle into careers and family life led the young couple back to Doug's native Calgary. Doug started with the law firm of Howard, Mackie where he specialized in Corporate and Commercial Law. Doug and Lois's family grew alongside their careers with the arrival of children Shelley, Steven, Sue Ann and Scott. Doug assumed increasingly senior positions with Howard, Mackie and took the leadership role. When the firm merged to become Borden Ladner Gervais, Doug also assumed responsibilities as national co-chair.

Throughout his legal career, Doug has continued to find ways to contribute to professional and amateur sport. After watching Canada sit out hockey competitions in the 1972 and '76 Olympics, Doug dedicated himself to reinvigorating the Canada Olympic Hockey program. He was instrumental in building the Calgary-based program and bringing the national team back to full force and onto the Olympic podium. During the early 1980s, Doug also served as a member of the National Hockey League Board of Governors.

In 1984, Doug took a five-year break from his law firm to serve as Commissioner of the Canadian Football League. For many years, Doug also provided colourful commentary for the Calgary Stampeders and, more recently, developed Legacy Sports Inc., which is a part owner of the Football Club. Throughout his career, Doug has played a leadership role in many other sports endeavours, including the 2001 World Track and Field Championships. He founded a national awards program, the BLG Awards, to honour Canadian University Athletes and has also served as a volunteer amateur football, hockey, soccer and baseball coach.

Although sports have been a great passion throughout Doug's life, it is not the only area to benefit from his leadership. He has generously shared his time and skills with a wide range of organizations, including chairman of the Southern Alberta Institute of Technology, the United Way of Calgary, The Calgary Booster Club, the Campbell McLaurin Foundation for the Hearing Handicapped, Theatre Calgary, the Calgary Zoo, chairman of the Calgary Chamber of Commerce and the Canadian Bar Association. He has also served as a leading advocate of Alberta's economic development as chair of the Alberta Economic Development Authority and founder of the Global Business Forum. Doug is proud to give back to his province and country as Honorary Lt. Colonel of the King's Own Calgary Regiment. Doug's exemplary record of community service has earned him numerous honours. He received the Lester Pearson Award as outstanding alumni of the Canadian Interuniversity Athletic Union. He is also a member of the Alberta Sports Hall of Fame. In 2004, Doug was named one of the most influential Albertans in the province's first 100 years. That same year, he became a Member of the Order of Canada.

When asked to offer leadership advice to young people interested in following in his footsteps, either in the field of sports or law, Doug offers the same guidance. His says, "Learn how to be a team player and be unselfish in putting the needs of others ahead of your own." Doug Mitchell has always lived that advice, and in doing so he has served as a consummate example of what it means to be a team player. He also offers an outstanding role model for anyone looking for a way to give back to his or her community, province and country.

Patrick R. Nixon

Inducted: 2007

PATRICK NIXON IS A LEADER in delivering compassionate and effective programs for the poor and the homeless. Pat's innovative work at Calgary's Mustard Seed Street Ministry has transformed lives and encouraged thousands within Alberta and across Canada to join him in building stronger and more engaged communities.

Pat Nixon was born in Vancouver on 24 November 1960 and raised in a troubled home. His tumultuous home life led him to act out, which led to trouble at school and with the authorities. His step-father kicked Pat out of the house at the age of 12. When he hit the streets, Pat was functionally illiterate and utterly alone.

Pat drifted around British Columbia, reaching lows that almost led him to end his life. Eventually, the police put him on a bus headed east. Pat arrived in Calgary at 15 and began panhandling to stay alive. One day, he was approached by four men from the First Baptist Church. Pat asked for money, but instead they offered him a meal and a place to stay. One of the men, Rod Derry, cared for Pat for a year before he slipped back into old patterns. By age 16, Pat was in provincial jail.

Two years later, Pat returned to Calgary to find that the same church community was ready to give him another chance. Pat reconnected with Lise, a young girl he had fallen in love with during his year living with Rod, and they were married in 1979. After a few false starts, Pat was ready to change his life for good. He found a job and began volunteering with Lise at the church's Burning Bush Coffee House. When he was laid off from his job as a construction worker, the church approached Pat about starting a street ministry. He was reluctant but soon began developing an approach that drew on his experiences with homelessness, fear and addiction. Pat was licensed as a pastor and in 1984 the Mustard Seed Street Ministry was born.

The mission started modestly, with 12 volunteers providing emergency food and shelter to 50 people per day. Pat understood how to mobilize volunteers, learning that the key to making the mission work was to give them the ownership of, and responsibility for, their volunteer duties. Pat also spent time counseling the broken people he found on the streets. The scope of the Mustard Seed's work has changed since those early years. The same sense of ownership that he hands to his volunteers Pat extends to the people who stay at the mission. They are encouraged and expected to move beyond emergency food and shelter services to the Step Up program, which involves education and counseling supports that lead to employment. They also find both encouragement and celebration as they pass each milestone. With Pat's vision and leadership, and with the dedication of the Mustard Seed board members, the mission has grown from an office in the basement of the First Baptist Church to a collection of downtown Calgary facilities that offer emergency care, training, job search services and transitional and affordable housing. It also includes Mountain Aire Lodge, which provides work experience and healing opportunities. In 2006, the mission saw more than 11,000 volunteers serve over 365,000 people.

In addition to programs for the poor and homeless, the Mustard Seed offers a public education component that ranges from primary school groups to post-secondary students in sociology, social work and nursing. People who take part are encouraged to look at their community differently and to consider the issues of poverty and homelessness from a broader perspective.

Pat Nixon's influence is not limited to his work in Calgary. He serves as a mentor and trainer for poverty and street workers across Canada, coaching them on building strong volunteer organizations and developing programs and resources. Pat has also been involved in advocating for social change at the national level as a member of the Evangelical Fellowship of Canada Council of Presidents and board member of the Canadian Round-table on Poverty and Homelessness. Working with Rick Tobias from Toronto's Young Street Mission, Pat developed Street Level, which is a national coalition offering training, networking and support for street and poverty workers across Canada. In 2001, Pat was invited to share his expertise with churches, universities and cultural centres in Poland and Latvia.

Pat has received many honours for his work. In 2001, he was named Calgary's Citizen of the Year, and in 2005 he became a Member of the Order of Canada.

Pat never forgets that his path in life was shaped by people who reached out to offer him help and who stood by him in his struggle to change. He faces the harsh reality that some of the people he tries to help may never escape the streets and yet he never falters in his commitment. He is willing to offer people in need as many chances as they are willing to accept. Pat Nixon's mission in life is clear, as he says, "I'll keep trying...I never give up on people."

THE ALBERTA ORDER OF EXCELLENCE

Upon the recommendation of the Council of The Alberta Order of Excellence The honourable Norman Lkwong Lieutenant Governor of Alberta and Chancellor of the Order grants Membership in The Order of Excellence to

Patrick Nixon

in recognition of service of the greatest distinction and of singular excellence for or on behalf of the residents of Alberta.

Given at Government house at Edmonton Alberta on the 14th day of June 2007.

Under the Seal of the Order by

The Honourable Norman Lkwong,
Lieutenant Governor of Alberta Chancellor of The Alberta Order of Excellence.

Dr. Robert C.P. Westbury,
Chairman Alberta Order of Excellence Council.

Accepted by Patrick Nixon
Member The Alberta Order of Excellence.

SEED
THE MUSTARD SEED STREET MINISTRY

YONGE STREET MISSION

centre street church

Artist Cora Healy-Tobin ©